THE ELIZABETH ICON, 1603–2003

The Elizabeth Icon: 1603–2003

Julia M. Walker

First published 2004 by
PALGRAVE MACMILLAN
Houndmills, Basingstoke, Hampshire RG21 6XS and
175 Fifth Avenue, New York, N.Y. 10010
Companies and representatives throughout the world

PALGRAVE MACMILLAN is the global academic imprint of the
Palgrave Macmillan division of St Martin's Press LLC and of
Palgrave Macmillan Ltd.
Macmillan® is a registered trademark in the United States,
United Kingdom and other countries. Palgrave is a registered
trademark in the European Union and other countries.

ISBN 1–4039–1199–1 hardback

This book is printed on paper suitable for recycling and
made from fully managed and sustained forest sources.

A catalogue record for this book is available
from the British Library.

Library of Congress Cataloging-in-Publication Data
Walker, Julia M., 1951–
    The Elizabeth icon, 1603–2003 / Julia M. Walker.
        p. cm.
    Includes bibliographical references and index.
    ISBN 1–4039–1199–1
        1. Elizabeth I, Queen of England, 1533–1603—Public opinion.
2. Great Britain—History—Elizabeth, 1558–1603—Historiography. 3.
Elizabeth I, Queen of England, 1533–1603—In literature. 4. Elizabeth I,
Queen of England, 1533–1603—In art. 5. National characteristics,
British, in literature. 6. National characteristics, British—History. 7.
English literature—History and criticism. 8. Great Britain—In art. 9.
Queens in literature. 10. Queens in art. I. Title.

DA355.W335 2003
942.05'5'092—dc22   2003062673

10   9   8   7   6   5   4   3   2   1
13 12 11 10 09 08 07 06 05 04

Printed and bound in Great Britain by
Antony Rowe Ltd, Chippenham, Wiltshire

For Mary Ann and Sarah

Contents

List of Illustrations

Acknowledgements

The four-century scope of this book has allowed me a sort of working vacation, as I've ventured to fresh woods and pastures new of history and culture far past my habitual "sell-by" date – Milton's death in 1674. I am most grateful to my friends and colleagues in later periods for their kind and unstinting help. The bloopers, of course, are mine.

As with all my academic work, the usual suspects deserve more thanks than I can render for help and support, moral, intellectual, and otherwise: Laura Doan, Celia A. Easton, Anne D. Lutkus, and (especially for the War of Jenkins' Ear) Dr. Judith Hunter.

I am most particularly grateful to Dr. Barbara Dixon, Provost, whose support and kindness encouraged both me and my work through bad times and good. At Palgrave Macmillan, Emily Rosser and Paula Kennedy combined encouragement with patience, to my eternal gratitude. Ron Pretzer's photographs add the key visual element to this study; he bravely battled with the biscuit tins. The multivalent Sandra Rohlfing came through with rescues on permissions, and Marie Henry and Michelle Feeley with all sorts of help. And SUNY Geneseo, producing and supporting excellence by alchemy, as far as I can tell, continues to rise above the fray of state schools even as it rose to this occasion, buying me my very own copy of Lady Florence Dixie's *Gloriana*.

A special thanks must go to the hard-working members of the Women's Studies Seminar, "From Paragon to Pop Culture," of the spring of 2002. They shall, as I promised them, not remain the traditionally unnamed entities of "my diligent students": Colleen Butler, my most excellent research assistant and her two companions in the nEXt generation, Whitney A. Crispell and Brynn Speer; Sarah Buzanowski, Jen Nuber, Princetta S. Self, Ilana Smith, and finally and mostly, the Three Fates: Jess*#! Seabauer, Lauren Walton, and Krista Zimmer.

As ever, the village of Geneseo is as magical a place to live and work as even Gloriana could imagine, and the court held in the (once and future) Around Back Café at least as scintillating as hers, thanks to Bob Wilcox, to Judith Hunter, Cindy Schmitt, Jim Memmott, Tom and Eileen Bushnell, the ever-matching Ellen, the Deni and Dan show, Louise and Will Wadsworth, the Hills, as well as Sherry, Emily, and Georgia Anderson, and to Tom the Lawyer, John the Voice of Doom, the Chanlers and other passing Republicans, and finally to the power-brokers – Alpha-Katie, Katie/Katie, Kari, Kat, Marianne, Rob, Emily, De'Von, Whit, Smitty, Lauren, and Krista.

On the home front, my son, De'Von McRavion, aka Super Kid, also of Around Back fame, has been not only generously supportive, but gleefully pro-active, as both a motivational coach/fetcher of fast food and historical researcher. It takes a brave kid to adopt a mother who's writing a book. The fur-covered members of the family – Rosemond Tuve, Tisbury Massachusetts, and Alice Fox – have variously contributed spaniel'd devotion, comic kitty fingers, and a very warm lap.

Finally, the beloved members of the movable house-party are perpetual sources of inspiration and felicity: Stuart Curran, Sarah Poyntz, Mary Ann Radzinowicz, Anne Shaver, Joe Wittreich, and Susanne Woods. Perhaps, if enough people buy this book, I can add yet another chapter to the narratives of Lancaster, Ballyvaughan, and Bologna.

Geneseo, New York
July 2003

Introduction:
History of an Icon in the Public
Space of Memory

24 March 1603
Richmond Palace

Elizabeth, Queen of England, departed this life, presumably in the "sure and certain hope of resurrection"[1] of which her 1559 *Book of Common Prayer* speaks, but with remarkably little drama for a monarch whose life was lived at the center of several stages. With her physical death, her carefully constructed public persona passed from her control and into an entirely new space: public memory.

In her 45 years on the throne Elizabeth had changed the image of monarchy forever. Yes, as all historians say, she brought England power and riches, peace on land and victory at sea, fostered arguably its greatest flowering of literary art, made a humanist attempt at religious compromise, and achieved for her island a position of world power that would last for centuries. But her most profound change was worked within the minds of her subjects and the generations to follow them. "Monarch" no longer meant only King. In a reign spanning six decades Elizabeth appraised, modified – first subtly, later radically – and finally claimed as her own the icons of rule: the human body with more-than-human powers externalized, the terrestrial globe and its cosmos, and the globe of heaven, the sun. By turning herself from a woman into a thing, Elizabeth was able to exist in a space no woman had ever filled: the human imagination's picture of supreme earthly power made manifest. In 1603 a woman died, a monarch ceded her kingdom to another prince, and a formidable intelligence lost control of the icon she had so carefully constructed.

We can see her carefully developed transformation from woman to mythic figure to icon in a chronological viewing of her portraits. She begins in the heavy-handed *Allegory of the Tudor Succession*, where her disproportionately large figure advancing on the public stage, leading Peace by the hand, the object of the gaze of her dead father and brother, the antithesis of her foreign-married sister who is shadowed by both Mars, god of war, and Rome. Soon after, *Elizabeth and the Three Goddesses* is a

1

logical episode from the thin history of powerful women, and in this re-making of the Choice of Paris, Elizabeth and her apple-like orb both banish and out-face the triumvirate of chief goddesses, Hera, Athena, and Aphrodite. Moreover, she accomplishes this by her mere presence; no action (or bribery) is required.

Although the Siena Sieve portrait addresses the specific topic of the queen's marriage negotiations, while the Armada portrait celebrates that victory, both paintings pick up the reference to Elizabeth's relationship to England and England's relationship to the world. In the most famous of the Sieve portraits (early 1580s), there is a large globe at the queen's left elbow, with England uppermost and enlarged. In the Armada portrait (1588), the globe is smaller, but is now in the foreground and under her right hand. In the Ditchley portrait of the early 1590s, the queen's more-than-life-size figure is straddling the globe, specifically standing on England, as little ships follow the Thames upstream under her spreading skirts. The body of the queen has become the land of England in the Welbeck portrait, with plants, animals, birds, and water creatures all cavorting on her gown. And, finally, the queen's image departs from the earthly sphere altogether, as Nicholas Hillyard's representation makes her the sun behind the rainbow, complete with the Latin inscription: "Non sine sole Iris" – no rainbow without the sun. In the 45 years of her reign, Elizabeth's image has morphed from that of a woman who was also a monarch, into that of a monarch who was also a woman, and finally into an image of a new concept – a woman, but not a realistic woman, rather a manifestation of earthly and heavenly power. Her body has ceased to become a sight at which to gaze (although the Rainbow portrait is hot not only in color values); it has become a site of power, a wholly unrealistic but instantly recognizable image of a particular emblem of power. Elizabeth had become an icon.

The light of the glowing sun-colored dress behind the rainbow shone brightly for the next 70 years, repeating the span of the queen's life. The tomb that James erected merely blurred the light of Elizabeth's icon in the first decades. Like any solid object too close to a source of light, it could partially obscure and diffuse the light of the source, but it did not yet cast a clear shadow of its own. But as the decades turned to centuries, the shadow of the tomb formed more sharp outlines, becoming itself the most recognizable element of this *luminare sans son*. As the centuries passed, however, even the tomb lost its clearly recognizable form, and all that survived was the iconic memory of a woman who was monarch. The hair, the ruff, and most of all the name – Good Queen Bess, England's Eliza, Elizabeth of blessed memory: Elizabeth.

It is one of the ironies of the Elizabeth Icon that its use in the sixteenth and seventeenth centuries requires more explanation than its use today. Not only did Elizabeth's image move into the newly created sphere of public memory, but her history and the history of her time were tied to the image. We require considerable background to recover the significance of Thomas Cecil's *c.*1622 print showing the queen mounted on a horse receiving a lance from Truth. To the citizen of London, the Armada reference in the print would have spoken directly to the debate about the proposed Spanish marriage of Prince Charles. Today, however, there is often no logical – let alone historical – relationship between the late queen's image and the manifestation of its use. A biscuit tin, a bath duck, a set of playing cards, a tea pot – these all say simply "England." Elizabeth has become an icon for her nation.

In the twentieth century, both before and after Elizabeth needed the designation "the First," if the person in the street were shown a pictorial succession of English monarchs, whom would she recognize, besides the current resident of the throne? Henry VIII, probably, although she may be a bit shaky on the numeral. "Isn't that the one with all the wives?" she might ask. He would probably be sure with Victoria, even if more for singularity of gender and her famous stubby figure clad in widow's weeds than for chronological proximity. But Elizabeth is always recognized, and not only in Britain and the Commonwealth nations; she is England's most recognizable royal export, with (perhaps) the current exceptions of the late Princess of Wales and Elizabeth II. In the "Renaissance Fairs" popular in the United States and Canada, while the activities are primarily pop-culture medieval, the publicity begins, more often than not, with the announcement that: "Her Majesty Queen Elizabeth the First [and that anachronism is only the first of many] invites you to her royal court for a day of jousting, feasting, dunking, ..." In this context, Elizabeth has become an icon of "Merrie Olde England," even if the England being so generally and generously imagined is a version of times several centuries before the House of Tudor existed.

In the half-century after her death, Elizabeth was a more potent political marker than she is today, when she has come to stand popularly for the glories of the English Renaissance and the comparatively innocent excitement of exploring a "new" world. Yet in the years between 1603 and 1660 we find a complex range of appropriations of the dead queen by artists, writers, preachers, architects, and politicians. In these varied appropriations, we see a significant transformation: the power of the brilliant icon of the Rainbow portrait first blurred, then casting an increasingly long shadow: the shadow of her tomb. The "late queen of blessed memory" has, in many ways, more power than the living monarch. After the Restoration, that shadow becomes sharper and is ultimately used to define a new icon: the England of Elizabeth. But, like the tomb that casts the shadow, the new icons of the following centuries have little to do with the reality of Elizabeth Tudor. The picture held in the sphere of public memory – a picture that still enables, to a great extent, the institution of the British monarchy – became (as are all icons) the picture of an idea. And that idea is England.

As we examine the final decades of the four centuries since Elizabeth's death, we might consider the observations of recent cultural commentators, who have observed how the relatively blank canvas of Diana, Princess of Wales, allowed private, public, and political figures to paint a glowing portrait of whatever image best fit their immediate needs. Ironically, the very full canvas of the life of Elizabeth I also allowed multivalent posthumous representation, albeit for the opposite reason. Like the Shield of Achilles, such accomplishment and political significance, so many powerful words and images, could never be incorporated into a comprehensive representation, making fragmented appropriations expedient and effective.

In the BBC's list of the Top Ten Most-Admired Britons, there are two women: Elizabeth and Diana. Like Lady Diana Spencer, the late Princess of Wales, Elizabeth Tudor is a guaranteed headline attraction, alive or dead. That she was used to further a variety of agendas, often conflicting, should hardly surprise us, for all that we have tended to cease studying the monarch at the very moment that her image passed out of her control. Some uses of the Elizabeth icon will require us to recover an historical context not readily at our mental fingertips. As we move in time from the clear shadow cast by the tomb that James built to contain Elizabeth's power, we lose the meaning of that shadow. One historical cliché – the figure of X casts a long shadow – is fascinatingly wrong when we speak of the history of Queen Elizabeth. Her authorized self-image, like her historical legacy, is a source of light, literal and symbolic. The shadows are cast by those of us who came after her, as, back-lit, we try to figure our own agendas on the surface of the public scene.

The best testament to the public's multivalent and perennial fascination with Elizabeth Tudor is that between the excellent scholarly study authored by Michael Dobson and Nicola J. Watson, *England's Elizabeth: An Afterlife in Fame and Fantasy*, and this book, there is very little common ground. While I have had the great good fortune to use their book as a source of both information and enlightenment, I've also been pleased (relieved?) that the two works are so essentially dissimilar. Both studies are chronological analyses of the re-presentations of the Queen from her death to the present; both works examine a variety of genres, written and visual; but neither work mines to any significant extent the same veins of material or uses the same subjects as set-pieces. Far from being a tribute to scholarly fair play, this fact is a monument to the mass of Elizabeth material available for study and analysis. The Elizabeth icon and the place it claims in the common sphere of public memory are, it certainly seems, rich enough to nourish any number of studies.

In 1603 Elizabeth Tudor, the woman, died. The afterlife of her icon, claimed by all manner of people and causes, gives evidence of the newly created public sphere of memory. Coming into being as Elizabeth passed to dust, this new public sphere has granted the queen a resurrection at once relentlessly secular and perpetually mutable.

1603–1620:
The Shadow of the Rainbow

The death of Elizabeth has become one of the major mile-markers in English history. Her passing puts a period to the popular conception of the Renaissance – never mind that Shakespeare wrote for another decade or that the Divine Right of Kings was not effectively challenged until the execution of Charles I in 1649. On a more pedantic level, 1603 makes a change from memorizing Tudors to memorizing Stuarts for those who are toiling their way through British monarchs. In one sense, the death of Elizabeth can be read as the end of English history, for with the beginnings of union with Scotland, England ceased to define itself as an individual national identity and began to articulate the language of collective power. This, in turn, generated a larger beginning, the first articulation of a collective identity that would grow naturally into the ideology of Empire. And, after all, when had England been truly English? The pre-1066 divisions were no less discrete entities than was the post-1066 definition of the country as including large chucks of what is now France. We should remember the telling fact that William the Conqueror made his oldest son Duke of Normandy; his second son got the land west of the Channel, showing the value placed on the newly-acquired England by the conquerors, if not the conquered. Even into the Stuarts, in the second half of the second millennium, the "English" throne claimed and reclaimed lands in France. And this is only the most clearly defined locus of national identity problems. Wales, Cornwall, and, of course, Ireland were at various times and with varying degrees of success defined as part of England. So rather than a national identity passing with Elizabeth, perhaps it is more fair to say that one idea of England died while yet another was conceived. Well worth noting is Paul Langford's lively study *Englishness Identified* (Oxford University Press, 2000), which has as its subtitle: "Manners and Character 1650–1850."

For all that it did mark the end of a dynasty, the transfer of Elizabeth's crown to James was accomplished very smoothly, especially when compared to earlier dynastic shifts. That most famous of changes, marked by the word "Conquest," allowed William of Normandy to overturn the House of Wessex in 1066. William II followed his father to the throne and was in turn succeeded by his brother, Henry I. The strife generated by the death of Henry I's male heir in 1120, leaving his daughter, the Empress Matilda, battling with his nephew Stephen for the crown of England, was not resolved in that generation, but with the establishment of the House of Plantagenet as Henry II, Empress Matilda's son (with the maddening redundancy of Henrys and Richards in Shakespeare's history plays, both Henry I's daughter and his nephew's wife were named Matilda), took the throne in 1154. While the crown passed in succession from Henry II to Richard I to John I to Henry III and then to Edwards I, II, and III, it can hardly be said to have passed smoothly. Still, there was no major disjunction within the House of Plantagenet until the deposition of Richard II by his first cousin Henry IV in 1399. This gave rise to the War of the Roses, but that was all in the dynasty (if not the family), as the Yorks and Lancasters quarreled over which plant was the proper off-shoot of Edward III. The brief and busy reign of Henry V left his infant son the supposed heir to France, before Joan of Arc took issue with the situation. When Henry VI (a Lancaster) was defeated by his cousin Edward of York, the historians barely blinked, at least in retrospect; Edward was crowned Edward IV in 1461. The popular myth of the Princes in the Tower murdered by their wicked uncle Richard makes much of the end of the Plantagenets, as Richard III died in 1485 on Bosworth Field, his crown in a hawthorn bush and the plea for a horse on his lips. His successor, Henry VII, six generations removed from Edward III (and arguably on the wrong side of the blanket), had the sound political acumen to claim the throne by right of conquest first, right of blood second. Henry's grafted Tudor rose wilted within two generations on the English throne, but his daughter Margaret's marriage to James IV of Scotland provided the continuity needed to make James VI/I the most logical, though not the only, choice for Elizabeth.

One of the most appealing aspects of James VI of Scotland for the English public was that he would come complete with all the accessories of a dynasty: a queen, an heir, a second son, and several daughters. His queen, Anne of Denmark, was neither Spanish nor French; his religion firmly Protestant; his bloodlines satisfactory both to the Tudor loyalists and to those who had cherished a theological or romantic fondness for his mother, Mary Stuart. That he was a humorless bi-sexual without the famed Tudor charisma, whose wife reportedly tried to induce miscarriage by beating her own bump, seemed, if noted at all, vastly outweighed by his outward trappings of conventionality.

James' formal entrance into London was delayed for nearly a year because of an outbreak of the plague. From a public-relations standpoint, this circumstance had the effect of a shrewd move. During that year, James conducted the business of government – not that he waited to reach that government's seat, drafting plans for new coinage and other matters on his trip down from Scotland. So it was as an actively reigning monarch of the city that James processed, not as an arriving foreign successor to the much-mourned Elizabeth. The long-planned spectacles of Jonson and Dekker thus celebrated an established monarchy rather than welcoming an uncrowned foreign prince. The famously unsubtle plan of Dekker to have St. George and St. Andrew make peace and greet James together had acquired a new significance: George and Andrew had had world enough and time to become well-acquainted, both with each other and with James. Furthermore, the rivers of ink and tears that marked the old queen's passing had long-since dried away, the ink to the shelf, the tears to legend, and people celebrated the established reign of a new king. While people speculated that James would change his name to Constantine or Arthur, the poets and artists gave him embellishments on his coined image of Augustus Caesar. James, it was clear, was bent on ruling a new country, at once new and ancient.

Arguably, James' focus on the idea of Britain prevented him from recognizing the political realities of the countries he was trying to rule. Problems with religion, far from being laid to rest, were foregrounded by the yoking of Calvinist Scotland to Anglican England, and the ever-present Catholic presence of Ireland only added to the competing agendas. Perhaps the perfect icon of this theological hornet's nest is a broad-sheet of Puritan propaganda printed on paper with a Roman Catholic watermark. And while James had hastened to design new money, he was less successful in getting it spent in the ways he desired. The Commons and James differed over taxes and appropriations for military actions, as well as over revisions of the Elizabethan Settlement and over all manner of foreign and domestic policies. And, meanwhile, Guy Fawkes was plotting (unknowingly) his own four centuries of flaming fame. Nothing generates bonds of sympathy like a common threat. The Gunpowder Plot, threatening the specific members of Parliament and that particular king as well as the established form of constitutional government, far from wreaking havoc in the land, made James one of the boys in a way that nothing else could. The celebration of deliverance from demolition found its way into all levels of the culture, from a rite in the Book of Common Prayer to the street-theatre still enacted today. Ironically, it is this November 5th celebration of the preservation of the monarch and the ruling body that generates Britain's only celebration to parallel the US Independence Day or the French Bastille Day.

By 1606 James had survived at least one theological summit, had commissioned the Bible that would immortalize his name, and had stitched the two major portions of his new Britain into a single icon: the Union Jack. The red cross of St. George does overpower the white cross, or saltire, of St. Andrew, but the blue field on which both rest derives from the Scots, not the English banner. Ceding the obvious point – the dominance of the St. George Cross, while making the rest of the flag a complete replica of the banner of St. Andrew, was very much James' style. Lacking the finesse of Elizabeth's political maneuvers, James had a good eye for an icon, and this compromise left most of his people happy enough and James with the knowledge that, symbolically, England had been grafted onto Scotland, not the other way around. Also in 1606, like any family recently moved into a new house, the Stuarts had the relatives over for a visit. Queen Anne's brother, Christian of Denmark, came on a state visit that enabled James to reify his rule by making it the subject of his entertainments.

In domestic policy, James set about attempting to homogenize his islands; the settlement of over 100,000 English and Scots in Ireland made the Jamestown settlement – on the edge of that swath of North America called Virginia after Elizabeth – seem a colonial afterthought. The opening of new lands for the new British coincided with ongoing riots over the enclosure of public lands the length and breath of England. Recusant Roman Catholics were barred by Parliament from holding public office, even as Queen Anne converted to Catholicism. James' chronic financial difficulties continued to obsess him. Certainly, living beyond his means in the unquestionably thrifty and arguably dour court of Edinburgh was not difficult to do; but James had celebrated his accession to the riches of the English throne by making a considerable dent in the assets piled up during the fiscally conservative – at least where the national budget was concerned – reign of Elizabeth. In 1610 James negotiated the Great Contract with his Parliament, trading a huge chunk of cash – £200,000 – for abolishing the custom of feudal tenures and wardships. This promising settlement, which would have done much to set James' house in order, fell apart when the king tried to double-dip, demanding what was essentially a payment for taking a payment.

As he came to the end of his first decade of rule, the year 1612 must have seemed to James – both as he lived through it and in retrospect – like a preview of the Apocalypse. Robert Cecil, that shadow of Elizabethan England and the most stable element of James' government, died in March. In September, Frederick V, the Elector Palatine, began his courtship of James' daughter Elizabeth, an alliance which would prove an eventual domestic success but an immediate political disaster; although defending the rights of his Protestant son-in-law on the playing field of Europe did James no good at all, the union did provide, albeit two generations later, the link between the defunct House of Stuart and the House of Hanover. Then in November, Henry Stuart, the much-celebrated perfect prince and heir, died. Providing one of the great "what if …" moments in history, Henry's unexpected death left his entirely secondary brother, Charles, as James' only heir. Unlike Henry Tudor stepping up to more than fill the shoes of his older brother Arthur, Charles had neither the physical nor mental endowments to allow even the most hopeful poet to praise him. When Henry was interred in the newly completed Westminster tomb of his grandmother, Mary Stuart, the practical hope of a dynasty to rival the Plantagenets went with him.

James spent the next eight years fostering and cleaning up after one favorite – Robert Carr, Vicount Rochester then Earl of Somerset, he of the Overbury poison plot fame – and (having sidelined him amid a scandal worthy of the current ruling House) began to heap attentions and honors on another, the inexplicable George Villiers. Still short of money, the king undertook to sell peerages at £50 a pop, even as Arabella Stuart, the most famous of the alternate claimants to the throne, starved herself to death in the Tower, sharing the family affinity for excess, albeit in the other direction. The second decade of the seventeenth century ended, like the season's last episode of a long-running television drama, with two ominous events. Jamestown, Virginia, saw the first meeting of a colonial assembly in 1619, and the Puritan Fathers (and, incidentally, the Mothers) landed at Plymouth Rock in December of 1620. The new empire that James' kingship was to presage was about to take on a life of its own.

Memory as a public sphere: making an Elizabeth icon

Of all the startling changes we associate with that remarkable period, the English Renaissance, perhaps one of the most profound was the changing perception of space. The perception of people's place and space in the world around changed with the discovery that there was a "new" world quite unknown to the ancients and seemingly up for grabs among the early modernists; the perception of the earth centrally occupying the space of the cosmos changed with Copernicus' treatise and Galileo's experiments; the space of human interaction changed as cities grew and towns prospered. And with the latter came the beginnings of the concept of truly public space.

While Jürgen Habermas presents theories useful to our thinking about changing social structures as related to the changing uses of space in early modern Europe, there is at least one social construction he fails to examine: memory. In saying that, I don't wish to diminish the force of Habermas' insights, especially those that dislodge us from our too-easy assumptions about the nature and scope of socio-economic change in Renaissance England. Among his less debatable points, Habermas makes the argument that "initial assimilation of bourgeois humanism to a noble courtly culture" has been over-emphasized by historians, social and literary.[1] "Over-emphasized" it has been certainly, if not actually misread by generations of students of the period, as we were taught from our first Shakespeare play to, and often through, post-graduate reading that there was such a thing as *the* Elizabethan world picture.[2] While the last few decades of scholarship have largely de-bunked the notion of ditch-diggers or even fishmongers raptly attending to the moral ambiguities of *King Lear* or of sonnet writers leaping out of bed into the dawn of a Renaissance morning, casting off the musty blankets of the Middle Ages even as they reached for their quills, the specter of schoolroom generalities has not been completely banished from our cultural history. Habermas continues his attempt to locate the fruit, if not the flower, of this new world-view by looking at money, that constant in any civilization's history. He argues that an economy still depending on, rather than transforming, the general model of agrarian feudalism and "the petty commodity production" of a class of urban craftspeople, would retain, at the least, "ambivalent characteristics."[3] In other words, for once the fish of the marketplace and the fowl of the farmyard had more in common with each other than either did with a true exchange of goods and services. One major factor signaling this ambivalence was the lack of truly public space, the agora of Athens, the forum of Rome. Not literally – or not only literally – a place for the exchange of skills and commodities, this public space would have been the locus and the occasion for an exchange of ideas. As society metamorphosed from the medieval to the early-modern, the need for a public space, a space controlled neither by the Church nor the monarch, began first to arise and then to manifest itself as a necessity.

While this seems obvious, once said, it is at odds with the charming notion of a rising merchant class clamoring for both economic autonomy and more books to read. And as for that crutch of the teacher whose students won't read *Julius Caesar* (the claim that dusty peasants eagerly grasped the manipulative political rhetoric of Marc Antony's "Friends, Romans, countrymen," speech) we must firmly, if regretfully, lay that in the dust of as-yet-unpaved roads and a working class unaware of theories about the globe or iambic pentameter in the Globe – or, indeed, notions of class, per se. So, no, we are not surprised to hear that a person did not go to sleep in the Middle Ages and wake up as the modern day dawned. If nothing else, the fact that Charles Stuart was executed after stepping out a window of the Banqueting Hall, his family's monument to privileged space of the dynastic few, should remind us that, even in 1649, London lacked a commonly recognized public space in which to execute a king.

But there is a crucial element of the early modern public sphere left unnoticed in Habermas' study. Not until England of the seventeenth century do we find a population sufficiently aware of the physical appearance of their monarch for that monarch's image to assume personal iconic status. Yes, Shakespeare's *Richard II* depends upon the central metaphor of an iconic monarchy for its theme; but it is the monarchy, not the monarch, that exerts iconic status. The king is the sun, the lion, the cosmic owner of the garden in need of a gardener. But Richard himself is unrecognizable. Even Bolingbroke, surely the most forceful figure of the play, and one who knows well how to play with icons ("he be the fire, I'll be the yielding water," he says as he puns on rain/reign), is physically unrecognizable to Hotspur. But the image of Elizabeth herself became recognizable the length and breadth of not only her own kingdom, but in Ireland, Scotland, and much of Western Europe. Besides her 45 years on the throne and her singularity as a queen regnant, there was her carefully developed metamorphosis through portraits, from a generically female crowned ruler in the 1558 coronation portrait to the sun itself, that icon of male kingship, in the Rainbow portrait. Furthermore, the image of Elizabeth's tomb, an engraving of which hung in so many parish churches, often with some other representation of the late queen, was thus able to play upon this public memory with the recognition necessary to manipulate an icon. But the simple image of the queen, the profile on the coin, was recognizable to all, even if distinguished from other such images only by her gender. For the first time in medieval and early-modern Europe, we find an individual image, a non-religious icon, recognized and identified by the majority of the population. By the end of her 45-year reign, the queen had become an English icon.

An icon, of course, is a picture. But we don't need to see pictures with our eyes to hold them in our minds. Words trigger pictures, as do scent and taste. Hearing words, seeing pictures, smelling lavender, tasting unusual flavors, all can summon mental images, whether positive or negative. Even touch, which would seem to defy picture making, can summon a memory – the grip of an elderly lady's primly gloved fingers transporting me back to greeting my grandmother's bridge club. But of all five senses it is sight, and words that describe sight, that give us the true fixed image that can most accurately bear the weight of the term icon. During Elizabeth's reign there were many literal icons generated, from the portraits to her face on coins to the allegorical Gloriana/Britomart in Spenser's epic poem. By the time her body was placed (for the first time) beneath the paving stones of Westminster Abbey, Elizabeth Tudor's iconic identity was firmly established in that public sphere common to all English-people: memory.

With the Stuarts, those master-builders, come a host of opportunities for exploiting that icon. Nor could the Stuarts be deemed mere opportunists in this venture, as it was James' shrewd removal of Elizabeth's body from her tomb and subsequent reconfiguring of the Henry VII Chapel in Westminster that generated one of the most powerful of visual Elizabeth icons, her tomb. With the manipulation of that putatively public but actually private space, James took his place at the head of a long line of political and social powerbrokers who would use the public's memory, triggered by an (often false) icon of Elizabeth, to generate debate, to disseminate propaganda, to promote or subvert issues social and political, all in the name of England. None of this would have been possible had not Elizabeth "of blessed memory" existed recognizably – as had no earlier monarch – in the public sphere of memory.

*c.*1606: tombs and wombs in Westminster Abbey

Beneath the coffin of Elizabeth rests that of her half-sister Queen Mary.
Westminster Abbey Official Guide, 1988[4]

Queen Elizabeth was buried in the unmarked grave of her sister Mary.
Edward Carpenter
The Official History of Westminster Abbey, 1966[5]

Queen Elizabeth. ... was carried, doubtless by her own desire, to the North Aisle of Henry VII's Chapel, to the unmarked grave of her unfortunate predecessor.
Arthur P. Stanley, Dean of Westminster
*Historical Monuments of Westminster Abbey,*1876[6]

Q: Who's buried in Elizabeth's tomb?
A: Elizabeth – but it's not her tomb.

Perhaps it is only as a joke that such a question can be entertained. But the politics behind the 1603 burial of the queen under the altar of the Henry VII Chapel, her exhumation and reburial in 1606 are certainly without humor, if not without irony. James Stuart, certainly one of England's most shrewd manipulators of ceremonial space, accomplished Elizabeth's double diminishment – buried with her sister, Mary Tudor, and over-shadowed by the tomb of her old enemy, Mary Stuart – so smoothly that it left no stone untrimmed in the history of the Abbey. Even 310 years later, the scholar who inquires about the provenance of Elizabeth's current resting place would receive a frosty reception in the Abbey's Muniments Room, the repository of the foundation's records.

The current Keeper of the Westminster Abbey Muniments Room, Dr. Mortimer, offered me – and with good reason – the shelves of books describing the Abbey's monuments, markers, and role in English history, all taking as a given the not unreasonable stance that Elizabeth's current tomb was her original resting place. Even in an institution which reveres it own historian, William Camden, just this side of canonization, the quote from his 1603 edition of *Reges, Reginæ, Nobiles* ... "Elizabetha Angliæ, Franciæ & Hiberniæ Regina ... eadem crypta cum Henrico 7, Auo conditur" (translated "Elizabeth, Queen of England, France and Ireland ... rests in the same tomb with her grandfather, Henry VII") could be dismissed, with impunity. Pronounced either metaphoric or all-encompassing – the entire chapel constituting Henry's tomb – Camden's chronicle derives its most powerful authority from being written in Latin. Only my subsequent discovery of the 1606 account sheet, including a line item for removing the queen from her original tomb – under the chapel altar with her paternal grandfather – generated serious doubt about Elizabeth originally having been laid to rest in what is now her tomb: "Item: more for removing of Queene Elizabeth's Body ... 46 shillings 4 pence."[7]

In a 1990 essay, "The Royal Body: Monuments to the Dead, for the Living," Nigel Llewellen matter-of-factly mentions that Elizabeth was first buried under the altar (citing Camden as his source), then moved to her present tomb.[8] Llewellen, using the fact as part of his argument about the power of funeral sculpture, evidently places his faith in Camden; nor does his rhetoric acknowledge that he is flying in the face of canonical Abbey. This essay, most unfortunately, was not part of the Abbey archives in 1993, nor had I read it. Instead I was faced down by a daunting pile of authority, some of it cited above, resting on the seeming firm foundation of the current tomb.

It is very difficult to argue with a life-size effigy under an elaborate marble canopy. There is permanence about the tomb, especially with the present walling of the chapel aisles, that renders speculation impertinent. That sense of historical inevitability, imparted by slabs and pillars of marble, by cleverly carved ruff and by gilding, is itself a tribute to the successful strategy by which King James marginalized Elizabeth. The text that James generated is now so central to the larger text of the Abbey that a number of powerful forces resist any re-reading. The unproblematic representation of the official guidebook, of the official history, of the grossly inaccurate work of the revered nineteenth-century Dean of the Abbey – all texts which give both heavy-handed and inaccurate readings of the text of the tomb – are the fruits of a stupendously effective act of political and historical revisionism authored by James I and reinscribed even today in the canon of English historiography and royal monuments.

On the face of it, all this may sound a bit like a plot for a novel by David Lodge or Michael Malone. Actually, my experience grew from relatively mundane causes: the result of an accident and a favor. As this implies, unlike conventional textual or archival scholarship, my work on Elizabeth's tomb was a personal adventure in time, space, history, and imagination. My story begins when an art historian friend, who works on French royal tombs, asked me once what Elizabeth's tomb looked like. I had no idea. At that point in my career, even though I had worked on the Elizabeth portraits in connection with Spenser's *Faerie Queene*, I had spent all my London visits in libraries and the Public Records Office, having no time for tourist attractions, under which heading I erroneously placed Westminster Abbey. Furthermore, while developing an argument linking James' and Shakespeare's views of Elizabeth I to *Antony and Cleopatra*, I had come across the following line in Thomas Millington's 1603–04 diary, saying that the queen was "buried in the Sepulchre of her grandfather."[9]

Even after reading that, I had never thought much about where Elizabeth was buried. And, although I did find some photographs and reproduced engravings of the tomb itself, a quick check of a number of scholarly works on the queen provided only detailed descriptions of the death, the mourning, the eulogies, and the processions; no one seemed to have written about the burial itself or the tomb's placement in the Abbey. So the next time I was in London, a blank slate with educated expectations, I visited Westminster Abbey. There I found the dead queen's memorial, not in the central location Millington had led me to expect – "with her grandfather" (who I found listed as under the altar of the Henry VII Chapel) – but isolated in the dark north aisle of that chapel, her body lying on top of her Catholic half-sister Mary, to whom she erected no monument during her reign. Not having been brought up on slide shows of or school visits to the Abbey, I was quite unprepared for this, and we can take as written my dismay. And so I began my research.

The first conclusion to consider, of course, is that Millington was wrong. After all, he was not even in London when Elizabeth was laid to rest, being more politically occupied by accompanying James on his trip from Scotland to London, and (more significantly) from James VI of Scotland to James I of Britain. But looking at the present tomb in relation to the rest of the chapel, reading it with not only an eye uninformed by received opinion, but one focused by that contemporary reference, I had to ask: is it *likely* that a queen so greatly loved and so lavishly mourned would have been put to rest in such relative obscurity? Is it *likely* that her Anglican nobles and clergy would have buried her with Mary Tudor, who had no monument of any sort during her sister's 45-year reign? No, it is not likely. Having decided that such an unlikely thing must have an interesting explanation, I began to search for one.

The accounts of Elizabeth's tomb offered by the various reference books in the library of the Abbey and elsewhere proved to be not only unsatisfactory, but actually misleading. No one, evidently, had ever questioned the likelihood of that tomb,[10] but the historians who described its present state had nevertheless celebrated the cultural and political implications of Elizabeth's burial with Mary Tudor. In other words, they had read as original a text which had been radically rewritten. And, to be fair, the text of the tomb itself was nearly all they had. After considerable library work, I can concur with the observation, in *The History of the King's Works*, that: "Henry VII's Chapel at Westminster is one of the most inadequately documented buildings in the whole of the King's Works."[11] The accounts from Stanley and Carpenter, which I use as epigraphs for this section, are not only a typical, but virtually a complete example of the existing histories that describe the royal tombs. The absence of contemporary records leaves room for considerable embroidery. The Keeper of the Abbey's Muniments offered me Stanley's study as the ultimate authority, even after I pointed out that lack of contemporary documentation evidenced elsewhere in the work and objected to the line "doubtless by her own desire" as being the very archetype of fictive scholarship. Dean Stanley, whose enthusiasm for the tombs in the Henry VII Chapel led him to take up bits of the floor and crawl around counting coffins, follows his statement about Elizabeth's "own desire" with the following editorial:

> At the head of the monument raised by her [Elizabeth's] successor [James] over the narrow vault are to be read two lines full of a far deeper feeling than we should naturally have ascribed to him – "*Regno consortes*

et urna, hic obdormimus Elizabetha et Maria sorores, in spe resurrectionis."
The long war of the English Reformation is closed in those words. In
that contracted sepulcher, admitting none other but those two, the
stately coffin of Elizabeth rests on the coffin of Mary. The sisters are
at one: the daughter of Catherine of Aragon and the Daughter of Anne
Boleyn repose in peace at last.[12]

As an example of Victorian sentimentality, this is striking; as an example
of logical political and historical analysis, it is almost willfully naive.

On the other hand, we overlook the influence of Victorian sentimentality at our peril when we read the Henry VII Chapel as it exists today,
for the imperialist, paternalistic attitudes of manifest destiny overlay the
monuments like a thick glaze. As a text, the entire chapel has been heavily
edited. It is a commonplace of history that architecture, particularly the
architecture of burial places, reflects the political agenda of any given era;
reading the architecture of the Chapel of Henry VII in Westminster Abbey
reveals the political and cultural agenda of nearly 500 years of one culture,
an agenda which privileges the male as warrior and the female as mother.
This is hardly surprising, considering that most of the other artifacts of
that culture – literary and artistic, social and political – also privilege
these same values. What is more noteworthy, however, is the extent to
which the monuments and architecture, as they exist today, reveal a
consistent and persistent desire to smooth over ruptures and disjunc-
tions in the political history of England (among which, evidently is
included the 45-year reign of the Virgin Queen), presenting instead a
nostalgic statement of peaceful patriarchal continuity.

As it has evolved, the Abbey as a whole, and especially the Henry VII
Chapel, is a series of revisionist narratives. The chapel's founder, the first
Tudor monarch, was making an architectural declaration of the end of
the War of the Roses; not only did he have the Tudor rose (red and white
petals uniting the roses of Lancaster and York) as the dominant theme
of the stained glass and the carvings, but he had his queen, Elizabeth York,
buried beside him, stressing the physical union of the Lancasters he represented with the Yorks he displaced, making concrete the indisputable
claim of their descendants. Their bodies in a single monument become
the generative text upon which Tudor history was based. James I – the
first Stuart monarch – authored his own version of revisionist history
through the tombs of Mary I, Elizabeth I, Mary Stuart, and his own
subsequent burial with the first Tudor. Nor was he the last to do so.

The iconoclastic damage to the chapel during the Revolution was
balanced by the destruction of Cromwell's tomb as Charles II had him

dug up and taken to Tyburn to be both hanged and decapitated. When the Royalist fervor of the Restoration abated, however, Cromwell's grave marker was rewritten, its text giving no hint that the represented body is absent. The chapel was largely neglected until the nineteenth century, but its restoration, which took the greater part of a century, is a testament to the British desire to glorify its past and to tie that past to its present, for the most recent revision of the chapel is the Battle of Britain Window in the RAF Chapel. In pride of place at the eastern end, behind Henry's altar, this stained glass celebrates not only the York/Lancaster/Tudor roses of Henry VII's agenda, but also, in the words of the Abbey's *Official Guide*, the insignia of the fighter squadrons that fought the Battle of Britain. While in the masonry below the window there remains a hole, now mediated by dingy glass, made by a fragment from one of the hordes of bombs dropped on London during September of 1940.

Buried here are the men who commanded this air battle: Hugh Montagu, 1st Viscount Trenchard, Marshal and "Father" of the RAF and Air Chief Marshal Hugh Caswall Tremenheere, 1st Baron Dowding, Air Officer Commanding-in-Chief of Fighter Command. Only the relatively neat and easily overlooked hole in the stonework speaks of the devastation visited upon London by the Blitz. Nothing speaks for the suffering and courage of the common English people, since the memorial represents only the twentieth-century version of their Knights of the Round Table.

This series of revisionist texts now is presented as a unified whole – even down to a plaque marking the spot where Cromwell was buried – the discontinuities subsumed by the complex totality of the statement implicit in the route marked out for the visitor. The visitor walks past the tombs of Edward the Confessor, Edward I, Eleanor of Castile, Edward III, Richard II (but not of the king who deposed him), Henry V (but not of his son who was deposed or Edward IV who did the deposing), past the Coronation Chair with the Stone of Destiny once, but no longer, beneath it, walks on eastward into the Chapel of Henry VII with a sense of the inevitability of English history that acknowledges the War of the Roses only in its resolution as a Tudor union of Lancaster and York. In the restoration programs from the nineteenth century to the present, the unity and continuity of patriarchy were clearly guiding principles. Nowhere is this nostalgia for the glorious continuity of the past more evident than in the chapel's final statement, that statement in the words of a poet from the time of James and Elizabeth, a poet writing about the time of Henry V: "We few, we happy few, we band of brothers." In the Chapel of Henry VII in Westminster Abbey, the historical realities of

English political upheavals are not merely glossed over, they are flattened by tons of marble and the gilded monuments of princes.

If the sentimental nationalism of the chapel can be laid primarily at the feet of a Victorian world-view, the impulse to revise history through funerary monuments cannot. Through the centuries of British monarchies, the Stuarts were among the most prolific builders; James I's building program in Westminster gives us ample evidence of this, while also displaying a personal and political agenda which has now become accepted as canonical history. When James VI of Scotland became James I of England and Scotland in 1603, he faced the problem of making a radical change seem like a natural sequence of events. He was not the heir of Elizabeth's body; he was not English. From his coronation through the first decade of his reign, James set out to take advantage of the first fact and to revise the second. Without directly disparaging the memory of Elizabeth, he set forth his gender, his heirs, and the unity of his two countries as evidence both of his destiny and of the benefits England would reap from the fulfillment of that destiny. The coronation medal depicted James wearing a laurel wreath, with a Latin inscription proclaiming him the new Caesar Augustus of Britain, while many of the pageants commissioned for his initial progress through London incorporated the Augustus Novus theme.

While these pageants and tableaux, generally presented at a stopping point along a royal processional route, once again remind us of the nature of public space – thoroughfares used for daily travel and business or small squares used for various markets – the Abbey would arguably constitute enclosed public space. The Abbey, however, and especially the space behind the high altar, where the Henry VII Chapel had been added, was not public space, being accessible only to the elevated few and only on certain occasions. We see in this a public sphere in transition: a space designed to make a statement, but not to allow an argument; a space defining the leaders of a people, but inaccessible to the vast majority of that people. Just as Westminster Abbey fulfills the dual role of coronation site and site of many royal burials – unlike the French dichotomy of Rheims for coronations and Saint Denis for burials – so, too, did it hold the ambiguous status of a space both public and private, for the public if not open to the public. Tacitly acknowledging the multivalent status of the Abbey, James Stuart, soon after his coronation, undertook a program of building designed to remind his new subjects and their descendants that his blood claim to the Tudor throne owed nothing to the Virgin Queen. In the Chapel of Henry VII in Westminster Abbey, James had Elizabeth moved from her original resting place in the central tomb of

Henry VII, and – reserving that spot for himself – commissioned the construction of a tomb for Elizabeth which marginalized her importance and foregrounded her childless state. Elizabeth's tomb was completed in 1606, just as Shakespeare was working on *Antony and Cleopatra*. In that play we can see both of James' agendas, the idea of the unifying super-ruler and the demystification of the cult of his female predecessor, clearly represented in the last act.

As soon as he entered London, James sounded the theme of dynastic continuity, not by foregrounding his real (albeit distant) blood tie to the deceased Elizabeth, but by stressing his direct descent from Henry VII. In his early speeches and in the iconography of his reign, James makes a statement designed to show that his presence on the English throne owed little to Elizabeth and much to his royal ancestor Henry VII. It was Henry whose policy he offered as a pattern for his own desire to rule England and Scotland as one country. Of the seven triumphal arches in James' formal entry into London (delayed almost a year because of the plague), two addressed this theme directly. The first arch linked the Stuarts to the Trojan line celebrated by Virgil as the ancestors of Augustus Caesar. In *The Golden Age Restor'd*, Graham Parry reminds us that James returned to that touchstone of Western European culture, the Troy story, to make the point that "he was the first modern king to restore the sovereign unity that the British Isles were fabled to have enjoyed in ancient times."[13] Like the Gawain Poet, the Tudors had also claimed to be descended from the survivors of Troy, and "since James' right to the English throne derived from Henry VII, he naturally appropriated the myth of the Trojan origin of the Tudors."[14] This claim made lighter the task of English poets celebrating James, not as the son of England's rejected Catholicism, personified by his mother Mary Stuart, but as a descendant of the Trojan Brutus and logical heir to the "claims of nascent imperialism" made repeatedly by the arches, "for the Trojans were the source of empire in the West, as Virgil had incontrovertibly established, and Britain like Rome was settled from Troy."[15]

The second triumphal arch on James' progress had a "central painting over the archway [which] emphasized the legitimacy of James's inheritance, showing Henry VII giving him the sceptre as the true successor to the Tudor line."[16] Elizabeth, on the other hand, was not directly depicted in any of these arches, although her presence was figured forth by images of Astrea and of the phoenix, both popular icons in her reign, now redesigned to represent James. Finally, leaving the City and riding down the Strand, the king "encountered one final tailpiece thrown up by Jonson at the last moment": Electra, represented as a human comet, "prophesies,

like an ancient Sybil," that the Stuart reign shall be safe from "'[a]ll …
That might perturbe the musique of thy peace' and at the climactic
moment James is hailed as the new Augustus."[17]

James himself continued to stress the themes of his triumphal entry.
He made these dual claims for historical and dynastic inevitability both
immediately and consistently, as in a speech to his first Parliament on
22 March 1604:

> First, by my descent lineally out of the loynes of Henry the seventh,
> is reunited and confirmed in mee the Vnion of the two Princely Roses
> of the two Houses of LANCASTER and YORKE, where of that King of
> happy memorie was the first Vniter, as he was also the first ground-
> layer of the other Peace … But the Vnion of these two princely Houses,
> is nothing comparable to the Vnion of two ancient and famous
> kingdomes …[18]

H. Neville Davies suggests further ways in which James Stuart's political
situation paralleled Augustus/Octavius Caesar's when he assumed control
of the power held by Antony and – in Shakespeare's play – by Cleopatra.
For even as James was represented in London pageantry and by his own
proclamation as Augustus Novus, Davies reminds us: "a great age had
recently passed with the death of Queen Elizabeth, and similarities …
between the behavior of Shakespeare's lass, supposedly unparalleled, and
Elizabeth … may reveal the dramatist's perception of a comparable diminishment."[19] Arguing that James continued to rely upon the Roman
paradigm of dynastic power and imperial unification Davies finds "incon-
ceivable" the suggestion that any dramatist writing in London in late 1606
(the probable date of *Antony and Cleopatra*), writing, moreover, for the
patronage of a king whose coronation medal depicted him "wearing a
laurel wreath, while a Latin inscription proclaimed him Caesar Augustus
of Britain," could have failed to associate the shift of Octavius Caesar to
Caesar Augustus with James, whose own "propaganda was making just
that connection."[20] The analogy, however, contained a serious flaw. James
was not subduing a female ruler of another country, both foreign and
dangerously exotic, a woman who any good Roman might rightly consider
to be the enemy; rather James was the foreigner, displacing a monarch
who had always and ever stressed her Englishness. Indeed, the Lancaster-
York references in this 1604 speech to Parliament were prompted by the
resistance of the House of Commons to the idea of Union.[21] Because
James was a Scot, indeed a Scot who was urging England to unify with,

rather than to subdue Scotland, he needed all the media support he could generate. In the second decade of the 1600s, two powerful media for shaping public opinion were coinage and the popular stage. James used both well, even as he built monuments to his new-minted dynasty.

Nor did James' problems with the English people diminish as his reign progressed. In a 1607 report by Nicolo Molin, ambassador to England from Venice, these problems are referred to as both serious and of long standing. Significantly, the ambassador compares James to Elizabeth:

> He does not caress the people nor make them that good cheer the late Queen did, whereby she won their loves: for the English adore their Soverigns, and if the King passed through the same street a hundred times a day the people would still run to see him; they like their King to show pleasure at their devotion, as the late Queen knew well how to do; but this King manifests no taste for them but rather contempt and dislike. The result is he is despised and almost hated. In fact his Majesty is more inclined to live retired with eight or ten of his favourites than openly as is the custom of the country and the desire of the people.[22]

Even allowing for the bias of a Catholic writer and audience (neither of whom, in any case, would have held Elizabeth in any special favor), this suggests that James had continuing problems subduing the shadow of Elizabeth's popularity. Indeed, that power was becoming less obscure as the first year of Stuart rule was followed by the next nine. And, as Davies points out, as early as 1607 there "is evidence ... some of it in plays and poems that ... the memory of Queen Elizabeth was being revived with affection." Quoting Bishop Goodman, Davies observes that

> although people were "generally wary of an old woman's government" by the end of Elizabeth's reign, experience of James soon prompted a revival of her reputation: "Then was her memory much magnified, – such ringing of bells, such public joy and sermons in commemoration of her, the picture of her tomb painted in may churches, and in effect more solemnity and joy in memory of her coronation than was for the coming in of King James."[23]

James countered this rising sentiment with a propaganda move which was a revision of his early self-fashioning and which was aimed directly at the veneration of Elizabeth's tomb. He had coins struck with the Latin legend "Henry [united] the roses, but James the kingdoms."[24] Here again we see James linking himself to Henry and his Tudor ancestry in a way which bypasses Elizabeth's life. James had further bypassed the importance of Elizabeth in his plans for the royal tombs in Westminster, marginalizing Elizabeth in death by the design and placement of her tomb in Henry VII's chapel.

With the irony we should be coming to expect, one of the most famous accounts of the queen's tomb, found in Fuller's seventeenth-century study, *The Church History of Britain*, describes and glorifies the very structure erected by James to diminish Elizabeth's iconic presence in the public memory:

> Queen Elizabeth, the mirror of her sex and age, (having above forty years, to the admiration of envy itself, managed this kingdom, finding when she began few friends that durst help, and leaving no foes that could hurt her,) exchanged her earthly for a heavenly crown; who, as she lived and died an unspotted virgin, so her maiden memory is likely, in this respect, to remain sole and single, seeing history affords no prince to be matched to her fame in all considerable particulars. Her corpse was solemnly interred under a fair tomb in Westminster, the lively draught whereof is pictured in most London and many country churches, every parish being proud of the shadow of her tomb; and no wonder, when each loyal subject erected a mournful monument for her in his heart.[25]

That the space created to diminish Elizabeth's place in English history could be praised as a monument to her greatness, a monument that would cast an oxymoronically brilliant shadow from Westminster to parish churches across London and the home counties, is more than ironic. James' tomb defines his own Englishness and right to the throne of England, revises Elizabeth's status as an English queen, and the tomb James uses to marginalize Elizabeth generates Fuller's archetype of the "mournful monument" that "each loyal subject" will erect in his heart. The real monarch is replaced by politically current but historically inaccurate icon. This is the first, and in some ways, the greatest example of an icon of the queen being co-opted directly from one posthumous re-presentation to another, with no connection of any sort between the icon – the picture of the queen's tomb – and the historical source of the image: Queen Elizabeth herself and the real tomb of Elizabeth, the altar of the Henry VII Chapel.

By identifying the Westminster tombs as the first example of the Elizabeth icon making a statement of English identity based on the queen's fame, if not the queen's history, we need to examine more carefully the circumstances of its creation. Elizabeth's death on March 24th at Richmond and her funeral on April 28th in London are both recorded in the diary of Lady Anne Clifford, the future Countess of Pembroke, who was 13 at the time and, on the 24th of March, living at Richmond, "sleeping on a pallet in the chamber of Lady Warwick, who was in charge of the arrangements."[26] Anne Clifford writes:

> my Aunt Warwick's man, brought us word from his Lady, that the Queen died about 2/3 o'clock in the morning ... About 10 o'clock King James was proclaimed in Cheapside by all the Council with great joy and triumph. I went to see and hear. This peaceable coming-in of the King was unexpected of all sorts of people. Within two or three days we returned to Clerkenwell again. A little after this Queen Elizabeth's corpse came by night in a barge from Richmond to Whitehall, my Mother and a great company of ladies attending it, where it continued a great while standing in the Drawing Chamber, where it was watched all night by several lords and ladies, my Mother sitting up with it two or three nights, but my Lady would not give me leave to watch, by reason I was held too young ... About this time my Lord Southampton was enlarged of his imprisonment out of the Tower. When the corpse of Queen Elizabeth had continued at Whitehall as the Council had thought fit, it was carried with great solemnity to Westminster, the lords and ladies going on foot to attend it, my Mother and my Aunt of Warwick being mourners, but I was not allowed to be one, because I was not high enough, which did much trouble to me then, yet I stood in the church at Westminster to see the solemnities performed.[27]

The queen's funeral, as this lengthy passage suggests, served a number of purposes. After a 45-year reign – the longest since that of Edward III in the thirteenth century – Elizabeth's person had indeed come to stand for the country she ruled. More than the commonplace of the monarch's two bodies, Elizabeth's public and private identity had taken on a unified and glorified singularity unprecedented in history and unsurpassed until the age of Victoria. Elizabeth was England in the newly developing public imagination and on the lips of every person under the age of 50, none of whom had ever uttered the exclamation "God save the King!" Furthermore, a significant portion of the population knew that with the queen died a dearly-held definition of England. More than the end of the Tudor dynasty, Elizabeth's death marked the end of England as the single definition of what Shakespeare's John of Gaunt calls "this stone set in a silver sea." After 1603, the English were forced not only to acknowledge that Scotland was also on that "demi-paradise," but they were also forced to recognize a new national identity, one which included Scotland.

Even as we marvel at the audacity of James for manipulating such a multivalent identity, we must also mark the circumstance of a royal identity so widely recognized that posthumous political manipulation had to incorporate some acknowledgment of the queen's accomplishments. Gone were the days when Henry VII's tame historian could write a history simply declaring Richard III to have been a wicked man. Shakespeare's Richard III is one of the great villains of history precisely because little was known about his person or his politics. People beyond the precincts of Westminster and the City knew of Elizabeth's foreign and domestic accomplishments as well as of her personal identity as the Virgin Queen. Any successful revision of her identity must therefore incorporate at least some version of those facts. Such a revision would therefore be at once more difficult and more invidious.

Elizabeth's burial took place before James entered London, and her body was placed, according to Millington, in the crypt beneath the altar, "in the Sepulchre of her grandfather,"[28] Henry VII, and where her father, Henry VIII, had initially planned his own tomb[29] and next to which her brother, Edward VI, was buried. The death of Elizabeth is chronicled in a number of sources, as is the reaction of her people to her death. Thomas Dekker writes:

> To report her death (like a thunder-clap) was able to kill thousands, it took away hearts from millions: for having brought up (even under her wing) a nation that was almost begotten and borne under her; that never shouted any other *Ave* than for her name, never saw the face of any Prince but her selfe, never understood what that strange out-landish word *Change* signified: how was it possible, but that her sickness should throw abroad an universal fear, and her death an astonishment?[30]

There are also elaborate descriptions of her body being brought by water to Whitehall,[31] of the lying in state, of the funeral procession – including a painted record "with paintings of the standards, banners, coats of arms, and the horses, a painting of the herse,"[32] and a listing of all who marched in the procession.[33] Again, Dekker's account is probably the most florid and famous:

> Never did the English Nation behold so much black worn as there was at her Funeral: It was then but put on, to try if it were fit, for the great

day of mourning was set down (in the book of heaven) to be held afterwards: that was but the dumb show, the Tragical Act hath been playing ever since. Her Herse (as it was borne) seemed to be an Island swimming in water for round it there rained showers of tears."[34]

We have a copy of the funeral sermon,[35] but of the interment itself we have little record beyond a rendering of the mourning tent erected in the Henry VII Chapel for this purpose. The tent is clearly in the nave of the chapel, and the altar is not visible.[36] In a letter from Thomas Lake to Robert Cecil, dated 24 April 1603, there is merely a passing reference to the ceremony and the breaking of the staffs of office:

> I am willed also ... to signify to y[our] h[onor] from the King who is now ready to go to horse that his pleasure is that after the staff broken at the funeral by T.[?] Thomas he shall notwithstanding bring a white staff to Thibalds so that if he need any ... warrants ether your Ho. shall use of the blanks you have, or send hither, & so a warrant shall be sent with all speed by the Lord Thomas ...[37]

Two circumstances are suggested by the wording of this letter. Most of the powerful men of the kingdom were now intent on meeting and pleasing James rather than on mourning the dead queen, whose name is not even mentioned.[38] The other circumstance to be inferred here is that the funeral was unremarkable. This is the reason why so few accounts mention exactly where in the chapel Elizabeth was buried. Everyone expected her to be buried under the altar; she was buried there; and so conventional a tomb called forth no comment, only a few scattered statements of fact. Had she been buried elsewhere, there would have been considerable comment, if only by way of justification. Like her grandfather, Elizabeth's memorial was to be the altar itself.

It was James who gave the orders for Elizabeth's memorial as we see it today, and the results make interesting reading. Not only is Elizabeth's monument now in the north aisle of the Henry VII Chapel; not only has she has thus been distanced from the central monument of Henry VII and buried instead with her half-sister and rival, Mary Tudor: but the choice of the exact spot was a sort of posthumous personal humiliation. We can infer this from the information in the *Westminster Abbey Official Guide* that tells us Elizabeth had so little desire to memorialize her half-sister that "The stones from ... broken altars were piled upon Mary's grave during the whole of her sister's reign."[39]

The monument which James ordered cost a total of £765.[40] As an index to the relative value of that sum, we know that in July 1587 Elizabeth spent £321 14s for Mary Stuart's funeral ceremony at Peterborough. James spent, therefore, little more than twice as much on Elizabeth – and, economically, her sister – as Elizabeth spent on James' mother. The equation will be worth remembering.[41] Elizabeth's tomb was completed in 1606 and is inscribed as follows (in Latin): "Partners both in throne and grave, here rest we two sisters, Elizabeth and Mary, in the hope of one resurrection." Even if this were all the evidence we have of posthumous disempowerment, it would make a powerful statement of James' intention to diminish Elizabeth by thus pairing her with her childless, unpopular, and Catholic sister. The effigy of Elizabeth (there is none of Mary Tudor) was gilded and painted – some records suggest by Hilliard – and certainly grand, but not so very grand when compared to another tomb James commissioned at the same time.

In the south aisle of the chapel James ordered a tomb erected for his mother, Mary Stuart, originally buried in Peterborough Cathedral. Her body was disinterred, then brought by Royal Warrant to Westminster "that the 'like honor might be done to the body of his dearest mother and the like monument extant to her that had been done to others and to his dear sister the late Queen Elizabeth.'"[42] "Like" does not here mean "same" or even "similar." Elizabeth's tomb (Figure 1) is, in the conservative words of the guidebook, "plainer and less sumptuous than that of Mary Queen of Scots."[43] In fact, Mary Stuart's tomb is both taller and wider than Elizabeth's, as the illustration shows, and the arch of Elizabeth's canopy does not cover her whole body, thus forcing bits of her – at the head and feet – into the visual margins of the structure. Mary's arch, on the other hand, frames her effigy perfectly, and, with the monument being so much larger, took much longer to complete and was much more expensive than Elizabeth's. The last recorded figure is an estimate of work yet to be done costing £2,000, and the monument was not completed until 1612. Court and household records of James' reign provide us with further insights as to James' agenda. For one thing, James seems to have been financing the building of Elizabeth's tomb out of the household accounts of his own wife. A letter from the queen's court dated 4 March 1604 to Sir Thomas Lake states that the queen's own accounts could not be paid, but "Rather than fail in payment for Queen Elizabeth's tomb, neither the Exchequer nor London shall have a penny left." The writer went on to "rejoice to falsify the prophecy that no child of Henry VIII should be handsomely buried."[44] And yet it seems that neither London nor the king were leaving their bills unpaid, but rather the queen's. This

Figure 1 The Tombs of Queen Elizabeth I and Mary Queen of Scots, plate 39 from "Westminster Abbey," engraved by Thomas Sutherland, pub. by Rudolph Ackermann (1764–1834) 1811 (aquatint) by Frederick Mackenzie (c.1788–1854) (after). © The Stapleton Collection/ Bridgeman Art Library

casts Queen Anne's notoriously overdrawn accounts in a somewhat different light.

In addition to size and cost, the placement of the tombs is invested with meaning, not just for us as twenty-first-century readers, but for James himself who so carefully claimed dynastic pride of place, the first Stuart with this great-grandfather, the first Tudor. As Jonathan Goldberg says of James' agenda in family portraits, here the "family image functions as an ideological construct."[45] Goldberg argues that James consistently presented himself as:

> Head, husband, father. In these metaphors, James mystified and politicized the body. With the language of the family, James made powerful assertions ... [resting] his claims to the throne in his succession and based Divine Right politics there as well ... [But] unlike his Tudor predecessor, James located his power in a royal line that proceeded from him.[46]

We can see this in the architecture of Westminster as clearly as in the portraits. Following the east-to-west orientation of ecclesiastical architecture, we find that Mary Stuart's tomb is next in line behind that of Lady Margaret Beaufort, Henry VII's mother, and buried in the vault beneath Mary's monument is an impressive collection of Stuart heirs, including Prince Henry and Elizabeth of Bohemia.[47] Behind Mary's tomb is the monument to Margaret, Countess of Lennox, James' paternal grandmother; indeed, James' father is one of the kneelers on the south side of that tomb and has a crown suspended a few inches above his head. James was placing his own mother in a line of fruitful dynasty, while Elizabeth and her equally childless sister were isolated from the line of inherited power. By his placement of Mary Stuart in line with Henry VII's mother Margaret Beaufort, James foregrounds the claim of the Queen of Scots to the throne upon which Elizabeth sat. Mary Stuart was the unquestionably legitimate great-granddaughter of Henry VII; Elizabeth had at one time been declared illegitimate by her own father and was always considered illegitimate by all Catholics. Even as he builds a tomb honoring the Virgin Queen, James reminds the public of this historical reality: virgins do not found or further the greatness of dynasties. Later Stuarts continued this architectural statement of the unity of dynasty (although ultimately fruitless), as the tombs of Charles II, William and Mary, and Queen Anne lie in the south aisle, continuing the line from Margaret Beaufort which was interrupted by those two barren (and now marginalized) Tudor queens.

That James was ultimately more interested in making a revisionist statement for history than for his subjects is borne out by the fact that his mother's second funeral was private, not public. In a letter from the Earl of Northampton to the Viscount Rochester, dated 10 October 1612, we find the following account:

> Though the King's mother's body was brought late to town to avoid a concourse, yet many in the streets and windows watched her entry with honour into the place whence she had been expelled with tyranny. She is buried with honor, as dead rose-leaves are preserved, whence the liquor that makes the kingdom sweet has been distilled.[48]

While it is perfectly clear which side the Earl is on, even he does not dispute the necessity of avoiding a "concourse." Elizabeth was, if anything, more popular in death than in the last years of her reign, and any statement that disempowered her had to be made with the utmost delicacy.[49]

But was that statement so delicately made that it passed unnoticed? James was proud of the tombs he had caused to be built. As Neville Davies notes, in the summer of 1606 when his brother-in-law, Christian IV of Denmark, paid a state visit to England, among the many festivities planned to honor the visitor was a sightseeing tour of London which included the royal tombs at Westminster. Davies argues that since in many of the state processions, records indicate that "'all our Kings Groomes and Messengers of the Chamber'" marched along, "Shakespeare, as one of the King's Men (and therefore ranked as a groom extraordinary of the King's chamber) can be assumed to have been present."[50] Shakespeare's presence may be less of a certainty for the sightseeing tours than for other royal entertainments, but he would certainly have heard of the trip, even if he were not actually present, which brings us to a discussion of one of the plays he wrote that same year. As we examine Shakespeare's *Antony and Cleopatra*, we find evidence that James' architectural revision of history did not go completely unnoticed in the London of 1606.

Greatly to be desired, in this context, would be a letter, diary entry or some other piece of paper with which we could "prove" that the playwright saw the tombs with the kings. But whether or not that was indeed the case, he would certainly have heard of, and could have seen at another time, the relative size and grandeur of the two monuments. In the final scene of Shakespeare's *Antony and Cleopatra*, Shakespeare departs from Plutarch – the source to which he was so faithful – by having Cleopatra carried from her own queenly monument and buried elsewhere as Antony's lover. Octavius (soon to be Augustus) Caesar orders that Cleopatra be buried "by her Antony." Caesar goes on to speak the uncharacteristically romantic lines about the grave which shall hold so famous a pair of lovers, rhetoric which masks the overtly political motives of the immediately preceding lines: "Take up her bed,/ And bear her women from the monument" (V. ii. 356–357).[51]

Queen Cleopatra will not be given the burial of a monarch of Egypt, in her own monument long prepared for that purpose; her burial with Antony, a defeated and disgraced Roman, assures that she will be remembered not as a queen but as a lover. Critics have recently acknowledged the influence on this play of James I's presentation of himself – particularly the so-called "sympathetic" presentation of Caesar in Act V. As we have noted, James, in his coronation pageants and later on coins, styled himself as "the new Augustus." This self-fashioning by James fits well with Shakespeare's portrait of an Octavius who resents the existence of Caesarion, the child of Cleopatra and Julius Caesar, whom, as he complains, "they call my father's son" (III. vi. 5). Octavius, of course, was the nephew of Julius Caesar, for all that he wanted to represent himself as the dead leader's son.

James had no illegitimate offspring of Elizabeth to contend with, but – like Octavius – neither was he the heir to the body of the great ruler. A male ruler whose presence on the throne accomplished the unification of England and Scotland, James felt the need both to acknowledge and distance himself from the female ruler whose death and spoken will made his new power possible. Sir Roy Strong points out that Shakespeare was one of the very few English writers who did not feel the need or desire to write a tribute to Elizabeth at her death in 1603. We have no explicit way of knowing, therefore, how the playwright might have viewed the subsequent apotheosizing of Elizabeth, having nothing but Cranmer's fulsome prophecy of her greatness when she appears as a baby in the final scene of *Henry VIII*, written (although possibly not by Shakespeare) in 1613. Questions of the Shakespeare canon aside, we can read the final scene of *Antony and Cleopatra* (written c.1606–07) as a much more realistic representation of Shakespeare's views on the death and burial of powerful female rulers. Especially since the date of the play's first production provides another link between the interpretation of Roman history and Jacobean politics, written as it was just as Elizabeth's was completed and while the much more elaborate tomb James ordered for his mother, Mary Stuart, was still under construction. Shakespeare's revision of Cleopatra's burial could, therefore, be seen as the first acknowledgement of the shadow of the queen's tomb, James' Elizabeth icon.

Like Elizabeth, Cleopatra's body is placed in a tomb chosen by the man who is taking over her kingdom. And, like James, Shakespeare's Octavius Caesar is concerned with making a statement about that dead queen. Shakespeare engages in a double revision at the end of his play: he has Caesar revise the long-set burial plans for Cleopatra, and while accomplishing this he undertakes a radical revision of Cleopatra's burial as it appears in his primary source, Plutarch's *Lives*.[52] In Plutarch we are never told that Cleopatra is taken from her monument. Antony is brought to her in her monument, he dies there, and Plutarch tells us: "Many Princes, great kings, and Captains did crave Antonius' body of Octavius Caesar, to give him honourable burial, but Caesar would never take it from Cleopatra, who did sumptuously and royally bury him with her own hands."[53] Later Plutarch describes Cleopatra being carried to Antony's grave where she speaks a long and emotional lament.[54] There is nothing to suggest, however, that this grave is not within Cleopatra's monument. Indeed, she seems never to have left the monument, for when she writes to Caesar just before her death, she sends the message, according to Plutarch, "written and sealed unto Caesar, and commanded them all [those who dined with her] to go out of the tombs where she was, but [for] the two women: then she shut the door."[55] Therefore, when Plutarch later states: "Now Caesar, though he was marvellous sorry for the death of Cleopatra, yet he wondered at her noble mind and courage, and therefore commanded she should be nobly buried, and laid by Antonius,"[56] we must conclude that this burial took place within her own monument. We must also note that Plutarch's version of Caesar's admiration for Cleopatra is a far cry from Shakespeare's Caesar who speaks not of her "noble mind and courage" but of grace and beauty and charm and who orders: "Take up her bed,/ And bear her women from the monument" (V. ii. 356–357), clearly implying that this grave, which will "clip" in it this pair unsurpassed, is very much elsewhere.

In Shakespeare's play we find a number of James Stuart's concerns and goals foregrounded by the Roman conquest of Cleopatra. While it is true that Cleopatra was not ruling a country independent of the Roman Republic, it is also true that James was not the conqueror of the queen he succeeded. The task of distancing himself from his predecessor was therefore more difficult and more delicate; his goal of diminishing her importance – a natural phenomenon of conquest – required that as much thought be given to tact as to tactics. Further and finally, we see that in both the play and the politics this hegemonic concept of male-defined dynastic continuity is both literally and metaphorically built upon the space created by the marginalization of a dead woman ruler of iconic status.

Nevertheless, in both the play and the politics we find the paradigm of displaced female power linked to male pseudo-dynastic empire building – "pseudo-" because James' thrice-removed Tudor blood was at least as problematic as Octavius/Augustus' indirect relationship to Julius Caesar; in both the play and the politics the paradigm of political self-fashioning is employed to give the illusion of historical inevitability.

How did James get away with all of this? The answer, I believe, lies in the function of Westminster Abbey – a semi-private space used for state occasions, but not readily or regularly visited by the more common of the king's subjects. Ironically, an official account of James' own funeral describes it by comparing it to Elizabeth's: "The Ceremonial was like Queen Elizabeth's (allowing for the different Sex) but more attended."[57] (And how, we might well wonder, does a burial "allow for the different Sex"?) As for the better attendance, we must remember that no one had to ride to Scotland to inform the next ruler that his day had come. King Charles would have attended his father's service in the Abbey.

Fuller's famous description of the veneration of Elizabeth's tomb refers to a tomb which was not hers, but made to diminish the queen's place in history. That Shakespeare's revision of Plutarch celebrates (without ever mentioning) that same tomb as an act of marginalization, is such a staggering irony that indignation (almost) evaporates in the face of wonder at such successful revisionism. We may be appalled at what James did, and dismayed at his success evinced by the centuries it has gone unnoticed, but both his efforts and his success are, in a round-about way, a tremendous tribute to the power of Elizabeth's own iconic presence. James had to remake that icon with one of his own; we find it hard to credit that anyone could have revised so powerful an image as the sun without which there is no rainbow.

By making his own tomb seem natural, James Stuart constructs the phenomenon of a powerful woman as unnatural. Here, sadly, he may still have history on his side. His Westminster monuments still constitute the primary texts; such correction as this chapter may accomplish will be but a scholarly footnote,[58] read as marginalia not marble. Elizabeth's image, here an effigy completed within three years of her death, is immeasurably removed from the political statement made by placing her body beside Henry VII's under the altar. We see an icon, the Westminster tomb, that conveys an implicit statement totally at odds with the political and personal power of Queen Elizabeth. We see Elizabeth's icon used both to serve the agenda of James I and to memorialize that misrepresentation with every print of that tomb. Even a mere three years past her reign, Elizabeth's iconic legacy has been taken over by others.

*c.*1620: London parish church Elizabeth memorials

As a site of state ceremonies, Westminster Abbey – especially the Henry VII Chapel, the space most distant from the western entrance – is a fine record of royal and noble agendas; the people of London, however, would have had no influence on the monuments in the Abbey and very little, if any occasion to see them. We must turn, therefore, to the parish churches of London to see the remains of Elizabeth as represented by her subjects. The Revolution, the Great Fire, the Blitz, and the IRA have sequentially removed all traces of memorials to Elizabeth in London parish churches. Fortunately, the 1633 edition of Stow's *Survey of London*[59] is itself a sort of Elizabeth text, as it records the iconic texts on all of the memorials to the dead queen in parish churches within the City of London. Through the lines recorded in Stow, we see Elizabeth the warrior, Elizabeth the heir to Arthur, Elizabeth the saint – or more-than-saint, as many of these memorials seem to fill the emotional, cultural, and physical spaces left vacant by the removal of the altars dedicated to the Virgin Mary, then absent for nearly a century. While many scholars – Frances Yates, perhaps first among them – have argued for an active attempt on the part of Elizabeth to replace Mary – much as Cate Blanchett does in the final scenes of the 1998 film – other scholars have challenged this. Helen Hackett argues that she is going to surpass the limitations of Yates and Roy Strong in their analyses of the relationship between the Cult of the Virgin and the Cult of Elizabeth, but that she will to do so by concentrating on the "literary evidence" of that misinterpreted conflation. Strong and Yates, as we all know, used the visual arts and records of spectacle at least as much, if not more, than they used literature to support their insights, so – while Hackett makes many excellent points in her work – she does not address the issue she acknowledges as central: the visual representations that required not literacy, but an awareness of the traditional uses of church space, to read.[60] Reading the memorials to Elizabeth in London parish churches requires both kinds of literacy – that of the word and that of the symbolic use of sacred space.

The question of the relationship between the images of and references to the Virgin Mary and the images of and references to Queen Elizabeth in London churches is not necessarily an either/or proposition. The arguments of Yates and Strong are impressive, but the questions that Hackett and others have raised – especially about the simple elision of one image onto another – are important. While it is unlikely that even a subconscious desire of seventeenth-century Londoners was the creation of a secular Virgin to worship, the Mary/Elizabeth paradigm still demands careful reading. The easiest point to make is that both are female icons. Any gentle-faced woman in a blue robe would be read as the Virgin Mary, while any proud-faced woman in a ruff, silks, and jewels would be read as the late queen. The cultural desire to provide an anthropomorphic female figure to balance out the non-anthropomorphic God the Father and the physically transcendent Christ the Son is a commonplace of European history of the second common millennium. What keeps the Cult of Mary separate from the Cult of Elizabeth is the decline of a single theology and the rise of nationalism. Not only because the Protestant reformers made the case was Mary ineluctably tied to the Roman Church. Mary, as immaculately conceived woman giving virgin birth, was a creation of the Roman Church in the early second millennium. As the Bible became more and more accessible to the people, both through translation and through printings, the absence of a biblical Maryology would have widened the gap between the Mother Church and a people who sought to confront directly the words in scripture. Mary, moreover, never having existed as she was represented, survived only in the two-dimensional elements of canonical narrative. She was always an icon only, because the historical Mary is all but invisible in the first Christian millennium, and presented in a very limited way in scripture. Elizabeth, on the other hand, far from being a mythic narrative that generated strictly controlled art, was a flesh and blood woman living during the period when Western Europe began to develop memory as a public sphere. Elizabeth had appeared in the developing public sphere of culture and politics, and her memory resonated with that reality. An icon of Elizabeth evoked the history of a real woman, not a theological mystery. As the Church of England distanced itself from the Church of Rome, the construct of Mary was one of the most available images at which to aim critical rhetoric. Indeed, Spenser's *Faerie Queene*, with the wicked Duessa working hand-in-hand with the evil Archimago, gives as vivid a picture as can be imaged of the Pope and his iconic woman, both always plotting to lead good Christians astray.

As the Church of England and more truly Protestant sects would have had little time for Mary, neither would the people of London have sought to identify their late monarch with the female add-on of the papacy. Nationalism, if nothing else, would set Elizabeth's icon not only apart from, but at odds with Mary's generally continental and specifically Roman origin. While many of the great cathedrals of France were Mary churches, the cathedrals of England were not. In addition to the theological problems generated by Mary, there was the larger issue of nationalism: Mary simply wasn't English. Elizabeth was entirely English.

"She was, and is/ what can there more be said?/ On Earth the Chiefe,/ in heaven the second Maid." This statement from the memorial, ironically or not, in the parish church of St. Mary le Bow does not replace Mary with Elizabeth, nor does it identify one with the other. In the Bible there is no talk of Mary as the Queen of Heaven. Here, by calling her a Maid, those who penned and carved this much-used epitaph were able to achieve a sort of hierarchical equity. Mary was an earthly Maid of no particular distinction save her spiritual worthiness. She is in Heaven before Elizabeth and arguably "higher" in heaven due to her role in Biblical narratives. Elizabeth was "Chiefe" Maid on the Earth, as Mary never could have been. In the great dichotomy of Earth as the shadow of Heaven, Elizabeth would thus come second in the afterlife. But second only to Mary.

That these representations of Elizabeth are very different from those found in the semi-private space of the Henry VII Chapel is telling. James' revision of Elizabeth may have had its effect within the court circles and within the larger frame of English history as read from monuments in public spaces, but the parish church memorials – erected between 1607 and 1631 – give us a reading of the dead queen more consistent with the representations produced in her lifetime than with those commissioned by her successor. Here we see not the shadow of James' icon tomb, but the light of the sun queen of the Rainbow portrait illuminating the memories of her people and their immediate descendants.

Here we turn from the texts of the Westminster tombs themselves – texts in marble, as are the Saint Denis tombs of which James would have been aware – to the words written on the tombs. These literal texts show that, while James was willing to make the radical revision of moving Elizabeth's body, he was more careful to bow to convention in the words carved on the revised tomb. The words James caused to be carved on Elizabeth's newly marginalized tomb are (literally) politically correct, if one overlooks the fact of the tomb's location, the spacing of the phrase "Principi incomparabili," and the left-handed compliment about her gender. Translated from the Latin in which they appear and with modernized spelling, we can read James' commissioned inscription. At her head:

AN ETERNAL MEMORIAL

Unto *Elizabeth* Queene of *England*, *France*, and *Ireland*, Daughter of *Henry* the eighth, Grandchild to *Henry* the seventh, great Grandchild to King *Edward* the fourth, the Mother of this her country, the Nurse of Religion and Learning; For a perfect skill in very many Languages, for glorious Endowments, as well of mind as body, and for Regal Virtues beyond her Sex

a Prince incomparable,

James, King of Great Britain, France and Ireland, heir of the virtues and the reign, piously erects this good monument

At her feet:

Sacred unto Memory:

Religion to its primitive sincerity restored, *Peace* thoroughly settled, *Coin* to the true value refined, *Rebellion* at home extinguished, *France* near ruin by intestine mischiefs relieved, *Netherland* supported, *Spaines* Armada vanquished, *Ireland* with Spaniards expulsion, and *Traitors* correction quieted, both *Universities* Revenues, by a Law of Provision, exceedingly augmented, Finally, all *England* enriched, and 45. years most prudently governed, *Elizabeth*, a Queene, a Conqueresse, Triumpher, the most devoted to Piety, the most happy, after 70. years of her life, quietly by death departed.

James, for a number of obvious reasons, needed to choose his words with care as he described both himself and the monarch whose death gave him the throne of England. If gender and virginity were her weak points, nationalism was his, as we see in the change from "England" in the lines about Elizabeth to "Great Britain" in the lines James tacked on about himself. Evidently, even in 1606, he still needed this emphasis, just as he had in that 1604 speech to Parliament with the Lancaster-York references at the heart of his argument. The Henry VII Chapel – indeed, Westminster Abbey itself – was not a place of public worship. This is why the memorials to Elizabeth in the City churches can give us a much better grasp of the public's icon of the dead queen. There is some disagreement among scholars as to the earliest revival of Elizabeth's popularity after the construct of a male monarch with children had ceased to be in itself a cause for uncritical popular approval. Neville Davies and others place the revival of Elizabeth's popularity around 1607, while Sir Roy Strong tells us that – after the flurry of images generated in 1603 – the 1620s marked the next "revival of interest shown in her as reflected in the engravings."[61]

There was little or none before that date as the country was entranced with the phenomenon of a royal family replacing a virgin queen. That revival coincided with the decline in popularity of Stuart rule and the outbreak of the Thirty Years War. Elizabeth then became a golden age ruler and the posthumous heroine of the Protestant cause.[62]

These dates correspond with the dates listed in the 1633 edition of Stow's *Survey of London* for the restorations of many churches within the City. Stow's listing, as valuable as it is, has two drawbacks: it does not say when a particular memorial to Elizabeth was erected, giving only the date(s) for some churches' general restoration, nor do the compilers of the *Survey* mention where in a church the memorial is placed. A partial listing of restorations with specific dates shows that most of the construction did indeed take place in or around the 1620s:

1605–09:	–	1620–24:	8
1610–14:	2	1625–29:	7
1615–19:	3	1630–33:	5

In only nine of the 32 churches listed do we find any direct reference to the official Abbey epitaphs, and those are always conflated and always translated and almost always shortened. The complete texts of the Westminster tombs were published in works by Camden, Stow himself, and others, so they were popularly available to be copied by persons who never entered Westminster Abbey. That fewer than a third of the City memorials listed in Stow include texts from the Westminster tombs suggests that James' revisionist representation of Elizabeth was less successful than he might have hoped, at least with Londoners, during his reign and the reign of his son. When we compare the two sorts of representation – the officially political and semi-private and Latin with the popularly political and public and vernacular – we find informative differences. Nor were these memorials limited to churches within the walls of the City. These City churches provide meaningful examples because Stow claims to provide a complete listing, whereas his records for other churches in what we might now call the greater London area are selective.

However different such public representations of the dead queen may have been in the first three decades of the seventeenth century, it is the Westminster tomb which makes the official statements and which has endured as the primary text. Fewer than five of the memorials listed in Stow survived the damage of the Revolution and the Great Fire, and those crumbled in the Blitz. The 1993 Bishopsgate bomb took out the oldest sections of the one church which claimed some remaining *c.*1620 bits. The resistance of the Abbey's present Keeper of the Muniments to the idea that Elizabeth's burial was not as Dean Stanley described crowns James' revisionist history with the success of canonical status. It has become tradition. And this, ultimately, was the same sort of recognition sought by Henry VII, who could not have hoped for his immediate background and the politics of the War of the Roses to evaporate from the minds of his subjects. The knowledge that the Tudor rose was a forced graft has faded with time. Although Elizabeth's fame has outshone her resting place, James I can also claim a great victory as a revisionist author of socio-history.

While Stow neither gives the date of (almost) any specific memorial nor makes the distinction between a church which was restored in the 1620s and a memorial that might have been added later, his *Survey* still remains our best – indeed, our only – guide to a valuable cultural parallel: texts forming a populist Elizabeth icon. The fact that only the 1633 edition of the *Survey* lists the tomb texts can be used in support of their currency, but it could also suggest that they had become such a conventional feature of churches that they needed to be catalogued. Or, to carry speculation further, the memorials may have become so popular that they were a selling point for this edition, which would explain their being mentioned on the extensive title page. All in all, there are many problems with basing chronological arguments on the listing in Stow, and we would be unwise in trying to build on such shaky ground. What we can do is to look at the public words in the parish church as they both reflect the light of Elizabeth's own image and skirt the shadow of James' own iconic representation of Elizabeth, the Westminster tomb.

So let us look at those memorializing texts. Of the 30 varied inscriptions in Stow's list, two elements of these memorial texts generate images of Elizabeth that could certainly be called icons: those which speak of Elizabeth's immortality in a way which passes conventional Christian discourse and those which speak of Elizabeth as a warrior. Actually, there is a third topic, but it is a topic which might be described as an absent presence: Elizabeth's famed learning. Only three of the memorials quote any version of the problematic lines from the Westminster tomb, "a perfect skill in very many Languages, for glorious Endowments, as well of mind as body, and for Regal Virtues beyond her Sex." The memorial in St. Anne Blackfryers quotes this exactly, praising the queen for her "perfect skill in very many Languages, for glorious Endowments, as well of mind as body, and for Regall Vertues beyound her Sex."[63] Similarly, the monument in St. Martin's Vintry translates the end of the line: "inbuded with rare Ornaments of Body and Minde, in all Princely Vertures above the Sex of Women."[64] Only slightly more promising is the memorial in St. Mary le Bow, which adds the somewhat ambiguously placed Westminster line: "A Prince incomparable,"[65] here referring both visually and grammatically to Elizabeth. No other church memorials evince the need to praise Elizabeth's intellectual accomplishments. Six churches have the following poem:

> Here lies her Type, who was of late,
> The prop of Belgia, stay of France,
> Spaines foile, Faith's shield, and Queene of State,
> Armes, of Learning, Fate, and Chance:
> In briefe,of Women ne're was seen,
> > So great a Prince, so good a Queene.

The phrase "Queen of ... Armes, of Learning, Fate, and Chance," seems to group learning with the latter two entities, leaving only Armes to be mentioned singularly. But if Elizabeth the intellectual was not a hot topic for memorial texts, Elizabeth the warrior was.

To represent Elizabeth as a woman warrior while she was alive was a delicate proposition. Spenser, perhaps, comes the closest when he gives us Britomart in the *Faerie Queene*. For all that we make much of the speech at Tilbury, we have no portraits of Elizabeth dressed in any form of armor during her lifetime. Even in the Armada portrait (1588) she is clad in one of the most elaborate of her fictive dresses, with a large pearl revising the iconic statement of her father's large codpiece.[66] After her death, however, we have the *c.*1625 engraving entitled "Truth Presents the Queen with a Lance." Here Elizabeth is mounted on a war-horse, dressed in armor and holding a sword and shield in her left hand as she receives the said lance with her right. Behind her is the Armada victory. Although this representation was produced in response to a particular moment in British history, the debate around the Spanish Match, by its very nature it was destined to become a popular icon. It is this representation of Elizabeth as Amazon, barely acknowledged in the conventional words of the Westminster tomb, that we find significantly exaggerated in the City church memorials.

By far the most popular text on these memorials is the passage from 2 Timothy beginning: "I have fought a good fight ... " Granted, this is a very conventional epitaph, but two elements of its use here need to be considered. First, it appears on all but nine of the 32 memorials. Second, it most often appears only as a fragment, ending with "I have kept the faith." If it did not appear so consistently, its significance would not support such emphatic attention. But since the passage is used in 23 of the memorials – 14 times as the only citation from scripture – its emphasis on the dead queen as a warrior (more than a merely spiritual soldier in the battle of life) is significant. Reading the passage with the second-most-frequently reproduced text "Spain's rod ... " certainly adds force to the argument that the citizens of London wanted to remember their queen as, at least in part, a warrior.

> Spaines rod, Romes ruine
> Netherlands reliefe,
> Heaven Jem, Earths Joy,
> Worlds wonder, Natures Chiefe.
> Britaines blessing, Englands splendor.
> Religions Nurse, the Faiths Defender.

Although worth noting in this text is the use of Britain and England as national entities that can be read as discrete or synonymous.

In the Stow listings, we find a number of additions to this representation of Elizabeth as the Rod which subdued Spain. More popular than the translations from the Westminster tomb, this ditty appears in eleven memorials, four of which also include some version of the Westminster texts. Also popular – appearing six times and, interestingly enough, never with either of the Westminster epitaphs or with "Spain's rod" – is this text:

> Here lies her Type, who was of late,
> The prop of Belgia, stay of France,
> Spaines foile, Faith's shield, and Queene of State,
> Armes, of Learning, Fate, and Chance:
> In briefe, of Women ne're was seen,
> So great a Prince, so good a Queene.

The description of Elizabeth as the "Queene of Armes, of Learning, Fate, and Chance" is perhaps the strongest praise we have seen, and owes nothing to the state tomb in Westminster. In three of these churches[67] we also find the only appearances of the Arthurian statement "She is not dead, but sleepeth," and in four churches "Here lies her Type" is followed by this six-line poem:

> Sith Vertues Her immortall made,
> Death (envying all that cannot dye)
> Her earthy parts did so invade,
> As in it wrackt selfe Majesty.
> But so her Spirit inspir'd her Parts,
> That she still lives in loyall hearts.

There seems to be no clear common ground between these five churches – St. Martin Orgars, St. Michael Queenhithe, St. Michael Querne, St. Laurence Jurie, and St. Michael Woodstreet – but we might speculate that the lack of a common bond between these churches indicates that this strong feeling for Elizabeth as a warrior was more general than other sources appreciate.

The next two texts are unique. Not only does each appear in only one church, but the people who commissioned the monuments in St. Mildred Breadstreet and All Hallows at the Wall evidently felt little or no need to reproduce texts used elsewhere. In the St. Mildred's memorial, there are no texts from other memorials; at All Hallows the only additional text is the ubiquitous "I have fought a good fight." The memorial in St. Mildred's is part of an extremely elaborate representation of English history. Stow describes a number of windows, one dealing with Elizabeth and the Armada. Each window evidently had a poem describing it.

> Marvell not why
> we do erect this Shrine,
> Since dedicated tis
> to Worth divine;
> Religion, Arts,
> with Policy and Armes,
> Did all concurre
> in her most happy raigne,
> To keepe Gods Church and us
> from plotted harmes,
> Contriv'd by Romish wits,
> and force of Spaine.

Here Elizabeth is credited with both "Policy and Armes" as she kept the country safe from "plotted harmes, Contriv'd by Romish wits, and force of Spaine." Although the facts set forth here are not radically different from those formal phrases on the Westminster tomb, the language is more colloquial and the presence of the stained glass turns the entire memorial into a popular history lesson. Furthermore, this victory over Rome and Spain is seen as Elizabeth's major accomplishment, an accomplishment which allows the author to call the queen "divine." And, as with Saint Peter's keys or Saint Catherine's wheel, the Armada was so associated with Queen Elizabeth that it becomes part of the icon itself.

The memorial in All Hallows at the Wall, although lacking the medium of stained glass, provides us with the most interesting representation of Elizabeth as a warrior.

> Read but her Reigne,
>   this Princesse might have beene
> For wisdome called
>   Nicaulis, Sheba's Queene,
> Against Spaines Holifernes,
>   Judeth shee,
> Dauntlesse gain'd many
>   a glorious victory:
> Not Deborah did her
>   in fame excell,
> She was a Mother
>   in our Israel.
>
> An Hester, who
>   her person did ingage,
> To save her people
>   from the publike [rage];
> Chaste Patronesse
>   of true Religion,
> In Court a Saint,
>   in Field an Amazon,
> Glorious in Life,
>   deplored in her death,
> Such was unparallel'd
> ELIZABETH.

In the first place, her reign itself is represented as a text: "Read but her Reigne," the poem begins. Furthermore, the text of her reign is represented as being filled with allusions to biblical texts of women leaders – the Queen of Sheba, Judith, Deborah, Esther. Of course Elizabeth had been compared to these biblical women throughout her reign – indeed, Helen Hackett, in her 1995 study, states that "biblical heroines like Deborah and

Judith dominated early Elizabethan royal iconography."[68] This Judith reference, however, moves beyond the boundaries of the conventional, or at least moves into another convention, for this allusion draws on the more violent aspects of the Judith narrative, and the paradigm of Judith the woman who kills is much less commonly represented than the paradigm of Judith, the humble servant of the Lord.

For a quick fix on the two Judith paradigms, we need a brief digression back to medieval France. In the thirteenth-century sculpture on the north portal of the cathedral at Chartres, there is an archivolt devoted to the Judith story. There, however, Judith is represented as a humble widow doing the will of the elders of the city, completing a task which was only possible for her because she was a beautiful woman. Later in the same century, when Blanche of Castile – who had been shown the newly completed Chartres sculptural program early in her marriage – collaborated with her son Louis IX on the stained glass for the Sainte-Chapelle, a much different representation was crafted. The Sainte-Chapelle windows graphically celebrate Judith's physical triumph over Holofernes; the bloody head is clearly visible both at the moment of decapitation and later – most unusually – displayed on the tip of Judith's sword. The archivolt at Chartres gives us a very different version of the story, with the most-often-reproduced voussoir figure being that of Judith kneeling, dressed in sack-cloth, putting ashes on her head, the humble servant of the patriarchy who is never shown holding the head of the dead enemy.

While these two French representations of Judith have no direct influence on the various constructions of Elizabeth as a Judith figure, we can easily make the same distinction between them. Early in her reign Elizabeth is the dutiful woman most unusually called on by God to serve her people in a public way. The Judith figure of the memorial text of this Elizabeth icon, however, fits better the fierce paradigm of the Sainte-Chapelle windows. Both representations are based on the biblical narrative, but the choice of emphasis makes an enormous difference. In the memorial in All Hallows at the Wall, Elizabeth is called a Judith who "Against Spaines Holifernes ... Dauntlesse gain'd many a glorious victory." Arguably the strongest female figure in Hebrew scripture (although banished from canonical bibles by the seventeenth century), Judith is one of the very few women in the Western canon celebrated for killing a man. To describe Elizabeth as a Judith who kills Holofernes is to go far beyond the more traditional biblical type of Deborah. Deborah, of course, also went into battle, and even the story of Esther (traditionally paired with the Judith narrative in medieval iconography) is here given more active overtones by the phrase "her person did ingage, To save her people." This martial reading of the texts is made inescapable by the strongest lines in the poem; near the end of this memorial, Elizabeth is called "In Court a Saint, in Field an Amazon." This representation of the dead queen is so far removed from the formal language of the Westminster tomb that we cannot read it as merely popularized or simplified: this is corrective. To conflate the hagiographic with the classical in so uncompromising a statement is to oppose the official Westminster representation of Elizabeth as an accomplished but unique woman. Among the ranks of saints many heroic women can be found, and, of course, the ranks of Amazons are wholly female. In this memorial verse we are asked to read her reign as we would read the stories of other great women warriors. She is "unparallel'd," but not alone.[69]

Similarly, we find in the inscriptions dealing with her immortality a sense of Elizabeth being one of a select company while having no peer among contemporary mortals of either gender. The text of St. John Baptist, "Vertue liveth after death,/ So doeth Queene Elizabeth," can be read as a simple statement of Christian life after death, as can "She is not dead, but sleepeth," in St. Martin Orgars, St. Michael Queenhithe and St. Michael Quern, although the Arthurian overtones of these deserve some consideration. The most radical statements are – "Queene Elizabeth both was, and is alive, what then more can be said? In Heaven a Saint, in Earth a blessed Maid" from St. Michael Crookedlane and "She was, and is/ what can there more be said?/ On Earth the Chiefe,/ in heaven the second Maid" in St. Mary le Bow – each appearing only once, and each in a different church. Both statements, however, so similar in syntax, appear in the political writings of the period as examples of public feeling about the dead queen, leading us to the conclusion that their representation as church memorials was the result, rather than the source, of their popularity. Frances Yates, in her nearly canonical study *Astraea*,[70] makes much of these texts in the literature of the period, as does Roy Strong.[71] Current scholarship on Elizabeth questions their easy equation between the cult of the virgin and the cult of Gloriana; in particular, Helen Hackett's study raises a number of valid objections to this simple reading of a complex relationship. Hackett, however, limits herself to literary representation – which makes her scorn for Yates and Strong a bit overstated, as they rely heavily on the portraits. While she makes a compelling case for revising our thinking on the notion that Elizabeth filled a sort of "post-Reformation gap in the psyche of the masses, who craved a symbolic virgin-mother figure,"[72] I would suggest that a text inscribed in a church cannot be evaluated in exactly the same light as a literary text.

This listing of memorials allows us to see how the wealthy merchants in the City parish churches may indeed have fallen back on older protocols when they tried to express their recognition of Elizabeth's place in the universal order. Such statements as these are hard to attribute to mere convention: from St. Mary le Bow,

> Fame blow aloud
>   and to the world proclaime,
> There never ruled
>   such a Royall Dame.

> The Word of God
>   was ever her delight,
> In it she meditated
>   day and night.

> Spaines rod, Romes ruine,
>   Netherlands reliefe,
> Earths joy, Englands Jem,
>   Worlds wonder, Natures chief.

> She was, and is
>   what can there more be said?
> Glorious in Life,
> On Earth the Chiefe,
>   in heaven the second Maid.

and from St. Mary Woollchurch and St. Mildred Poultrey,

> Th'admired Princesse [or Empresse]
>   through the world applauded,
> For supreme Vertues
>   rarest imitation;
> Whose Scepters rule, Fame
>   loud voic'd Trump hath lauded,
> Unto the eares
>   of every forraigne Nation,
> Canopied under
>   powerfull Angels wings,
> To her immmortall praife
>   sweet Science sings.

and yet another from St. Mildred Poultrey,

> If prayers or teares
>   of subjects had prevail'd,
> To save a Princesse
>   through the world esteem'd,
> Then Atropos
>   in cutting here had fail'd,
> And had not cut her thred,
>   but been redeem'd,
> But pale fac'd Death,
>   and cruell churlish Fate,
> To Prince and people
>   brings the latest date.
> Yet spite of Death and Fate,
>   Fame will display
> Her gracous Vertues
>   through the world for aye.

Although I would say that, by providing such textual tributes to the icon of Elizabeth, the vestries of these City churches "may indeed have fallen back on older protocols," I do not think that Maryolotry is necessarily the intended paradigm. The figure of the life-giving lady goes back through Persephone to Gaia. The reference to Atropos, the classical personification of the third Fate, the woman with the shears who cuts the thread of life, is part of an older trinity than that associated with Mary. It is the prayers and tears of her subjects that would protect Elizabeth from the cut of Atropos "and cruell churlish Fate"; Elizabeth's own fame – for virtues gracious, not specifically Christian – will spite Fate and Death (Fate having nominally no place in a Christian paradigm) and eternalize the queen's greatness throughout the world forever.

No, I'm not suggesting that this is a deliberate attempt to elide classical values onto a Christian monument. But, while the public sphere of Christian memory offers only one woman in a position of some power and much glory, the classical world offers a wider field. What I think we see here is the attempt to assemble an Elizabeth icon from the available materials of cultural history, so to speak. That there are more useful allusions in the classics than in the Christian canon should not lead us to conclude that the latter system is being rejected in favor of classicism. What we do need to acknowledge, however, is that – other than Mary – Christians had no specifically New Testament females on which to draw.

That Mary is indeed "alone of all her sex," makes her, I would suggest, a default choice, not a pattern.

Pictures, of course, would be extremely helpful at this point. Stow's descriptive record of the monuments is not analytical (except in a relative sense – i.e. this is the biggest or the finest or the most ornate monument), but to the reader who has some knowledge of church architecture it is clear that these monuments were constructed both physically and imaginatively – if not theologically – to replace the lately displaced Lady chapels. Scholars have long cited the tag line of Elizabeth's apotheosis: "on Earth the first maid; in Heaven the second." Yes, but, as I have argued, what choice did the authors of such texts have in an ecclesiastical setting? Similarly, while the removal of Mary chapels and altars may well have provided appropriate space for the later Elizabeth monuments, this does not mean that one was meant literally, or even metaphorically, simply to replace the other. And the cultural artifacts recorded in Stow allow us to see that this concept – even if problematic – may have been literally a social construction. In a period where political and religious lines were blurred, conflated, re-drawn, and re-blurred, the texts of Elizabeth's tombs and memorials allowed her to be re-constructed within agendas grounded more in socio-theology than political history.

That the iconic texts of the people differ from the icon of James Stuart is a point that hardly needs a chapter for its making. Each set of representations grows from social and political circumstances of which we are aware in other contexts. Reading Stuart history as we read the tombs of the dead Tudor Queen gives us another slant on the issue of the feeling of Londoners for their king. Reading the words of the memorials – almost lost to us by the passage of time – in relation to the enduring and now canonical images of the Westminster tombs gives us some insight into the political uses men can make of powerful women, even in death. Icons, as we shall see, are not always constructed for veneration.

1620–1660:
The Shadow of Divine Right

Elizabeth as an icon of monarchy

As James spent nearly two decades establishing his place as both the rightful and logical monarch of England by constructing himself as the heir of Henry VII, he simultaneously rendered Henry VIII and his children as a dynastic dead-end, a splendid sideshow in the fabled parade of English history. But, as the elaborately painted ceiling of the Stuart Banqueting Hall was meant to illustrate, the main force of dynasty, destiny, and domination was now back in control of an enlarged and enlightened kingdom. A kingdom, after all, is still quintessentially a kingdom, even if it is temporarily ruled by a queen or two. The next logical move for James – not that he waited until nearly two decades of rule had passed – was to make a place for himself as a, if not the, major power on the European scene. Approving the marriage of his daughter Elizabeth to Frederick was a gesture in this direction, albeit a gesture that backfired. The plans that James had built upon the future of his heir, Prince Henry, had to be reconstructed – literally downsized for the diminutive younger brother – for the new heir, Prince Charles. Making a power-laden marriage for Charles was an obvious first move.

In the long-running debates over the Spanish Match, a multifaceted dispute which concerned nearly all politically-aware people of Britain for the first half of the seventeenth century's third decade, we find the Elizabeth icon fashioned by the late queen herself in conflict with the iconic tomb James constructed, and both iconic evocations immediately appropriated for conflicting agendas in politics, art, and religion. Although the main focus of this debate was a proposed marriage – which generated negative reactions combining anti-Catholic and anti-Spanish feeling and positive responses based on economic and royalist issues – the religious and the political elements of the dispute spilled over into a wider range of both related and seemingly unrelated topics. From ballads sung in the streets, to stage plays and imaginary heavenly dialogues, the topic of the possible marriage of Prince Charles to the daughter of the King of Spain was one of those topics upon which everyone had an opinion, informed or not. King James was so acutely aware of his subjects' heated opinions on the topic that he issued in August of 1622 the *Directions to Preachers*, officially banning the subject from pulpits; the king subsequently asked John Donne, the Dean of St Paul's, to preach at St. Paul's Cross on 15 September in support of this gag order.[1]

While scholars tend to think of and discuss the Spanish Match as a topic of the 1620s, it was in 1611 that James first raised the question of Prince Henry marrying a Spanish princess. Nothing came of that suggestion, but the arrival of a new Spanish ambassador in 1613, Don Diego Sarmiento da Acuña (later and more famously known as the influential Count Gondomar) revived the question, although the groom was now, of course, Prince Charles, Henry having died the year before. A number of political conflicts caused the discussion to fall by the diplomatic wayside, but when Gondomar returned again to London seven years later, he was quickly able to place the issue back on the table.[2] Gondomar's influence is almost impossible to overestimate, combining as it did very considerable personal charm with wit and shrewd political judgment.[3] Both generally and specifically, Gondomar made his mark on English politics – negotiating significant concessions for English Catholics and bringing about the execution of Sir Walter Raleigh – furthermore, he successfully kept peace between England and Spain at a time when people of both countries were inclined toward war. Gondomar encouraged James' dependence on the Duke of Buckingham, while charming Buckingham into carrying out an agenda calculated to make both Englishmen look foolish. The one thing that both Gondomar and Buckingham had in common was power; and that made them both unpopular with the people beyond their immediate charmed circle. Bald asserts that Gondomar was genuinely fond of the English.[4] If that were true, he had a strange way of showing it.

The proposed marriage between Prince Charles and the Infanta of Spain was certainly an ongoing issue during in the first half of the 1620s, but its importance in the greater scheme of English politics is a matter of some debate. In his painstaking and relentlessly focused study of the actions of Stuart Parliaments,[5] Conrad Russell downplays the concern over an actual marriage, making the discourse of marital union into a stalking-horse for other issues, especially in 1621. Suggesting that the "chief concerns of the members of the court were with three things which never happened," Russell presents the issue of the Spanish Match as a more personal conflict between James and his son, Charles. While Russell names the three concerns of the court as "a war which did not happen, … an attack on the Duke of Buckingham which never got off the ground," and any sign that Prince Charles might be leaning toward Rome, he goes on to observe that, popularly, the "mystifying phenomenon" of a dearth of silver coinage, both extremely unnerving and evidently inexplicable, was the county's greatest single focus of concern.[6] When James asked Parliament, early in 1621, to find the reason for this shortage, a reason which had eluded both king and Council, all those involved "seized the chance to blame their favorite scapegoats, ranging from Catholics sending out money to educate their children abroad to smokers allowing their money to be carried out of the kingdom for the import of tobacco" to the foremothers of ladies who lunch for coming to the capital to spend too much change on frocks and rocks.[7] As Parliament adjourned for the summer on 4 June 1621, Sir Edward Coke interrupted the cool and cultured prose of the Book of Common Prayer's invocation for the safety of the king's children with a heated ejaculation to "'Almighty God, who has promised to be a Father to thine Elect', and the House cried 'Amen, Amen'."[8] This theatrical outburst was a sign not of reasoned concern, but of emotional reaction to a conditioned stimulus: the threat of Spain, and behind Spain, Rome. Most of these men had been alive during the time of the Armada, and it was to that image they responded: to an icon of what it is to be English. Russell compares this frenzied view to the phenomenon of Foxe's *Book of Martyrs*, saying that this popular mix of the Protestant and the patriotic was "something familiar to fall back on as a touchstone in time of strong emotion."[9] Russell caps this shrewd bit of cultural analysis by concluding that if James were carefully observing this session of Parliament, "his reluctance to go to war [with Spain] can only have been increased."[10]

Nor might that have been James' only problem with the question of war. Even with the death of King Philip III of Spain in March, the expiration of Spain's Twelve Years' Truce with the Dutch in April, the new Spanish government's increase in the size of its fleet in the Atlantic, and the November advance of General Spinola (commissioned by the Emperor and paid by Spain) to invade the Palatine, the most serious issue in James' eyes may have been the Emperor's decision to go ahead and deprive his son-in-law, Frederick, his claim as Elector of Palatine. Between the threat(s) to his son-in-law's positions, present and future, and the question of his son's marriage in this, the third year of the Thirty Years War, James, perhaps understandably, claimed illness and stayed in Newmarket with fast horses and Buckingham. It was in this climate that the issue of a Spanish marriage took on the weight of a debate over free speech and the king's power to curb it.

Ironically, it was one of Parliament's more outspoken proponents of a general war with Spain, John Crew, who, in the fall of 1621 – while making it clear that he wasn't speaking for the king – was the first member of the House to mention "the taboo topic" of Prince Charles' proposed marriage. Russell points out that the Commons' silence on James' hopes and plans for a Spanish match had lasted since February, despite both public and political opposition. Even when Crew mentioned the topic in November of 1621, he prefaced his one sentence on the subject with the (admittedly disingenuous) disclaimer: "but this is not fit for me to enter into ... " The ensuing debate gives evidence that neither the members' desire to negotiate with nor to mount a war against Spain was very enthusiastic, although war seems to have had the lead by a short head. But nothing in the debate suggests that those who spoke had any intention of telling the king what to do.[11]

Indeed, the next morning, 27 November, only one member tried to raise the vexed issue again, but was silenced by general consent and a collective desire to get back to other bills. As Russell points out, such silencing "is a sharp contrast to the tolerance shown to similar exuberant speeches in Elizabethan days."[12] Saying that without the benefit of "hindsight, the debates of 26 and 27 November suggest that the anti-Spanish brigade in the Commons were neither large, powerful, nor determined," Russell embarks on a nuanced dissection of the parliamentary exchanges in late November, observing that at their most critical, the speakers merely pointed out that the plans for war and the plans for marriage were incompatible. We might, in fact, suspect that James was looking for a fight, since the issue does seem to have been at least as much one of the king's perception as the Commons' intent. Even the subsequently (in)famous petition of 3 December had only one add-on clause: in a document primarily about fishing was a clause merely expressing the wish "that the prince should be 'timely and happily married to one of our own religion.'"[13] But, as "members at Westminster were still in blithe confidence that they were following the official line ... James at Newmarket was losing his temper."[14]

On 3 December – before receiving the petition from the Commons and only twelve hours after its passage – James composed his angry letter of response, saying that "our distance from the Houses of Parliament ... hath emboldened some fiery and popular spirits [in the Commons] to argue and debate publicly of matters far above their reach and capacity" approaching a "breach of prerogative royal."[15] Although James might not have been able to make up his mind whether to fight with Spain or arrange a Spanish marriage for his heir, clearly he didn't welcome the members of Parliament weighing in on either side.

Of the many questions arising from James' outraged response, perhaps the most interesting is the question of how he knew of the clause so quickly. Sir Edward Sackville, who had warned against the inclusion of the clause in the first place, suggested "that James had been informed 'by a stranger,' [implicitly] Gondomar. [But, by the account of] Sir Richard Weston, Chancellor of the Exchequer, the informant was much nearer home: Charles, Prince of Wales."[16] Russell supports this suggestion, saying that had Charles been the one to express anger to James, feeling that the personal topic of his marriage plans should not be debated in the Commons, this might explain the rapid and furious eruption of the royal temper.[17] Nor is Russell willing to lay this open dispute at the feet of Buckingham, another popular historical reading. Stressing the likelihood of a letter from Charles to James – although he offers no documentation for such a theory and ignores the somewhat disingenuous role in which it casts a Prince of Wales who would think his marriage a private matter – Russell is willing only to allow that: "Buckingham, faced with an angry King on one hand ... may have been tempted to try to keep the quarrel going when it began. He had, after all, no reason to love this Parliament."[18] While Russell argues strongly for Charles as the fuse that ignited his father, other historians think differently. Nevertheless, the outcome, rather than the flash-point, of this anger is of much greater import.

While Russell places the responsibility on Charles, Simon Schama, on the other hand, sees Buckingham as the force manipulating not only James, but also Charles, saying that the Prince's opposition was more likely to be a problem than that of his royal father. Schama suggests:

Charles might have been a tougher nut for Buckingham to crack, being so reserved in his demenour and alienated from the unbuttoned bonhomie of his father, but a special feast that Buckingham gave for him took care of that. Together, Charles and Buckingham managed to persuade James – over what was left of his better judgement – that a way to nail the match was for them to go to Madrid, woo the infanta in person and confront the court there with a *fait accompli*. James was so anxious to avoid a war that he agreed to the hare-brained plan.[19]

Whoever was responsible for James' anger and subsequent decision to seek love, not war, there is no debate over the results of this particular conflict between king and Commons. Deciding not to seek war, that time-worn remedy for domestic problems passed down the centuries from Pericles to Thatcher to George W. Bush, James overlooked the fact that dynastic alliances can cause more lasting conflicts than can combat. So outspoken was the opposition to the marriage that James felt the need to silence it officially.

The issue of free speech (from the Parliamentary point of view) or the right to control debate on the highest matters of state (the king's point of view) became more important a conflict than any of the historical specifics which sparked it. Although neither side had intended for free speech to become a, if not the, crucial issue in this conflict, the very care which the Commons had expended on trying not to offend the king now produced an understandable resentment, matching James' expressed outrage that his royal right to have the last word was being questioned. As Russell reminds us, it was no small issue for the Commons to "sign on the royal dotted line, and announce that they had no right to discuss issues which did not please the King," for if they abandoned their claim to freedom of speech, they could find they were abandoning their power to make law. [20]

And where is Elizabeth in all this?

Everywhere.

In the link with Spain, we see clearly how the image of the late Gloriana became such a powerful marker on both sides of this dispute. Gardiner tells us of the House of Commons' 1621 opposition to the possibility that "a Spanish Infanta was to become the future Queen of England, and the mother of a stock of English kings. In the course of nature her child would within forty or fifty years be seated on the throne of Henry and Elizabeth."[21] But James, in his attempt to stop protests from the Commons – an attempt which culminated in the dissolution of 1621 – also cited Elizabeth, but as an authority for restraining debate in the House, as she did in both 1588 and 1593. As Gardiner points out, however, these dates did not constitute fair parallels to the situation with which James was coping.

> In times of excitement, as in 1588 ... and in 1593, when the shouts of triumph were still ringing in the ears of her subjects, [Elizabeth] had had her way. Such a view of the case, however, was not likely to be taken by James. The right to interfere had been maintained by his predecessor. His dignity would suffer if he abandoned it on any pretext whatever.[22]

As the situation worsened in the summer of 1622, the question of the opinion of the people, as well as the opinion of the House of Commons, arose. Lacking BBC *News 24*, the people of England were not aware of every nuance of this situation. But, they did have a sense that, rather than elevating Britain to Imperial status on the world stage, James had diminished the standing of the English crown to such an extent that England's very laws were being dictated by foreign politicians with Roman agendas (read "Gondomar") and that the king was "thus undoing the sense of national identity so carefully cultivated by the Tudors," to say nothing of their religious reform: "the great cause of which Henry VIII and Elizabeth had been the champions. In the eyes of posterity, the rhetoric of the Commons predicted, James would be found guilty of defiling the sacred cause of religious liberty by making bargains over it for Spanish gold and Spanish aid."[23]

Perhaps the most telling of the public reactions is John Reynolds' 1624 pamphlet *Vox Coeli, or News from Heaven*, in which he wittily presents a discussion (later "published in Elisium") among Henry VIII, Edward VI, Mary and Elizabeth Tudor, Anne of Denmark, and Prince Henry on the topic of Charles' proposed marriage to the Infanta. In this text Elizabeth speaks of the victory of her country "against the pride and malice of Spane, who grew mad with anger and pale with griefe, to see this his great and warlike armado beaten, foyled, and confounded," while lamenting that James has now let "my royall-navy lye rotting."[24]

With so specifically Spanish a conflict between the king and his subjects, we should not be surprised to find references to and the iconic display of the Armada used by both sides. As Woolf contends: "The conclusion seems unavoidable that Elizabeth was, as a propaganda symbol and source of precedents, valued as much by King and Court as by Parliament and Puritanism."[25] If James tried to usurp the precedent set by Elizabeth's control of debate in the Commons, then it should come as no surprise that the populist response to this 1621 strategy also focused on iconic representation of Elizabeth. "Along side the ghost of Elizabeth the wise and cautious, there now grew up – or rather returned – a *doppelganger*: Elizabeth the Protestant warrior and uncompromising enemy of the Antichrist of Rome and his minions. This was an image unacceptable to the eirenic and peace-loving James."[26]

Despite this seemingly obvious problem, some historians contend that James could never have seen any image of Elizabeth as a threat, even those obviously constructed to be critical of his Spanish policies. Speaking of the "Foxean image of [Elizabeth as] the lost Deborah" as "being revived in response to the perceived foreign policy failures of the 1620s," Woolf still claims that this image was not critical of James, but merely "intended to set the King straight."[27] Let us recall that this is the man who flew into a rage after hearing of one mildly suggestive sentence from the Commons. James was indeed between a rock and a hard place, since to invoke Elizabeth's right to override Parliaments was also to invoke her defeat of Spain and refusal to allow the growth of Roman influence in her kingdom.

Nor were the images of Elizabeth in this debate confined to verbal icons. Two pictures – one an oil painting and one a print – appeared in the first half of the 1620s: Gheeraerts' "Elizabeth with Time and Death," and the Thomas Cecil print "Truth Presents the Queen with a Lance." While the Cecil print of Elizabeth receiving a lance from Truth, with the Armada formation in the background, can barely sustain so mild a reading as "setting the king straight," other Elizabeth images of the period employed elements of the Armada as well, some aimed, perhaps, at "setting straight" the voices of the Commons. The parish church references to Elizabeth as a Deborah, a Judith, and "Spaines Rod" take on fresh significance in the context of the Spanish Match conflict. Any invocation of Elizabeth in a debate involving things Spanish – even if the focus of the debate were freedom of speech – would inevitably invoke the threat of and subsequent victory over the Armada. Within a three-year period, we see three examples of literary uses of the Elizabeth icon in various works speaking directly and indirectly against the Spanish Match. The voice of Elizabeth herself, in Reynolds' 1624 *Vox Coeli*, is, of course, the most strident of these anti-Spanish protests. The indirect references to the queen in the sermon John Donne preached in response to James' 1622 *Directions to Preachers* is the most immediate of the three, and, in many ways, the most dangerous, as Donne was responding directly to James' request for a sermon supporting his ban on the topic by raising the topic with a marked, if learned, anti-Spanish bias. And other than the portraits, the most traditionally iconic is Middleton's 1624 play, *A Game at Chesse*, a defense of Faerie Land against the attack of Babylon, heavily and obviously influenced by Spenser, but with the Gloriana figure named Titania. Here on stage, Titania (along with other equally obvious manifestations of the personae of the current conflict) actually appears before the people, unlike Spenser's invisible queen or the personae of the Donne and Reynolds texts, which appear in the mind's eye. The play was so popular that it was shut down by James' government after only nine days. Clearly, it was not only the people of London who were reading/seeing Titania as an Elizabeth icon speaking against the king's current agenda. While the textual icons are all anti-Spanish Match, in the visual images from the same period we get both sides of the debate: Marcus

Gheeraerts' pseudo-portrait, "Elizabeth with Time and Death," and the Thomas Cecil print "Truth Presents the Queen with a Lance" evince the crafting and use of a second generation of posthumous Elizabeth icons.

*c.*1622: the Spanish Match and the ghost of Gloriana

Out of all of these Elizabeth icons employed in the debate over Charles' possible Spanish marriage – the voice in the ghostly debate in heaven, the character in Middleton's play, the Deborah of Donne's sermon, and the pair of visual icons – it is the two most widely separated by genre, the sermon and the print/painting, that most draw my interest. Sermons had long, indeed we might say always, been used to disseminate the views of those in positions of power; art, on the other hand, tended to be a celebration of times past, as in the Roman Forum or a statement of hopeful identity, as Michelangelo's David figured the doubts and desires of Florence. King James was so acutely aware of his subjects' heated opinions on the topic of the Spanish marriage that he issued what amounted to a gag order in August of 1622: the *Directions to Preachers*, officially banning the subject from pulpits. The king subsequently asked John Donne, the Dean of St. Paul's, to preach at St. Paul's Cross on 15 September in support of these *Directions* – in other words, Donne was to speak out against speaking out. In this climate of dis-ease over matters of free speech and the power of a ruler over that speech, Donne chose for his sermon a text that emphasizes order. This does not, however, put him as squarely on the king's side as it might appear, for the order within the text he takes from the Book of Judges is one in which the former queen, Elizabeth, has a very clear place. Certainly the fifth chapter of Judges is one of the most obvious texts in all of scripture for discussing a woman in a position of both earthly and spiritual authority – but a text in which the place of the current king and his immediate actions is at best obscure and perhaps absent. By his use of the text from the song of Deborah the judge and prophet and of the general Barak in Judges, Donne stresses both order and the breaking of order through the special circumstances of gender. Furthermore, Donne's references to Elizabeth I within the sermon show us that (while he did not make a line-in-the-sand public statement about the Spanish marriage) Donne chose to emphasize, rather than to ignore, the irony of preaching on a document limiting the scope of political preaching.

As we have seen, James never invoked the icon of Deborah in relation to his predecessor, but the monuments of the people as evidenced by the parish church memorials do figure the late queen as, in general, "Spaines Rod" and, more specifically, a Deborah. "Against Spaines Holifernes,/

Judeth shee,/ Dauntlesse gain'd many/ a glorious victory:/ Not Deborah did her/ in fame excell … In Court a Saint,/ in Field an Amazon …"[28] So let us return for a moment to Woolf's insistence that James would not have been threatened by minatory allusions to the late Elizabeth as a Deborah figure.[29] Once again, I strongly question this judgment. When we turn to Donne's famous sermon as yet another Elizabeth icon in biblical garb, we see that James – hearing or reading the sermon – would have been hard pressed not to feel, at the very least, uncomfortable.

How did John Donne, Dean of a cathedral that stood in the midst of all those Elizabeth-praising, Spain-hating parish churches in the City, respond to the possibility of a Spanish wife for the next king and still follow the instructions of his present king? He chose the very words of Deborah herself as she sings with Barak about the death of Sisera, whose armies had oppressed Israel "until you arose, Deborah, arose as a mother in Israel" (5:7) to prophesy the death of Sisera at the hands of a woman. Yes, Donne's text, Judges 5:20, "From the heaven fought the stars, from their courses they fought against Sisera," must be read in the context of the story of a cosmic order which has produced the exceptional circumstance of two strong women as saviors, Deborah the Judge and prophet and Jael the executioner. As a figure defending his country, James has no place in this paradigm. Barak acted upon the advice of Deborah, but it is Jael's action that kills the enemy. And if he is not Barak, that leaves only one role for James: the enemy Sisera, he who fatally assumed that the politics of a wife should be the same as those of her husband.

That this is one of only three sermons in which Donne makes direct reference to Elizabeth strengthens my argument that Deborah is here an Elizabeth icon. At both the beginning and the end of his preaching career, Donne makes flattering references to the queen, first in a sermon preached on 24 March 1616/17, anniversary of both the day that James came into the crown of England and the day Elizabeth died. There Donne uses Elizabeth's virtues only to compliment James,[30] while in the last Easter sermon he preached, in 1630, he uses the example of the queen to support his argument that women do indeed have souls.[31] But interestingly, only in the 1622 sermon, with its context of the Song of Deborah, does Donne actually use Elizabeth's name.

John Chamberlain's contemporary response to the sermon in relation to James' decree was that the biblical text seemed "somewhat a straunge text for such a busines"; he goes on to further critique the sermon by observing "how [Donne] made yt hold toghether I know not, but he gave no great satisfaction, or as some say spake as yf himself were not so well satisfied."[32] Jeanne Shami speaks of "Donne's claims to be in the service of uniting the Church both in itself and with the godly designs of James," observing that it may have been "the uneasy dichotomy between the dual intentions that helped produce the vague feelings of dissatisfaction recorded by Chamberlain."[33] Shami goes on to judge the choice of text as inherently problematic: "the text is a text of resistance, albeit an orderly one, the very stars of heaven being enlisted in the fight against Sisera ..."[34]

Shami, like the other scholars who have published on the sermon, is interested in placing it within the context of Donne's preaching or of James' influence on speaking from the pulpit, the context in which it is most usefully examined. Without doing violence to that context, however, I think it is also possible to see the sermon as yet another example of the subtle use of the icon of Elizabeth I to make a political point. As he opens his remarks, Donne foregrounds the context of the passage from Judges, "the Song which *Deborah* and *Barak* sung" (4:179). Donne goes on to say that "The children of *Israel*, sayes *God*, will forget my Law; but this song they will not forget" (4:179); after cataloging important songs in scriptures, from the song of creation to the "Song of *Moses* at the *Red Sea*, and many *Psalms* of *David* to the same purpose" (4:180). Donne declares that "this Song of *Deborah* were enough, abundantly enough, to slumber any storme, to becalme, any tempest, to rectifie any scruple of Gods slackness in the defence of this cause" (4:180). Interestingly, although he almost always refers to the passage as "the Song of Deborah and Barak," he never identifies it with only Barak's name, although he several times designates the song as only Deborah's. This song of Deborah's, Donne reminds Londoners of 1622, proves that God will come to the rescue of even a people who have done evil in his eyes. God's means of rescuing the people of Israel from the threat of Sisera is constructed as entirely feminine.

> God cald up a woman, a Prophetess, a *Deborah* against him, because *Deborah* had a zeale to the cause, and consequently an enmity to the enemie, God would effect his purpose by so weake an instrument, by a woman, but by a woman, which had no such interest, or zeale to the cause; by *Iael*: And in *Iaels* hand, by such an instrument as with that, scare any man could do it, if it were to be done againe, with a hammer she drives a nayle through his temples, and nayles him to the ground, as he lay sleeping in her tent. (4:181)

There are two elements of this passage which interest me. The construction of Deborah – the woman who leads but who does not kill, who has "interest" and "zeale to the cause" – as different from Jael – the woman who uses an instrument that no man would use but who has no zeal or interest in causes – is a significant one, I believe. Deborah's prophecy is the generative force which contextualizes Jael's act within the Judges passage. No motive is given for Jael's actions; those actions are merely seen as fulfilling Deborah's vision. Jael, then, is Deborah's instrument, but Deborah is God's. Furthermore, Donne says that God called up "a Deborah," implying that she is a type, not a unique entity.

Now sometimes a Deborah is just a Deborah. But in a 1622 sermon aimed at mediating between the differing opinions of a king and his people on a foreign alliance, *a* Deborah is impossible to read as completely unrelated to that Deborah of England, Elizabeth. Nor does Donne content himself with indirect references to the queen. Very shortly after the passage I just cited, Donne constructs a hierarchy, saying that "*God* in this Song of *Deborah,* hath provided an honoralbe commemoration of them, who did assist his cause; for, the Princes have their place ... then, the *Govenours* ... after them, the *Merchants* ... And in the same verse, the *Iudges* are honorably remembered ... And lastly, the whole people in generall" (4:182). In a sermon which stresses order in its text, this is a very interesting list, quite worthy of a paper in itself.

Donne works references to Elizabeth into two categories of this unusual hierarchy. First we find a reference to the queen in the explication of the place of merchants in the larger order. Donne seems to be defending both the actions of merchants and their place in this hierarchy when he says: "The Merchants have their place in that verse too," going on to state how greatness of merchants is evidenced throughout the world, then making the shrewd thrust that "certainly, no place of the world, for Commodities and Situation, is better disposed then this Kingdome, to make Merchants great" (4:188–189). Answering the implicit criticisms of merchants, Donne says "It is but a calumny, or but a fascination of ill wishers. We have many happy instances to the contrarie, many noble families derived from you; One, enough to enoble a World; *Queene* Elizabeth was the great grandchild of a *Lord Maior of London*" (4:189). The "you" here seems to be the merchants, the merchants who paid for all those Elizabeth memorials in parish churches within the City. When Donne turns to speak of the general people, three paragraphs later, he again uses the "you" to draw the audience into the text, here to bring the hierarchy full circle. "You, sayes, Saint *Paul,* you who are the Stars in the Church, must proceed in your warfare, decently, and in order, for the stars of heaven, when they fight for the *Lord,* they doe their service, *Manenets in Ordine, containing themselves in their Order*" (4:192). Elizabeth's place in the order of her people is strongly paralleled to Deborah's, but here the subject of the song – the object of the fighting – is not made clear. Donne moves cautiously toward that in the second part of the sermon.

After a careful build-up to the question, Donne addresses James' right as a ruler to limit words spoken from the pulpit. He asks, is this "out of order"? Is it new? He answers: "That is not new then, which the *Kings of Judah* did, and which the Christian *Emperours* did, but it is new to us, if the *Kings* of this kingdome have not done it. Have they not done it? How little the *Kings* of this kingdome did in *Ecclesiasticall* causes, then" (4:200). But, ah, he goes on to say, of course they have done such things. For Henry VIII "the true jurisdiction was vindicated, and reapplyed to the Crowne ... and those who governed his Sonnes minoritie, *Edward the sixt*, exercised that jurisdiction in *Ecclesiastcall* causes, none, that knows their story, knows not" (4:200). Surely, Donne imples, no one would quarrel with the actions of Henry VIII and the guardians of Edward, actions which broke and kept the English church away from Rome. The actions of Elizabeth, however, are constructed very differently. "And," Donne continues, "because ordinarily we settle our selves best in the Actions, and Precedents of the late Queene of blessed and everlating memory, I may have leave to remember them that know, and to tell them that know not, one act of her power and her wisedome, to this purpose" (4:200). Unlike the actions of Henry and of Edward's men, however, the action of Elizabeth is not implied, but spelled out, and spelled out in a very limiting way. Donne goes on to recount in some detail how the queen heard that various opinions were about to be delived in a sermon, a sermon which she stopped by "Countermaund" and "Inhibition to the Preacher"; but this is described by Donne as carefully different from the actions of Henry VIII. "Not that her *Majestie* made her selfe *Iudge of the Doctrines,* but that nothing, not formerly declared to be so, ought to be declared to be the *Tenet,* and the Doctrine of this Church, her *Majestie* not being acquainted, nor supplicated to give her gracious allowance for the publication thereof" (4:200–201). This is very careful language. Elizabeth was not a judge of existing doctrines, it seems, although she and only she could graciously allow the addition of anything that didn't yet exist but was proposed as a Tenet. Elizabeth, is, then, constructed as was Deborah, one who has interest and zeal, but one who is an instrument of God. The foundation upon which Donne lays James' authority is therefore constructed of various sorts of building blocks. The next sentence reads: "His Sacred *Majestie* then, is here in upon the steps of the *Kings of Judah,* of the *Christian Emperours,* of the *Kings of England*, of all the *Kings of England*, that embraced the Reformation, of *Queene Elizabeth* her self; and he is upon his *owne steps* too" (4:201). Very much on his own steps,

I'd say, considering the varied powers and actions of this list of authorities. Neither the "Kings of England that embraced the Reformation" nor the queen who served as a zealous Deborah against the Spanish foe would approve of the ends to which James wished to apply his powers. Donne reads Deborah as an instrument of God and Elizabeth as a modern Deborah. So far so good, but where does that leave James in the equation? He does not sing of the order of the stars with Deborah, so he is not Barak; but I also agree with Shami's dismissal of Gosse's reading of James as Sisera.

The choice of text is so powerful a marker for a preacher's intentions, that we cannot ignore its significance. If we have trouble placing James in the paradigm of cosmic order generated by the reading from Judges, we might do well to consider the possibility that this is a deliberate act on the part of John Donne. He emphasises order, the defeat of an enemy of the people, and the role of a woman leader in both the conflict and the subsequent celebration. Like Deborah, Elizabeth had "interest" and "zeale to the cause," but her cause was to save England from Rome and Spain. In Donne's sermon, James' cause is less clear. Only near the end of the document do we find the preacher creating what could be a place for James in the paradigm of scriptural explication. In the dedicatory epistle to Buckingham, Donne says that for the "Explication of the Text, my profession, and my Conscience is warrent enough," but for the second part, "the Application of the text, it wil be warrent enough that I have spoken as his Majestie intended" (4:178–179.) And it is near the second part of the sermon that we find the authority for the king's intentions, in the discussion of the 39 Articles. In a careful set of parallel analogies, Donne brings the 39 Articles into an analogous relationship with the stars God sets in the heavens. He then goes on to point out that in the 39 Articles, the king's role is that of a father – analogus to the role of God. After defending James from any sympathy with either "the Superstition of the Papist" or "the madness of the Anabaptist" (4:208), Donne states: "We have him now, (and long, long, O eternall God, continue him to us,) we have him now for a father of the Church, a foster-father" (4:208). Donne then offers a coda to his text about ordered stars, but of stars which do not behave as God approved:

> And therefore, to end all, you, you whom God hath made Starres in this Firmament, Preachers in this Church, deliver your selves from that imputation, *The Starres were not pure in this sight* [Job 25:5]: The Preachers were not obedient to him in the voice of his Lieutenant. (4:209)

Are we then to see bad preachers – those who would talk about the Spanish Match – as bad stars? Perhaps. This would solve the problem of reading James as Sisera, since the stars in Deborah's song were good stars, doing the will of God and fighting against a bad man. But this pushes the place of James in this equation very close to the place occupied by God. There is no biblical precedent for this – indeed, Judges is full of statements against having a king usurp God's power – but Donne senses this danger, and supplies this final biblication citation from the Psalms, saying:

> And with that Psalme, a Psalme, of confidence in a good King, ... I desire that this Congregation may be dissolved; for this is all that I intended for the Explication, which was our first, and for the Application, which was the other part proposed in these wordes. (4:209)

I want to offer the suggestion that the phrase "this is all that I intended" is somewhat disingenuous. The careful elision from biblical authority to the authority of the 39 Articles, the hints that if James has the right to tell preachers what to say he is assuming a more God-like role than even this authority will grant him, coupled with the references to Elizabeth, whose authority *could* be paralleled in the text – all these elements suggest that Donne may not be agreeing with the *Directions* after all. Like the series of "if" clauses with which he concludes his discussion of James and the 39 Articles (4:208), Donne is saying that while we find only one foundation for an earthly leader's authority in scripture – here we see the model of Elizabeth as a Deborah who is the instrument of God – that in the present moment of 1622 there are two foundations of authority for an earthly monarch's actions, the second being the 39 Articles. So if we equate the 39 Articles with scripture, and if we agree that this put James in the position of a Father, then if we are to obey our earthly father, we must let him direct our thinking, and thus "heere is no abating of Sermons, but a directon of the Preacher to preach usefully, and to edification" (4:209).

After this string of subjunctives, let me ask but one more question: if defending the king's authority were really "all that [Donne] intended," why would he pick so problematic a text? Why a text which brings Deborah into such a central position, thus allowing him to mention Elizabeth I by name for the only time in his preaching career? How could he speak against speaking against the Spanish Match when his controlling metaphor specifically invokes the image of a contemporary monarch whose most famous act was repelling the Spanish enemy? My answer, obviously, is that he would not and did not do any such thing. To haunt James with the ghost of Gloriana dressed in the gown of Deborah is to question on every level James' actions, both in the *Directions* and in the Spanish Match itself.

Two icons of Elizabeth from the 1620s, Thomas Cecil's engraving of a youthful queen in armor (Figure 2), and Marcus Gheeraerts' painting, *An Allegorical Portrait of Queen Elizabeth I in Old Age* – more commonly called "Elizabeth with Time and Death" (Figure 3) give us evidence of an imaginative and political opposition between which other posthumous representations of the queen can be read. The weary old woman (a luxury item for the nobility) and the triumphant warrior (populist, mass-produced) both produced in the 1620s, provide a key to the multivalency of Elizabeth's image in the third Stuart decade, showing how potent a marker for political commentary Elizabeth remained. As James tried to

Figure 2 "Truth Presents the Queen with a Lance," Thomas Cecil, *c.*1622. Reproduced courtesy of the British Museum

arrange a Spanish marriage for his son Charles, the various reactions of a number of factions in English politics are interestingly concentrated in these two images of the dead queen. In the Cecil print the gloriously armed queen subdues the seven-headed beast of Revelation, a monster

Figure 3   An Allegorical Portrait of Queen Elizabeth I in Old Age. Courtesy of the Methuen Collection, Corsham Court. The credit is the official description of the painting rendered in accordance with permission to reproduce the work. The more commonly used title of the work is "Queen Elizabeth with Time and Death." Recent scholarship, however, places the date nearer 1622 and suggests that the artist is Marcus Gheeraerts.

which is visually linked to the Spanish Armada depicted in the background: a political stance which recalls the dangers of Spain and thus implicitly opposes the Spanish Match. The Gheeraerts portrait, on the other hand, is a deliberate parody of the 1588 Armada portrait (Figure 4), a record of one of Elizabeth's greatest triumphs. In the portrait of the 1620s, however, the queen is no longer triumphant and powerful, but old, tired, indeed clearly dead. This portrait unmakes the composition and iconography of the Armada portrait, arguing with striking visual effect that the age of Elizabeth is long past and that those who form new paradigms of power should not seek for her precedents in the dust of the tomb. That both the royalist and populist factions turned to images of Elizabeth to make a statement about the proposed Spanish marriage of Charles Stuart gives evidence of just how powerful a political icon the dead queen remained, even two decades after her death.

The heart of this reading of two posthumous representations of Elizabeth I lies in the disparity between the royal revision of her position in English history, best exemplified by the removal of her body from under the altar of the Henry VII Chapel in Westminster Abbey and its relocation in the marginal space of the north aisle, and the populist celebration of her reign evinced by the memorials in parish churches within the City of London. These well-thought-out and significantly documented representations of the dead queen provide the larger cultural and historical context for reading these two images of Elizabeth from the 1620s, the first a luxury product for the nobility, unique and not widely circulated, while the second is a more populist artifact, mass-produced and thus more widely known. Like the memorial texts, the two images show us that the split between discreet (and discrete) royal disrespect and populist praise of the death queen continued from 1606 through the 1620s. As we have seen that the texts of the people differ from the texts of James Stuart, we see this dual agenda – with the same class-defined split – more radically furthered when we examine two images of the dead queen.

The Cecil engraving is a very strong populist statement, with the elements of Elizabeth the warrior foregrounded in an historically apocalyptic context. Elizabeth is seated – one could hardly say mounted – on the horse which tramples the seven-headed dragon described in Revelation, as she received her lance from Truth, interestingly framed by a cave of light. That the dragon is related to both Spain and the papacy is suggested by the background of the Armada fleets, very clearly influenced by the representation of that conflict in the Armada portrait. This gives an apocalyptic overtone to Elizabeth's victory over Spain and makes the engraving an extremely strong statement of Elizabeth's power both in

Figure 4 Queen Elizabeth: The Armada Portrait. Attributed to George Gower, c.1588. By the kind permission of the Marquess of Tavistock and the Trustees of the Bedford Estates. © Marquess of Tavistock and the Trustees of the Bedford Estates

67

life and after death. A spray of Tudor roses springs from the top of the queen's helmet, a symbol both of eternal feminine life and of the dynasty of which she was arguably the flower; that there are three roses in the spray could be a conventional gesture to the Trinity or a more specific reference to the three generations of Tudor monarchs. Elizabeth holds a sword and shield in her left hand, while she accepts the lance with her right, a traditional prelude to righteous action. When we look at the queen's portraits from the late 1560s until her death, we see that no consistent use was made of the symbolism of left and right hands, although we might argue for the increasing importance of the traditionally empowering right hand. In the 1569 Allegory of Elizabeth and the Three Goddesses, she holds the scepter in her right hand, but the more important prop, the apple-colored orb, is held in her left. In the 1572 Allegory of the Tudor Succession, Elizabeth leads Peace with her left hand as she gestures toward the figure with her right hand, while in the 1583 Siena Sieve portrait, she holds the sieve in her left hand, while her right hangs limp at the base of that Virgilian column. In the Armada portrait, however, her right hand rests on the globe, and in the 1603 Rainbow portrait, the rainbow is extended in her right hand.

We need to keep this inconsistency in mind as we read the Gheeraerts painting "Elizabeth with Time and Death." Both of Elizabeth's hands are occupied here, with the left holding a neglected book and the right holding her drooping head. However fabled her learning might have been, it is evidently of little benefit or comfort to her now. In fact, as hard as it may be for us to acknowledge in the twenty-first century, the appearance of the book itself may have negative connotations. In the Westminster tomb text, Elizabeth's learning was problematically represented, and in the parish church memorials – as I have already remarked – it was not a popular topic for praise of the queen. More significantly, none of the portraits after the very early 1560s have a book or books in their iconography. Only in the portrait of Elizabeth as princess, painted in the late 1540s during the reign of her brother, do we find her learning foregrounded. There we find a small book clasped in both of her hands and a much larger book on a lectern at her right elbow. Her left hand supports the small book, while her right rests on top of it, almost in the manner of one taking an oath. We see Elizabeth's learning as her defining characteristic, a very proper and safe characteristic for one who was only second in line for the throne after a younger brother who was still publicly figured as carrying on the dynasty. In the years during which Elizabeth constructed her own royal image through her portraits, we find no evidence that she, or any of her nobles who might have commissioned portraits, wanted to stress her extraordinary learning. Her hands hold gloves, fans, flowers, if not more iconographically charged objects, but no books. That "Elizabeth with Time and Death" features the queen holding a book suggests one of two implicit statements. The most obvious is that her learning, unnatural in her sex as all have observed, has taken the place of her more natural activities as a woman and thus she is left, not with the fruit of her body in the form of heirs mourning at her tomb – heirs which might have benefited her nation – but with an effete and somewhat inappropriate way to pass eternity by reading, an activity which evidently gives her little satisfaction. The more convoluted reading of that book in her left hand would be as a reference to the portrait of her as a princess, a role which the Stuarts would suggest she should never have abandoned. When the early portrait was painted, and indeed for most of Elizabeth's reign, no Stuart supporter would have described her as anything other than an educated, illegitimate daughter of a king. In "Elizabeth with Time and Death," the book held limply in her left hand has sinister implications on many levels.

Similarly, the queen's head held in her right hand is at odds with the other right-handed actions in the portraits, as this pose suggests not action or control, but the abandonment of all active pursuits, including learning. Although her body is oriented to her right as it is in the Allegory of the Tudor Succession, the Siena Sieve portrait, the Armada portrait, the Ditchley portrait, the Rainbow portrait, and in Cecil's engraving, her head is turned to her left, her sight-line down and to the left, as though she had just lowered the left hand holding the book. Death, the more prominent of the two background figures, looms over her left shoulder, and – even though it requires considerable contortion – both of the putti hold the crown with their left hands. Again, the orientation toward the sinister is difficult to overlook.

Formally, the painting is a deliberate revision of one of the most powerful of Elizabeth's portraits, the Armada portrait. Here, as in the 1588 painting, we see the queen seated before a table (a pose not used in any of the other portraits) with two important elements of the composition over her right and left shoulders. Rather than the English and Spanish fleets and that God-sent storm, however, we see Time behind her on the right, mirroring the queen's pose by propping his head with his left hand as he supports himself with his right arm, his hour-glass broken before him, and Death leaning over her left shoulder holding an emptied hourglass in his right hand, his left arm over the back of her chair. The chair and pillow are similar to the Armada portrait chair and pillow, although in the earlier portrait the pillow is behind the queen's left side as mere decoration, while in the posthumous portrait the pillow becomes a seemingly necessary support for her right arm. Not only are the pillow and the chair structurally similar to those in the Armada portrait, but they are very nearly the same rich shade of crimson. With the exception of that earliest portrait of the Princess Elizabeth, painted during the reign of her brother Edward and over which she would have had little if any control, this is the only portrait of Elizabeth in red – a color she would have avoided wearing for its obvious links to sexuality[35] – although it is sometimes present in details of the paintings: the orb she holds in *Elizabeth I and the Three Goddesses*, the rose and intaglio of the Phoenix portrait, and in the table-covering as well as the cushion and chair of the Armada portrait. The Armada portrait figures forth Elizabeth's greatest achievement in the eyes of both her successor and her subjects: victory over Spain. It is her Crécy or Agincourt, all the more significant because the sceptered isle itself was actually threatened by invasion and all the more remarkable because, as Venus said of Carthage, *dux femina facti*. The victory was marked by an explosion of images and symbols of the queen,[36] and became a key element of the memorial texts celebrating her reign. That the Cecil engraving is organized around the mythology of the Armada victory shows us how important it would have been for those who wished to diminish Elizabeth's reputation to diminish the memory of that victory. The subliminal elements of the Gheeraerts portrait are as powerful as any of the iconography used for or by Elizabeth in her own portraits. Here, however, the power of art works toward a very different end.

If we see this posthumous portrait of Elizabeth as a disempowering remake of the Armada portrait, the representation of her face becomes a fascinating issue, for what we see here is not the face of the Armada portrait, but essentially the face of one of the other two portraits we know Elizabeth agreed to sit for: the Darnley portrait painted by Zuccaro in 1575 and used as a face-pattern for many royal portraits of the next decade, most famously in reverse for the Siena Sieve portrait. If the intent behind "Elizabeth with Time and Death" was to represent the queen negatively, why not use the older face from the Armada portrait or the even older and more worn – indeed, haggard – 1590s face of the Ditchley portrait, both also painted from life? I would suggest that the use of the younger and arguably most famous face of the queen anteriorizes the agenda of the 1620s painting to Elizabeth's reign not only in life, but in her prime. In "Elizabeth with Time and Death" we see an exhausted and depressed woman, a woman at the mercy of forces she cannot control. That the portrait was long misidentified as having been painted during

Elizabeth's troubles with Essex is, I think, a significant error. Yes, the dead Elizabeth might arguably look exhausted (although this doesn't say much for the power of resurrection), but to represent the queen as worn out and losing control in a revision of her Armada portrait with an only slightly aged version of the Darnley face is to call into question – to call with great subtlety but also with profound effect – the power she held and used in life.

The political potency of the Armada in each representation of the queen cannot be understated, for not only was this the defining victory of the last Tudor's reign, but it was, of course, the ultimate Janus-faced icon for the debate of the Spanish Match. Setting James and Charles straight on the subject of a Spanish marriage is certainly the very least that can be said of the Cecil print. The parish church references to Elizabeth as a Deborah, a Judith, and "Spaines Rod" take on fresh significance in the context of the Spanish marriage conflict. Likewise, it seems more than a possibility that "Elizabeth with Time and Death" was commissioned not merely as a parody of the queen at her most powerful, but as a dismissal of Spain as the natural enemy of England and English monarchs, substituting instead the more universal Time and Death. Elizabeth's victory over the Armada is figured as ultimately pointless, as the greater forces that finally overtook her know no national boundaries.

As emphatically as the revision of the Westminster tombs and the texts written for her marginalized memorial, this portrait gives us a graphic example of the politically potent usurpation of the iconic Elizabeth I by her powerful survivors. Here we see the power of art furthering the agenda of the Stuarts and their supporters who needed, for a variety of pressing reasons, to erase the shadow of a generally popular queen by representing her as unnatural, alone, powerless, and ingloriously dead. That the portrait has the trappings of regal glory keeps it from appearing an open desecration of the memory of the queen; that these trappings are all so seductively familiar and yet so ultimately sinister makes it a very powerful tool of negative propaganda, a disrespectfully revisionist view of both a monarch and a reign. That the icon of the dead queen was used by both sides in a fierce debate about what was and wasn't English lays down yet another layer of public memory associating that queen with the ongoing history, politics, and daily life of her country.

*c.*1650: what Milton didn't say

Charles Stuart, after 1625 King Charles I, far from learning the strength of public opinion on a Catholic marriage from the debacle of the Spanish Match, chose instead to believe that the issue was entirely one of national alliance, not one of religion. With James' approval, a different marriage was negotiated, complete with treaties, in December of 1624. Encouraged by Buckingham, Charles proceeded to marry the French Catholic princess, Henrietta Maria, by proxy in Paris on May Day, 1625, roughly five weeks after his father's death. She arrived at Dover – escorted, of course, by Buckingham – on 12 June of the same year. Her cradle-Catholicism and lifelong devotion to Rome was to prove both the proverbial nail that lost the shoe that lost the horse that lost the battle of her husband's reign and the last nail in the coffin of the Stuart dynasty. As Marshall Grossman so wittily observes, Charles' reign was doomed by a surfeit of Marys:

> [In *Eikonoklastes*] Milton consistently distinguishes the image and the reality of the king by presenting Charles with a choice of mothers: the Parliament ... and three papistical women, his grandmother, Mary Stuart, his (in the roundhead view) overweening wife, Henrietta Maria, and her mother, Marie de Medici.[37]

Indeed, *Eikonoklastes*, Milton's anti-tyrannical tract, written at the behest of Parliament after Charles was judicially executed in 1649, could well have placed ultimate blame on the over-arching Mary, the Virgin Mother of Christ. As he attempts to make the civil case for the right of a people to execute a tyrant (as with the terms Civil War and Revolution, political stances are encoded in the adjectives "regicide" and "tyrannicide" as used to describe the militant factions of the pamphlets and tracts written in the 1640s), Milton is careful to include the shortcoming of Charles the Head of the Church of England along with the shortcomings of Charles the King, and Charles the man who could not control "his" women. Although the Virgin Mary was styled "Queen of Heaven," neither Henrietta Maria nor Marie de Medici was a queen regnant – although Mary Stuart most certainly was. Even as he critiqued the principles of monarchies and their abuses of power, Milton did not look much beyond the specific target of Charles Stuart. While Milton, unsurprisingly, has little to say (and none of it positive) about either Mary Stuart or the English queen regnant, Mary Tudor, his remarks about Elizabeth surprisingly defy easy expectation. Although he did not support the extreme view of some Protestant sects, the Diggers, for example, on the natural inclusion of women in the political process, neither, it seems, did he consider mere sex to be the deciding factor.

For iconic fame as a supporter of the English Revolution, John Milton may be second only to Oliver Cromwell. Milton sacrificed over a decade of his life as Latin Secretary to Parliament, during which time he lost the last of his failing eyesight. Those years spent in what he called "the cool element of prose" written for the Revolution and the "darkness visible" of total blindness thus reduced both the span and the scope of the canon of his carefully planned and arduously prepared-for career as a poet. And in this "cool element," so powerful from his pen, but never in his own mind as glorious as the element inhabited by the poet, "soaring in the high region of his fancies with this garland and singly robes about him," he also wrote the equivalent of Parliament's official position paper on the execution of King Charles I, *Eikonoklastes*. Taking the time to tease out Milton's use of the Elizabeth icon can, therefore, provide us with cultural assessments both authorized and canonically representative of this crucial period in English history.

The authoring of *Eikonoklastes* – along with *The Tenure of Kings and Magistrates*, written immediately after the execution – could be considered a double ideological burden for Milton insofar as he had, less than a decade before, set as his poetic goal the writing of an English epic about King Arthur, presenting the monarch as one who "might be chosen … to lay the pattern of a Christian hero."[38] Such an epic, he reasoned, would not only raise the English king to and above the ranks of the heroes of Homer, Virgil, Ariosto, and Tasso, would not only allow him "to fix all the industry and art I could unite to the adorning of my native tongue," but would also assure his own fame:

> that by labor and intent study (which I take to be my portion in this life) joined with the strong propensity of nature, I might perhaps leave something so written to aftertimes, as they should not willingly let it die. (III, 236–237)

But, although *The Reason of Church Government* (1641), from which that passage is taken, now may be contextualized in Milton's intellectual odyssey from post-medieval/Renaissance habits of thought to a startlingly modern political sensibility, such a radical change of world-view could not have been taken lightly by a man who wrote in a 1633 letter to a friend that studying and thinking, so as to develop a coherent body of work, was not only far from the sleep of Endymion, but was actually the preparation of Athena putting on her helmet to prepare for war. The invisible act of preparation made the concrete goal of achievement possible. For Milton, the thought, the continued education, the planning of a poet's career were as crucial to the act of writing as are the parallel actions of political response, intelligence gathering, and military strategy to the undertaking of warfare. Milton's involvement in the English Revolution, specifically his authorship of *The Tenure of Kings and Magistrates* and *Eikonoklastes*, left him a changed man. While we could reasonably ask "how could it not?" we would all do well to remember the single-minded devotion to study and contemplation expressed by Milton throughout his life. No, this re-vision of his world was not the carefully thought-out change of a scholar devoting years of study to the issue; rather it was the intellectual and emotional epiphany that the goal of personal freedom could never be reached if one person were elevated over another by any merit other than accomplishment. This realization set the poet directly at odds with the doctrine of the Divine Right of Kings.

While Milton has as his immediate target both the life and errors of Charles Stuart and *Eikon Basilike* (the text defending the late king's right to live that life and make those errors), he frames his condemnation to include not only monarchs of the past, but also those subjects who honored bad kings rather than the people who challenged them. This, of course, puts him squarely into the midst of the ideological struggle of the English Revolution, since he is telling the public that the long-revered Divine Right is nothing more than a social construction set up to benefit the few and made possible by the belief of the never-enfranchised many who automatically cried "God Save the King/Queen!" In a passage evincing considerable intellectual struggle on the part of the author, Milton writes in *Eikonoklastes* (1649):

> Kings most commonly, though strong in Legions, are but weak in Arguments; as they who ever have accustom'd from the Cradle to use their will only as thir right hand, thir reason always as thir left ... But the People, exorbitant and excessive in all their motions, are prone ofttimes not to a religious onely, but to a civil kinde of Idolatry in idolizing their Kings; though never more mistaken in the object of their worship; heretofore being wont to repute for Saints, those faithful and courageous Barons, who lost their lives in the Field making glorious Warr against Tyrants for the common Liberty. (V 63, 66–67)

While Milton may have defended the execution of King Charles, it is still difficult to imagine him championing the rule of the (very) common man, having here and elsewhere expressed his doubts in the collective intelligence of any but a "fit audience, though few."

Even more famous than Milton the Republican, certainly in our last and current century, is Milton the misogynist. While rivers of apologist ink have floated the carefully decontextualized hypotheticals from the divorce tracts, in which Milton argues that only a union of equal minds constitutes a true marriage, none of these torrents of prose has sufficed to wash away this brief phrase from *Paradise Lost*: "Hee for God only, shee for God in him." And yet, while John Milton wrote a great deal – one way and another – about kings and kingship, his views on female monarchs are less clearly articulated. The title of this section addresses not only the absence of what we might expect to read of Milton's commentary on a woman who was also a monarch, but could more accurately be extended to read: "what Milton didn't say about Elizabeth in poetry and barely said in prose." There is only one minor challenge to the statement that Milton's poetry is Elizabeth-free, as it were, and that is based on an imaginative reading of an extended metaphor about Eve in *Paradise Lost*, not on an allusion or a direct reference.[39] The editors of the Columbia edition of the works of John Milton, since 1938 the standard edition and still unchallenged, identify 28 prose passages in which Milton mentions Elizabeth, with the most frequent references occurring in *The History of Moscovia* and the Commonplace Book. In the same index, the word "queen" has 50 entries, none of which refers to Elizabeth, although there are many unindexed passages where the title is linked to her name. While the Columbia index is not a concordance, since it does not index every word of the author's writing, it does have a strength which concordances lack. Unlike the rigidly precise extraction of every usage of, for example, the word "wind" – whether a useful or dangerous movement of the air or a verb meaning something quite different – the Columbia indexers do acknowledge context in addition to mere iteration. So, for a quick take, the proportions of the ballpark figures are not only interesting, but perhaps more accurate than the listings in a concordance.

From that indexing we might conclude that Milton was not much interested in queens – or at least in the word "queen" as distinct from "sovereign," "ruler," or "monarch"; we might further conclude that he takes note of queens only when forced to by a pre-existing narrative or by history. The more precise numbers in the prose concordance confirm this, with 11 entries for Elizabeth's name and 131 for "queen," although some of those do refer to the last Tudor. While it goes without saying that we must remember that fewer queens, especially queens regnant, would have come to the attention of any writer in the seventeenth century, that makes the next tabulation all the more interesting. The index of the Columbia edition, with its 28 entries citing Milton's references to Elizabeth, records fewer than half that number of passages about her sister, Queen Mary Tudor, about her Catholic cousin, Mary Stuart, or about the much-despised Queen Henrietta Maria. There are, moreover, only 14 passages mentioning Elizabeth's father, Henry VIII. Considering that it was Henry who broke with Rome, neither religion nor gender seems to be the determining factor in Milton's attention to Elizabeth. While many of Milton's references to Elizabeth Tudor are certainly a function of the periods and topics of English history upon which he focuses, there are a number of clusters of allusions and iconic associations for us to examine for surprising – in context – descriptions of Elizabeth as a good monarch. When we recall that the translation of Charles' tract is *The King's Icon*, and that the translation of Milton's tract is *Icon-Breaker*, we see that both sides, once again, focus on the idea of an image of the monarch existing in the minds of the people. Ironically, Milton's faith in the power of this sphere of public memory may have been stronger than the king's, for his text contains no illustration, while Charles' text (authorized, if not actually authored by Charles) contains an extremely elaborate print with every possible space filled with royal iconic representations of every sort. Of course nothing is about as strong an anti-icon as one can imagine, but Charles' perception that his book's readers required visual reinforcements is both part and parcel of his Stuart heritage and surprisingly insecure. Also surprisingly, Milton takes considerable care not to include Elizabeth as one of those condemned monarchs "strong in Legions, are but weak in Arguments ... accustom'd ... to use their will only as thir right hand, thir reason always as thir left." Is this because, in Milton's eyes, she is not a king? The answer, as we shall see, is "no."

Milton refers to Elizabeth in the same style of prose and with the same sorts of descriptors that he uses for all English rulers. When he is discussing the history of religion in England, he speaks of Elizabeth with detachment, not dogmatism. The passages in *Of Reformation* and *The Ready and Easy Way to Establish Free Commonwealth* show both Elizabeth and the Bishops to be powerbrokers, but it is the Bishops who are described as inventing an authority which is not theirs; Elizabeth, like her father before her, is the traditional monarch. If anything, she gets some credit for paying attention to religion and religious freedom and for being, as he says in *The Ready and Easy Way*, "so good a Protestant" (VI, 142). Michael Dobson and Nicola J. Watson, in their analysis of the image of Elizabeth during the Revolution, point out that, while the theatres (which had been filled with Elizabeth figures) were closed in 1642, the simultaneous "collapse of Caroline censorship unloosed a flood of discussion about her in print."[40] They continue, enlarging upon points made in passing by other scholars of the period:

Her image, encompassing crown, country, court, Church, and City alike, was by now far larger than any of the factions into which the state had split, and its residues haunted them all. For many of its leaders, not least Cromwell, the English Revolution was an attempt to restore the supposed constitutional balance of the Elizabethan age (just as many Cavaliers felt that they were above all defending the Elizabethan Settlement), and politicians on all sides debated her legacy throughout the twenty years' conflict.[41]

Once again, we see a conflict – this time, of course, much larger than that over the Spanish Match – with the icon of Elizabeth as part of the intellectual and political currency of both sides.

In his posthumously published brief work, *The History of Moscovia*, Milton again resists editorializing about the queen (a position in and of itself), for his references are essentially factual, namings of the monarch of England who sent ambassadors and letters, and the title to which, in turn, various officials and nobles responded. In Milton's Commonplace Book, however, the references are more varied, more problematic, and more interesting. While many of the Commonplace Book references are as incidentally historical as those in *Moscovia*, others are almost willfully singular. Some scholars suggest that the Commonplace Book is "peppered with approving references to Queen Elizabeth."[42] Although "peppered" as a verb implies a stronger presence and greater frequency of references to the queen than the Commonplace Book actually offers, the general flavor of those notations is certainly positive. Although we might find this hardly surprising, when we note that nearly all have William Camden's numerous and multi-lingual histories as their source, we need also to acknowledge that Milton chose Camden to annotate, and not for lack of other historians. While Camden is ranked as one of the commentators who "stressed the importance of remaining impartial and steering away from the imaginative,"[43] we must still count Camden as a strongly pro-Elizabeth historiographer. As David Lowenstein points out, taking care to separate Milton from Elizabethan historians:

> Surveying English Reformation history, Milton discerns only a pattern of thwarted progress … Milton considers the Elizabethan Settlement particularly disappointing precisely because the divines of that day were 'moderate' – that is 'neither hot nor cold' (1, 533) – while Puritan reformers suffered imprisonment, ridicule, and disgrace. We need only recall Foxe's view of Elizabeth as the culmination of Constantine's positive historical influence to realize how far Milton's radical

apocalypticism diverges from the more orthodox vision of that sixteenth-century historiographer.[44]

Nevertheless, it is to these laudatory passages by Milton and their contexts that we should turn our attention. They are of interest, not merely because they exist at all, but primarily because they may serve to help us to trace a neglected byway in a famously revolutionary writer's thinking, study, and analysis of two vexed topics: monarchy and gender. In these examples, we find that even John Milton, republican and misogynist, could look beyond the shadow of the falsified tomb and acknowledge, however briefly and factually, that the real Elizabeth was neither the comfortable myth of "Good Queen Bess" nor the blank slate of a shadowy memory, ready for the doctrinaire dialogues of the Jacobean stage or the vilification of Puritan pamphleteers.

Begun sometime in the 1630s, Milton's Commonplace Book includes an Ethical Index containing 64 entries under 24 headings, an Economic Index with 67 entries under 14 headings, and a Political Index with 210 entries under 32 headings. John T. Shawcross links the Commonplace Book to Milton's decision to "emulate the great poets of all nations" as part of "a threefold program to be fit": the beginning of "a notebook of poetic writing," which we now call the Trinity MS; the setting-up of "a notebook of *topoi* drawn from his extensive reading with an eye to possible future use in the great literature envisioned [that is to say, the Commonplace Book]; and [his] ... sojourn abroad from around April 1638 – August 1639."[45] Introducing her study *Toward Samson Agonistes: The Growth of Milton's Mind*, Mary Ann Radzinowicz takes the organization of the Commonplace Book as a model. "As a young student," Radzinowicz remarks succinctly, "Milton began keeping a Commonplace Book, a habit itself commonplace in his day."[46]

While commenting on the nature of the text, Radzinowicz makes the point that, while the purpose of such a book was the recording of ideas, "[i]t is notable, however, that he recorded no appreciative or critical literary insights."[47] This is a point not simply notable, but well worth stressing, and a generalization not confined to the literary, I would suggest, but one which may explain many of the historical and political entries on Elizabeth, as well. In the words of a now-standard disclaimer, the views expressed in this Commonplace Book are not necessarily those of John Milton. Susanne Woods slides over this issue, while Ruth Mohl, in her 1969 study *John Milton and His Commonplace Book*, goes even further afield, suggesting that the laudatory entries "shed considerable light on Milton's attitude toward women's exercise of authority, whether in the home, in public affairs, or in the government of a nation."[48] Both Woods and Mohl, I suggest, need to consider the possibility that the approval they assign to Milton may be largely transcribed from his sources, especially Camden, or from passages which must be decontextualized to apply to Elizabeth, the most obvious example of this being Milton's description of "the falsehood of the Salick law,"[49] a defense of female inheritance that was made not in reference to Elizabeth, but to the claim of Henry V[50] to the throne of France. In such a context, it is difficult to see any positive comment about queens regnant.

Nor, indeed, are all of the references to Elizabeth primarily about the queen. Under the heading of "Virtue," for example, Milton's first (and only) entry reads:

> All that is fair to see does not at once deserve to be called virtue. Thus, Philip, the husband of Queen Mary, did not go so far as to get rid of Elizabeth, not so much because he was scrupulous and merciful as is generally believed, or of a gentle disposition, but because he foresaw that the result would be that if by chance Mary of Scotland, who was betrothed to a Frenchman, should succeed to the throne, she would add the realm of Britain to France.[51]

In this passage Elizabeth is merely the object being manipulated by Philip of Spain, whose actions, while in seemingly unproblematic control of his wife's state, are found by John Milton to be shrewdly Machiavellian rather than virtuous. Similarly, under the heading "The Tyrant" Milton notes that "The Scottish nobles sent envoys to Elizabeth after Mary had been driven from the realm, and maintained by many examples that this had been done legally" (XVIII, 182). Here, of course, the emphasis is on the legal deposition of a monarch, not essentially on Elizabeth or her actions. In other sections, however, Milton speaks specifically of Elizabeth and praises the queen, as when he speaks of her "excellent care to furnish her fleet with implements out [of] her own country" (XVIII, 208). And on the same page as his mention of the Salic Law (the first entry under the heading "The King of England") we find the fifth entry noting "the wealth of the crown without oppression of subjects may be seen in the expences which Q. Eliz. was at in maintaining warre with her monies in divers places abroad, and at the same time paying her debts at home" (XVIII, 185).[52] Yes, the source here is once again Camden, but the context does imply approval of Elizabeth, especially as the next entry (in Latin) arguably rebuts French thinking: "A Book entitled *Franco-Gallia* ... shows that women have regularly been excluded from all public administration of affairs" (XVIII, 186).

Under the heading "King," we find an interestingly matter-of-fact reference to Elizabeth in the entry "On naming the heir."

> If the King intends his son to succeed him on the throne, the best course is to make his son believe that his father gives the succession not to his years but to his merits ... not as hereditary booty but as a reward of excellence ... [The king should publicly] leave the matter somewhat in doubt. By this course he will save the youth from arrogant behavior, from a crowd of flatterers, and from plotting against the life of his father ... For this reason Elizabeth was unwilling to declare Mary of Scotland her heir. (XVIII, 171–172)

Here Elizabeth's behavior – although actually different insofar as Mary was not her child, a lack that made the succession a deeply vexed question – is mentioned simply as an example of a prudent ruler.

But, if the proof of the pudding is in the tasting, surely the significance of the note-taking may be in the writing. As Janet E. Halley argues of Milton's poetry, his very choices of topic and source text generate a homosocial poetics, presenting us with "single women enmeshed in male worlds."[53] As I have suggested elsewhere, Milton did try to avoid, insofar as was possible, writing about women in his poetry.[54] Keeping the focus on the prose is, therefore, doubly important. In the famously "cool element of prose," then, we may hope to find more measured judgments on women rulers, separated from the soaring fancies of the poet. From Boadicea to Henrietta Maria, Milton supplies the Jerry Falwells of today with historical misogynist sound-bites. In the *History of Britain*, as Woods points out: "[Milton's] notorious statements ... confirm current attitudes toward gender roles and female authority ... Women dressing in men's clothing and fighting as warriors reaps Milton's particular scorn; he rejects the notion outright, even suggesting that the tales about Boadicea were fabricated."[55] The passage from the *History* is worth citing in its (rather heated) entirety:

> The Greek Historian setts her [Boadicea] in the field on a high heap of Turves, in a loose-bodied Gown declaming, a Spear in her hand, a Hare in her bosome, which after a long circumlocution she was to let slip among them for lucks sake, then praying to Andate the British Goddess, to talk again as fondly as before. And this they do out of a vanity, hoping to embellish and set out thir Historie with the strangeness of

our manners, not careing in the mean while to brand us with the rankest note of Barbarism, as if in Britain Woemen were Men, and Men Woemen. (X, 68)

Shawcross admits, in a discussion condemning misreadings of Milton's women by scholars as varied as French Fogle (the editor of the *History* for the Yale Prose edition), Virginia Woolf, and Sandra Gilbert,[56] that "Milton is severe with the overconfident Britons and with Boadicea," but somewhat contradictorily offers the explanation that Milton criticizes Boadicea "'for her usurpation of a man's proper role of military leader and for her inefficiency in military planning and exercise of command' *as Fogle states.*"[57] Having barely one page earlier judged Fogle as one who "sometimes misses the point," I find Shawcross' use of the Yale editor a bit arbitrary. All commentators on this passage, however, at least acknowledge the difficulties generated by great historical distance between Milton and the woman warrior and the possibilities of multiple editorial agendas.

Not surprisingly, Milton claims no such historical distortion when he condemns the power exercised by Henrietta Maria in *Eikonoklastes*:

Examples are not farr to seek, how great mischief and dishonor had befall'n to Nations under the Government of effeminate and Uxorious Magistrats. Who being themselves govern'd and over-swaid at home under a Feminine usurpation, cannot but be farr short of spirit and autority without dores, to govern a whole Nation. (V, 139–140)

Milton goes on to say that the letters taken at the Battle of Naseby were "of greatest importance to let the people see" the king as he was: "to summ up all, they shewd him govern'd by a Woman" (V, 251). Yes, for Milton, whose last hero, Samson, sees his greatest failing as giving up his "fort of silence to a woman," being ruled by a woman has a predictably horrible ring. But being ruled by one's wife – the case with both Charles and Samson – is not, as we shall see, the same as being ruled by a reigning monarch, female. But the woman must be the monarch, not a queen matrimonial. Even a power more symbolic than political on the part of a ruler's wife is condemned when Milton describes Claudius showing mercy to the brave family and entourage of Caractacus, who spoke movingly before the Tribunal in Rome:

Caesar mov'd at such a spectacle of Fortuen, but especially at the nobleness of his bearing it, gave him pardon, and to all the rest. They all unbound, submissely thank him, and did like reverence to Agrippina the Emperors Wife, who sat by in State: a new and disdained sight to the manly Eyes of Romans, a Woeman sitting public in her Female pride among Ensignes and Armed Cohorts (X, 60).

(Worth mentioning in passing is Milton's frequent spelling of woman as the literal "woe man." While orthography was still not standardized, this spelling was becoming obscure in general usage.)

More ambiguous still is the case of Queen Martia, whose entry in the Commonplace Book and story in the *History of Britain* are used by scholars to support a full spectrum of views. Under the heading "Laws," Milton's fourth Commonplace entry reads: "Alfred turn'd the old laws into english. I would he liv'd now to rid us of this norman gibbrish. the laws of Molmutius. as Holinsh[ed], p. 15. and of Queen Martia. see Holinshed." Mohl's notes in the Yale edition provide us with Milton's source material.

> Milton's entry on Queen Martia adds one more to the list of noble women in the *Commonplace Book*. Holinshed (1587, I 19) records her time as the 430th year after the building of Rome. At that time, since King Sicilius of Britain was not of age to rule, his mother, "that worthie ladie called Martia," governed for him.[58]

Mohl goes on to quote Holinshed as having praised Queen Martia's learning in the sciences, her excellent keeping of the existing laws, and her prudent making of new laws, called for centuries the Martian Laws in her honor. Woods, who uses the Yale edition, supports Mohl's evaluation, stating that Milton "presented Holinshed's admiration of Queen Martia without comment."[59] That is true of the Commonplace Book entry, but not of Milton's use of Holinshed in the *History of Britain*. The passage there includes the facts listed in the Commonplace Book, but Milton's narrative continues, offering the following invective in the same paragraph:

> In the minority of her Son [Martia] had the rule, and then, as may be supos'd, brought forth these Laws, not her self, for Laws are Masculin Births, but by the advice of her sagest Counsellors; and therein she might doe vertuously, since it befell her to supply the nonage of her Sone: else nothing more awry from the Law of God and Nature, then that a Woman should give Laws to Men. (X, 26)

Fogle, in his notes for the Yale edition of the *History*, reads this passage much as I would, a response which elicits from John Shawcross a furious rebuttal. "At times Milton is sarcastic and subtle of tone, although French Fogle ... sometimes misses the point."[60] After quoting the Martia passage above, Shawcross continues.

> The sarcasm of the last sentence blares out surely in viewing woman's laws given to men as being the most "awry" possibility to confute the Law of God and Nature. Milton's reference to the laws of Queen Martia in the Commonplace Book ... seems fully approving.[61]

I, however, cannot find support within the *History* – or indeed elsewhere – for a sarcastic reading of that passage on queens and gendered laws.

And yet almost as famous as the Boadicea and Martia passages (if much less-quoted) is Milton's praise of Queen Christina of Sweden. Mohl remarks tartly: "In *Second Defense*, Milton seems to forget that he ever wrote a word about the unfitness of a woman ruler." She calls his "unbounded admiration" of the Queen "a four-page eulogy."[62] Woods also remarks the passage, noting:

> The panegyric is particularly interesting from a feminist point of view since it constitutes a digression for which Milton was criticized and serves no better purpose than to praise someone who had admired his work.[63]

Willing to admit to the inconsistency Shawcross refutes, Woods concludes from a comparison of these prose passages that "Milton appears to have mixed attitudes toward female authority, despite his famous condemnations."[64]

I would suggest a less diplomatic explanation, but one which goes some way to explain Milton's views on Elizabeth Tudor. As Milton presents her, Boadicea is the wife of a king, as of course, is Henrietta Maria.[65] Martia is a queen regent, but essentially a wife and mother. Queen Christina and Elizabeth I, on the other hand, are monarchs in their own right. This distinction, I believe, will provide us the key for Milton's general view of Elizabeth Tudor. Milton sees a hereditary queen as a monarch first and as a woman distantly second, if at all. It has taken quite a time to build up to this point, so let us remember where we started. Milton's famous misogyny and his equally famous support of the execution of a reigning monarch make it seem unlikely, on the face of it, that the Elizabeth icon would be for him anything more than easy target practice. That this is not the case speaks to both the complexity of the times and to the adaptability of an Elizabeth who now exists – even less than 50 years after her death – so completely in the public sphere of memory that she can be realized by any strong imagination. Add to that Milton's fabled brain, and we have an icon of great force emerging from this prose.

The passage that I offer in support of this judgment does not mention Elizabeth directly. Under the heading "Various Forms of Government" we find a notation reading "James Kennedy, Archbishop of Saint Andrews, in a long address assails and rejects government by women" (XVIII, 200). The source is George Buchanan's 1582 history of Scotland. Mohl's notes provide us with the text, in which Buchanan (once the tutor of Mary Stuart) cites the fifteenth-century Archbishop Kennedy as saying: "If you search all the names of things, you will not find among them the word for 'rule by women' ... So to this very day there has been no rule by a woman in public administration."[66] Although I have rendered them here in English, both Kennedy's statement and Milton's Commonplace entry are in Latin,[67] a circumstance which allows Mohl to make the following crucial observation: "It is interesting to note that, whereas Buchanan uses the Latin phrase '*muliebre imperium,*' Milton's entry, as if to correct Kennedy's statement that there is no name for it, uses the word '*gynae-cocracy.*'"[68] In her study of the Commonplace Book, Mohl speculates:

> Perhaps it was the very falsity of the statement that attracted Milton's attention. In his own summary of it he supplied the word declared lacking, namely *gynaecocracy*; and he must have recalled, as he did so, the several examples of women rulers, both ancient and modern, whom Archbishop Kennedy should have known as well as he.[69]

Here, far more than all the quotes from Camden, I suggest we find Milton's evaluation of the reign of Elizabeth I.[70] By supplying the word that refutes the linguistic argument against the rule of women, Milton puts hereditary queens on the same level as kings. He gives Elizabeth, indirectly, that word which was always lacking in her reign – a feminine word for kingdom. That he rejected the rights of both female and male monarch is less significant than the fact that he – however briefly – considered them to have coexisted. The distinction for Milton, therefore, was not whether the monarch was male or female, but that the person sat on the throne by birth, not because of the more problematic circumstance of marriage. So what Milton *didn't* say about Elizabeth I is that she couldn't rule England because she was a woman. Milton, the icon-breaker, has not only left Elizabeth's public memory unshattered, he actually has gone some way towards arguing that a good queen and a good revolutionary may share some civic values as they both serve the England they love.

1660–1837:
The Shadow of a Golden Age

Restoring without re-empowering

Although 1660 is held out as one of the watershed years in the history of Great Britain, like many such history-book dates, it lacked both a defining moment and a precise cause. We can say that in 1660 the Revolution failed (or that the Civil War ceased). Or, we can argue that the idea of a Commonwealth sans monarch was something which the majority of the people – or the majority of the people whose views were knowable – did not really want; in that light, 1660 was the beginning of mending a largish rip in the fabric of the commonweal of the sceptered isle. (The best argument supporting this latter point, of course, is the survival of that monarchy through the nearly three and a half centuries from the Restoration to the current Golden Jubilee of the monarch whose Annus Horribilis – unlike those of her people – had nothing to do with Margaret Thatcher.) Or we can combine the two arguments and see 1660 as marking the end of or the recovery from an idea whose time, at least in England, had not yet come.

The politics behind the restoration of the monarchy, of Charles I's son being crowed Charles II, are obviously complex and nuanced, as well as open to a number of interpretations. The chronology, however, is clear. Oliver Cromwell died in 1658, and despite the attempt of his son to step into the paradigm of the Protectorate, the revolutionary government never recovered from that death. As Simon Schama quips: "The extraordinary irony about the restoration of Charles II is not that he became king because the country desperately needed a successor to Charles I. He became king because it desperately needed a successor to Oliver Cromwell."[1]

If images of Elizabeth were thin upon the ground during the Interregnum, they are even thinner at the historical moment of the

Restoration. It was not, after all, Elizabeth's England that was being restored. Resolution might be a better tag. The republicans resolved to limit the power of the returning monarchy; the royalists resolved to have a monarch, even at the price of some increase in the power of the people. What we have, then, is a compromise, not an anti-revolution. What we do see, however, blurring the line of demarcation between the Elizabethan age as a golden past and the Restoration as a golden future was that old obsession: the shadow of Rome. The seventeenth-century Elizabeth icon, as we have seen with the Spanish Match, is ineluctably tied to an historically anti-Spanish, an arguably anti-European, and a clearly anti-Papist mind-set. Those who welcomed the Restoration did not wish to evoke the Protestant sentiments tied to the Elizabeth icon, while those who opposed the Restoration were even less likely to summon into the public memory the image of a successful monarch.

Charles II, it was widely believed, was heavily influenced by his Catholic mother, Henrietta Maria, as heavily influenced, perhaps, as his more outspoken (and less politically astute) brother James, the Duke of York. Yet, ironically, the marriages of the two brothers were the reverse of what we might expect in the circumstances. Charles married the Catholic Catherine of Braganza, daughter of the King of Portugal, promising that which he never delivered – a Protestant heir. (Although he did invest his illegitimate son by Lucy Walter, James Crofts, with the title Duke of Monmouth a bare 20 days after he married Catherine at Portsmouth.) James, on the other hand, made an uncharacteristically cautious match with the daughter of Clarendon, the Lord Chancellor: the already-pregnant Anne Hyde, with whom he had two daughters, the future queens Mary and Anne. (Although James more than made up for this uncharacteristically sensible move by marrying, upon Anne Hyde's death, the rigidly Catholic Mary of Modena, with whom – of course – he had a son.) The Stuart dynasty looked to be ending even less tidily than had the Tudor dynasty.

And then there was the issue of sex. Elizabeth had tried to make this a non-issue during her reign, and James hid away with Buckingham et al. in the heavy shadow cast by his multiple offspring. Charles I, once past his own Buckingham phase, famously presented himself in the bosom of his attractive family. So not since Henry VIII had London seen a monarch indulge his sexual appetites as openly as did the Stuart brothers. Nor did multiple marriages figure in Charles' agenda, cloaking appetite in the trappings of dynastic concerns, as did Henry. Queen Catherine survived her royal husband by 20 years, but they had no child. Charles could not have been giving his marriage bed his full attention, as –

scattering jewels and illegitimate children in his wake – he amassed a collection of mistresses to rival in number the wives of Henry VIII. Three of the most famous of these women were Barbara Plamer, Lady Castlemaine (who often made decisions about who got audiences with the king), the Protestant actress Nell Gwyn, and the French Catholic emissary for Louis XIV, Louise de Kéroualle. While Charles was indulging in these and other pleasures, his brother was making, if possible, an even greater spectacle of his personal life. Mercifully, there were no telephone tapes.

As horrified as the former supporters of the Revolution and former or quietly right-wing Puritans must have been at the turning of their new Jerusalem into Sodom, to take a frequently employed metaphor, even they could take no pleasure in being justified by the year 1665–66. In February of 1665, the Second Anglo-Dutch War began, and before it ended in 1667, the English experienced the humiliation of the Black Day, when the Dutch fleet sailed up the Medway as far as Chatham, sank three ships, and towed the flagship back to Holland. Between April and December of 1665, the Great Plague of London took over 70,000 lives, driving the Court and Parliament to Oxford in the hope of safety. And in September of 1666, the Great Fire of London burned 13,300 buildings in the City, including St. Paul's Cathedral. All this, a mere half-dozen years after a Restoration. And, if Charles' diversions outraged the politically radical and religiously narrow, his behavior was almost equally incomprehensible to the old county families, who had thought that their steadfast, if low-key, support was to be repaid by a king who would embody the seventeenth-century version of Family Values. Recalling the image of the Virgin Queen was hardly appropriate in such an atmosphere.

But another aspect of Elizabeth's public image did play well during the reign of Charles: Elizabeth, foiler of Popish plots. While those loyal to Rome actually had been trying to kill Elizabeth, political rabble-rousers during the reign of Charles found it very easy to play the Pope card, even though Rome's threat to England via Charles was more from within the man himself than from external assassins. In 1668, a demented gadfly named Titus Oates advanced, through various channels, the conspiracy theory that (wait for it) Catholics urged on by the Pope were planning to kill the king. More for lack of other energizing causes than because Oates offered political reality, the Parliament and the people of London went into a frenzy. The Popish Plot, as it was called, became the Armada threat revived. If the Plot could be overthrown, then England would be saved. Well, not quite, but it was a very popular idea for those who didn't ask too many questions.

Seeking the help of a clergyman with the astonishing name of Dr. Israel Tonge (one of the numerous adherents of the theory that the Great Fire had been started by Catholic arsonists), Oates managed to get an audience with Charles and, eventually, with the whole of the Privy Council. The October 17th murder, on Primrose Hill, of Sir Edmund Berry Godfrey, the magistrate in whose ear Oates had first sown the seeds of his fancy, was taken by all to be proof positive that killer-Catholics were once again loose upon the land. And that, of course, blew the cork out of the bottled-up anti-Catholicism of the people of London. Instead of the traditional Guys burning in effigy on that 5 November, the celebration of the overthrow of the famously Catholic Gunpowder Plot was marked by Pope Burnings, some attended by hundreds and some by thousands of people. And now, enter the Elizabeth icon. The 110th anniversary of her accession, 17 November 1668, was the occasion for yet more Pope Burnings and the invocation of Good Queen Bess, she who had once survived Popish Plots and defeated the Rome-backed Armada.

It mattered not one bit that all of this plotting had grown from Oates' warped mind. Even after he was revealed as the poser he was, the impetus that would power the Glorious Revolution had been set forth. For all that Charles did take the precaution of sending James and his even more Catholic second wife abroad, he refused to authorize the Act of Exclusion, which would have barred James and any child of James and Mary of Modena from the order of succession. There was, in 1683, an attempt to try to name the king's oldest son, the Duke of Monmouth, as Charles' heir (by saying that Charles had married Sarah Walters in Paris); but this attempt (known as the Rye House Plot) to put the Protestant Monmouth on the throne – killing, by the way, both Charles and James – failed, and Monmouth went into exile in Holland. He did return in 1685 (four months after his father's death and two months after the coronation of James and Mary at Westminster), trying to raise a revolt, but he ended up being beheaded on Tower Hill.

Charles died without legitimate heirs. James succeeded him, promising not to meddle in religious or military appointments, but James' own lack of judgment did him in. Within two years of his coronation, he was appointing Catholics to positions of power, suspending the penal codes in their favor, and receiving the papal nuncio – who arrived at Windsor in a formal display consisting of 36 carriages. Even this, however, James might have survived, had his wife not given birth to a son. Ironically – considering all the reigns that teetered or fell for the lack of a male heir, it was the birth of James Francis Edward Stuart in 1688 that proved the chief cause of his father's loss of the throne. On Guy Fawkes Day of that year, William of Orange (husband of James' Protestant daughter Mary) landed in England, and by the end of the year it was all over. James was in exile on the continent; William and Mary acceded to the throne of England in early 1689. When Mary died in 1694, her sister Anne returned to court to act as hostess for the seven years before William's death. Anne came to the throne in 1702. The death of her oldest (and only) surviving child in 1700, the relentless plotting of the exiled Stuarts, and the nation's fear of a Catholic monarchy had lead, in 1701, to the passage of the Act of Settlement, declaring that Anne should be followed to the throne by the great-granddaughter of James I, Sophia, the Electress of Hanover; no heir of James II would ever wear the crown of England.

Although physically exhausted by attempting to extend the Protestant strain of the Stuart dynasty (she survived at least 19 pregnancies), Anne ruled until her death in 1714; even in ill-health she was arguably a more attentive monarch than her great-grandfather, grandfather, or uncle. Sophia of Hanover died only two months before Anne, and her German-speaking son, George Ludwig, became heir to the crown and then king of England. It was left to the House of Hanover to clean up the last of the endlessly plotting Catholic Stuarts. Charles Edward Stuart had succeeded his father, the "Old Pretender," as claimant to the English crown, and spent much time and other people's money trying to back-door himself onto the throne through the loyally Stuart shores of Scotland. Bringing disaster to all who helped and supported him, the Young Pretender, Bonnie Prince Charlie, hopped a boat (complete with that Stuart pre-req, a pretty girl) out of the country after the clans who rose to his cause were slaughtered at Culloden. While he went back to France, the Scots, defeated by the Duke of Cumberland, were left to experience the inglorious results of a failed revolution.

As we move into the eighteenth century, we will see that the references to Elizabeth, and such uses of the Elizabeth icon as can be found, require progressively less and less historical background. Unlike the Spanish Match or even the Popish Plot (both of which demand at least a few pages of background information to appreciate), the later occasions for which Elizabeth's icon was deployed gradually had less to do with specific political events and more to do with popular responses to general social issues, both foreign and domestic. An excellent example of this is that fabulously named moment of comic relief for the student of history: the War of Jenkins' Ear. Although we cannot dismiss the name as a factual referent (as with the Holy Roman Empire's schoolroom tag: wasn't holy, wasn't Roman, and wasn't much of an empire), the conflict was certainly more about the perennial Spanish-phobia than about the ear of one Captain Robert Jenkins. Jenkins' ear – which rapidly became Jenkins' Ear – was presented to Parliament as having been cut off by Spanish coast-guards while the Englishman was trading in Caribbean waters in March of 1738. The ear thus became the occasion, rather than the cause, of an upsurge of the always-simmering anti-Spanish sentiment in the hearts of the Crown's loyal subjects. Over the objections of Walpole, the current Prime Minister, Parliament increased funding for the navy, the traditional response to any perceived or actual threat from abroad, especially from Spain. In November of 1739, Edward Vernon, Vice Admiral (and later Member of Parliament), seized the Spanish port/loading dock of Porto Bello, near what is now the Panama Canal. Out of all proportion to the significance of either the War of Jenkins' Ear or the victory of Porto Bello, Britain celebrated, renaming houses, streets and whole villages in honor of the triumph. The war did not end well, but it brought down Walpole, and – predictably – spawned more Elizabeth icons. The anonymous, two-volume 1740 *History of the Life and Reign of Queen Elizabeth* (London: Printed for F. Noble, at Otway's-head in St. Martin's Court) contains little, if anything, new, but the climate of the time generated a need for another Elizabeth fix. In the same year, a more interesting publication also appeared: *The Chronicle of Kings of England* (a bizarre little work to which I will shortly return.)

The War of Jenkins' Ear may be the sort of trivia that sticks in the minds of students, but the conflict that it ushered in was of more lasting significance. With Walpole out of power, there was little to stop those elements of the government who wished to undertake any of a variety of wars. Simon Schama's characteristically dry insight on this situation perfectly encapsulates the historical moment: "Just as sixteenth-century England's national identity had been beaten out on the anvil of fear and hatred of Catholic Rome and Habsburg Spain, so the British identity was forged in the fires of fear and hatred against Catholic, absolutist France."[2] While King George was off tending to matters of continental interest, the south of England fell into a panic, sure that the French were planning a replay of 1066. And as we are all aware, this fear was far from groundless, as the next 50 years were to prove.

The change to the House of Hanover itself was a cause for some disease, for while the threat of Rome had supposedly been avoided, the people were not exactly sure how a German, even one bearing the name of England's patron saint, came to sit on their throne. There were, of course, better ways of spreading public information than there had been in the days of the Tudors, but it was still a long leap from accepting the

Act of Settlement to actually getting a king whose father, grandfather, and great-grandfather had not spent their youths in the palaces and streets of London. Much as the English felt when the first thrill over James I, arriving complete with a spouse, and heir, and a spare had died down and turned into a mild longing for the good old days, the idea that the crown was back on the head of a man who could produce sons created only a brief sense of relief. Surely, people began to murmur, someone must have pulled a fast one.

Always open to a conspiracy theory, especially one involving foreigners, the vocabulary of plots and secret pacts arose. How to talk about this without being openly treasonous to King George? Talk instead about Elizabeth. The flood of secret histories and curtain-twitching tales of highly impassioned disputes became first a release valve and then a popular genre. And the life of a Virgin Queen certainly offered considerable scope for the narrative of the secret. As the new century dawned, so, we might say, did the beginning of tabloid journalism. No, not reporters peeking through Georgian windows, but writers offering what was not and could not have been available in Elizabeth's day – a tell-all narrative. Most of the secret histories – for there must be secrets hidden in so complex a fusion of the public monarch and the private woman – were sensationally written and focused on one of two topics: the Virgin Queen's love life, or frustrated lack thereof, and her relationship with that eternal anti-heroine, Mary Queen of Scots. Some of the texts, however, presented more carefully thought-out examples that did attempt to examine the paradox of a monarch with a public and masculine body who also possesses a private and feminine body. This, in itself, was nothing new. Spenser had been there and done that with Gloriana, Belphoebe, and Britomart (and, on the dark side, with Duessa) in the *Faerie Queene* of the 1590s. But that date is part of the problem. One reason for these new narratives being "grafted on to a body of Elizabethan artistic and literary representations of the Queen" was, as Dobson and Watson observe, precisely because these older icons "were fast vanishing into the unreadably archaic."[3] An additional advantage of these narratives is that they required no detailed knowledge of history on the part of the reader; the books and plays themselves aimed to take care of that. All that was required of the reader/audience was a clear sense of what, if not who, Queen Elizabeth was.

An issue that arose along with the House of Hanover was the question of Englishness. While the Stuarts had been primarily Scots who married Europeans, James I had done a good job of selling the concept of the union of Scotland and England, along with his own direct descent from Henry VII, thus allowing the dynasty to represent itself and to be perceived as English, both politically and in the sphere of public imagination. George I, however, was quite a different problem. Aside from his famous lack of spoken English, he was not perceived as English, and, for once, public perception bore some resemblance to the facts. Keeping in mind that George came to the throne of England via his descent from his great-great-grandfather James I, who was himself one-quarter English, George's genealogical math makes him one-sixty-fourth English or something like 1.5% the descendant of Henry Tudor and Elizabeth York. Nor did the Hanoverian monarchs take English wives. To anteriorize the scoff of "being more English than the English," we must realize that, in the eighteenth century, almost everyone was more English than the king. Indeed, after Henry VIII it was not until George VI – who never expected to be king – that another queen matrimonial was born in Great Britain. Being English – or being British, for that matter – became a vexed intellectual and emotional question in the eighteenth century. Although the colonizing of what was to become the Empire had begun under the rule of Elizabeth, the process had now reached a crucial stage. With English settlements in North America, on the islands of the Caribbean, and increasing throughout Africa and southern Asia – in addition to the Indian subcontinent and Australia – it became necessary (at least in the minds of the people in these outposts and those with dreams of Empire) to distinguish clearly between the colonizer and the colonized. In other words, who was "them" and who was "us"? If it had been merely a question of skin tone, the element of nationalism might not have been so much in the forefront of people's minds. But England was far from being the only Western European country planting flags and picking produce in the far reaches of the world. So it was not only a racial issue; nationalism was key to identity.

So, they were English? What did it mean to be English? In the London of the Georges – at least before Britain found itself in a state of war with most of the continent in the 1780s – that was not an easy question to answer. In fact, London itself became the clearest image of what it was to be English. But soon people from the colonies were appearing in London as well. Did that make them English (a disputed question even now, many generations after they first arrived)? What did the English have that these people could not share?

History.

The answer had to be history. Not King Arthur or the Crusades, but history that lived within the early modern sphere of public memory: to be English was to know about the golden age of Good Queen Bess.

The conflicts with France and other European nations that marked the end of the eighteenth-century British history spring more readily into the public memory than do the details of Popish Plots or even the War of Jenkins' Ear. The French Revolution and the Napoleonic Wars constitute relatively recent history. Having survived, one way or another, three Georges and the revolt of the American colonies, the sphere of English/British public memory could now accommodate the redefined sense of national history required by so radical a shift in dynasty and government. Furthermore, as the Industrial Revolution began to begin, almost all of England's pre-industrial history was packed away in a golden glow labeled "once upon a time … " At the end of the eighteenth century and the beginning of the nineteenth, Elizabeth seemed no more distant than did the suppression of the clans that changed the face of Scotland. Although radically different, both the reign of the queen and the purging of lands and people of at least legally identical national status, could now be willfully incorporated into the narrative of a nation working to make not only its own people, but most of the world around it see that to be British was to be right. And from this it follows that the British could do no wrong. It was this comfortably self-righteous self-sufficiency that ushered in the nineteenth century, and with it, the Age of Victoria.

*c.*1680: King Elizabeth and the Pope

Although the late seventeenth century was short on visual icons of the queen, her image was resurrected in various avatars. She appeared most frequently, of course, as a proto-Protestant in the literature prefacing and surrounding the Glorious Revolution or, indeed, any time a strong reference to a Protestant monarchy was needed. "Appeared," may not be the perfectly correct term for this period. Unlike the dueling images of the Spanish Match dispute, the Restoration and eighteenth-century uses of the imagery are more verbal or performative than strictly iconographic. But these invocations of the memory of Elizabeth on page, stage, and in song fall into the two paradigms established by "Elizabeth with Time and Death" and "Truth Presents the Queen with a Lance." An excellent example of a Protestant invocation is the short – 22 quarto pages – play *The Coronation of Queen Elizabeth*, published in London in 1680, just after the furor of the Popish Plot. Because it is both really funny (although perhaps unintentionally) and such a great example of anti-Catholic propaganda, I'm including extensive quotes, and the entire ending, with a few of my own annotations.

<u>The Coronation of Queen Elizabeth, with Restauration of the
Protestant Religion:
or The Downfal of the Pope.</u>
Being a most Excellent Play As it was Acted Both at Bartholomew and
Southwark Fairs, This present Year 1680. With great Applause, and
Approved of, and highly Commended by all the Protestant Nobility,
Gentry and commonality of ENGLAND, who came to be Spectators of
the same.
London: Printed for Ben. Harris,
at the Stationers Arms under the Piazza in Cornhill.
1680.

Act I scene I
[The play opens with Bishops and Cardinals crowning Elizabeth, who,
once crowned, tells them to leave immediately as they are loyal to Rome]

> Queen.   ... First then, To settle Religion, the dearest part of
> Government, and surest Rock for Princes to build upon, shall
> be my speedy care to begin: I'll reform my own House, and
> after that the nation. therefore all you who pay obedience
> to the See of Rome, or think Supremacy due to the Pope, we
> here discharge you and banish you our Court ...
> > Bloodshed and Rapine shall to Rome retune,
> > Murther and Luxury which feed the fire
> > Shall to the Scarlet Beast for Succor fly,
> > And unimploy'd within his Bosom die ...

[The Cardinals are furious and call, in prayer, upon the pope]

> I. Card.   O Pius Quartus, assist us with thy Prayers, and Hell, if
> thou hop'st a glutting Harvest, protect the best Religion.

[Note that they are praying to the Pope and to hell, not to Christ or God,
for the protection of this "best Religion"]

Act III scene I
The Scene opens, and discovers the Pope and Nun sitting upon a couch
> Pope.   Now thou lookest more lovely Fair than Venus ... and
> now my Dulcementa, in a Dream, when soft Slumbers close
> her Eyes, may by the force of Fancy, be well pleased with what
> timerous Virgins wish, but have not known. Is not this better

than poring upon Religion? Thou art the only Book I'll ever read, unless to cheat the prying Eyes of Rome.

Nun.   I must confess you have taught me to forget the thorny way, which I poor fool once wandered in, being misled; but now by your Advice, return to taste of Pleasures and Delights, I had not else been capable to understand. They cannot sure be ill, that you the Universal God on Earth vouchsafe to try ...

Enter the Devil in the shape of a Jesuit

[He warns the nun to flee, but she gets caught by Cardinal Moricena who condemns both Nun and Pope and stabs the nun, who dies]

Pope.   Damn'd Incarnate Devil, what hast thou done, thou hast slain that Angel in thy Daughters Shape, that shall deny thee thy Salvation ...

Morice.   Talk on, talk on, Lascivious Pope, thou Head of Hell, no Rome: How can'st thou look upon an Angry Father, whose Daughter thou hast so basely defloured, and caused him to kill?

Pope stabs Cardinal, who dies. The Pope leaves and the devil/Jesuit follows.

scene II
[Some English types come on – Tim, a tinker, Honey-Suckle, a cook, and others. They sing of Elizabeth and do a dance and say anti-Catholic things, then leave]

Enters the Pope, lead by the Devil in his own shape.

Pope.   Where hast thou brought me, through these gloomy shades of Night?
Devil.   Ask thy self ...

[Suddenly there are devils and popes and cardinals with ghosts of Moricena and Dulcementa]

Enter one who singes in Answer to a Noise behind the Scenes

SONG

Voice.	Where, where's the Pope
Answer.	Come to die in a Rope:

Or his breath expire, but the flames of hot fire.
To meet the just Plagues that his sins to require.

Voice.   Pray what is his Crime?

Answer: For coming to Popedom before 'twas his time;
For Murther and Whoredom, for Poison and Rape,
For killing the Father and making escape,
From the Chair of St. Peter to a Heretick City;
Mid'st the Rabble, to suffer without any pity.
Around, around, round, inclose the Pope round;
Push him and toss him on Prong; all yet quicker,
Till he cryes there's no hope, for bloody, bloody
Pope,
And a cheating old fool of a Vicar.

{Exit Singer.}

Pope.   Cursed dissmal fate, must all my glories and incumbent
Honours sink into the dust! O popedom, thou gilded Pill,
whose outside seems enticing fair, but being took, thou hurriest
Mankind upon his sure destruction.
Oh, I could curse thee, but 'tis now too late,
And I with patience must endure my fate.

*As he is going out, Tim, Bursh, Honey-Suckle, and others of the Rabble
come running in, and almost beat him down.*

Tim.   Pray Sir, if a man may be so bold to ask, what are you
Sir?

Voice.   He's a pope—

Tim.   Ha, – hark ye there Neighbours, there's something says
he is a Pope.

All.   O law!

Tim.   Pray, Sir, are you a Pope?

Pope.   No.

Tim.   Why then you might have told a body so at first.

Voice.   He lies.

Tim.   Ha, there's something says he lies, but I don't know
what
It is … Pray Sir what Pope are you?

Voice.   He's the Pope of Rome.

Tim.   Ha, – hark you there Neighbours; – nay, if he be the Pope of Rome, he shall quickly know his doom.

All.   He shall, he shall.

Tim.   For now I think on 't Neighbors, we are to have Bonfires tonight, for the victory over the Spanish Armado, and this pope having been the cause of the burning of many a Heretick; what say ye if we should return him like for like, and burn him? Hold, stop the Pope there.

[Much to and fro action, then]

The Queen, Enter, her General, Lords and Attendants

[There's much honorific exchanging by General & Lord: "long live … etc." Tim and the others come back]

Tim.   Here's King Elizabeth. Down on your Marrow-Bones ye Dogs, Down on your Marrow-Bones, I say.

[They kneel]

Queen.   What would these Supplicants?

Tim.   Ha, what does she Invite us all to Supper.

All.   O, ay; O law!

Queen.   What is your request?

Tim.   We the Tatterdy-Mallion head of the Body Politick, an't shall please your Majesty – We are your True-born Subjects, as Arrant hereticks as ever piss'd: and it shall please your Majesty, we have been a fighting against the Pope, An't please your Majesty, and have beaten the Pope, and taken the Pope; and now we are come to get your Majestie's leave to let us burn the Pope.

General.   And where will you get one?

Tim.   O, we have a Pope, a lusty Pope, a strapping Pope, a Rumping Thumping Pope, a Pope that will fry like Bacon, an't please you.

Queen.   Use your freedom, you have our leave; but do it with discretion, without Riot or Tumult; lest Grace once given and then abused, should turn the Sword of Justice against my Friends.

Tim.   Hark you there, she calls us all Friends.

All.   O law –
Tim.   O 'Tis brave king Elizabeth; I'll warrant your Worship
           we'll have use him as we ought. come, come, to burn the Pope,
           to burn the Pope; Away, away.
{They go out leaping and shouting.}

Queen.   Thus heav'n showers Blessings on the head of Kings,
           And does protect them with Immortal Wings.
           Rome may Conspire, and Hell with her Combine;
           Yet cannot harm, though Pope and Devil join.
[They go out.}

Enter six Dancers, who Dance a Set-Dance, which ended,
They go out, then a Woman Enters and Dances a Jig.

The End of the PLAY.

Although this reads like Monty Python – or Michael Keaton playing
Dogberry in Branagh's *Much Ado* – there is somewhat more subtle political
manipulation than immediately meets the eye – or ear. Tim the Tinker
and Honey-Suckle the cook strongly evoke *A Midsummer Night's Dream*,
a play redolent of the English countryside, good if simple English folk
and the basically benign English fairies who play tricks on them – for all
its putatively Athenian setting. (But, as it has often been said, almost all
of Shakespeare's comedies are set in England, although only *The Merrie
Wives of Windsor* has that location.)

   In *The Coronation of Queen Elizabeth*, there are at least three points we
need to examine – three beyond the obvious, that is. First is the unity
of purpose between Elizabeth and her people. She banishes Cardinals and
Bishops, saying "I'll reform my own House," and England is her house.
At the end of the play, it seems that she has done so effective a job that
Tim and the others are not sure what a pope actually is, although they
are more than willing to burn one, especially for "the victory over the
Spanish Armado." And, although they seem not to know exactly what
the words mean, they recycle proudly the words of the Catholic propa-
gandists into self-identifying pride: "We are your True-born Subjects, as
Arrant hereticks as ever piss'd." Elizabeth, in her turn, does not actually
rebuke them, but offers what might be read as a caution: "Use your
freedom, you have our leave; but do it with discretion, without Riot or
Tumult." What we see here is very like the situation in London at the
time of the so-called Popish Plot; the people were frenzied in their

antagonism, even if they were not sure exactly who to burn or why. The monarchy – even though it was the king's life that was supposedly at risk – expressed alarm and dismay, but did not encourage wild riots in the streets.

The presentation of the Devil as a Jesuit was not only fairly conventional, but was also a direct reference to the Popish Plot, when Oates had claimed that it was a Jesuit who killed the magistrate and the Jesuit Order that was implementing the Pope's plot to kill the king. Here the Devil/Jesuit comes to warn the incriminating nun (to flee, not condemning the dalliance, but rather preserving the Pope from either inopportune exposure or censor). The only odd note in this scene is that the Pope is indeed rebuked by Cardinal Moricena (Dead Dinner), whereupon the Pope kills the nun and, subsequently, the Cardinal. So the Pope himself is so bad that even the Church of Rome will not countenance his activities, as he acknowledges when he says to the nun: "Thou art the only Book I'll ever read, unless to cheat the prying Eyes of Rome." In fact, he calls the papacy "thou gilded Pill, whose outside seems enticing fair" but leads to destruction. He seems to regret not his acts, but the "fate" that made him Pope. Even the Devil – although no longer dressed as a Jesuit – condemns this Pope by leading him to the shades of hell, where a Voice promises that he will be burned or hanged.

Why this delicate separation of Pope and Church? Well, what seems to be suggested here is that there are (if not good) some not-so-bad Catholics and some really evil Catholics. There are Catholics whom even the Jesuits condemn. Considering the number of Catholics in the government, to say nothing of the royal palaces, this is a shrewd bit of back-pedaling. Unlike the Protestant propaganda of Elizabeth's day, including Spenser's *Faerie Queene* where the Pope is the arch-villain of the piece, there is some wiggle room in this little drama.

Which brings us to the third point in need of examination: King Elizabeth. Now this may, of course, simply be the sort of misspeaking for which Bottom and Dogberry were famous – rehearsing "obscenely" rather than "obscurely," for example. Tim calling Elizabeth "King" is certainly on par with the rest of his speech. Or it may be, coupled with the Armada reference, an allusion to Elizabeth's Tilbury speech. The other possibility returns us to the vexed paradigm of gender and rule. A kingdom has a king. Unless the ruler of the kingdom is a queen. For Tim and Honey-Suckle, re-gendering Elizabeth's title is easier than working through that political paradox.

Although the play – skit, really – is tiny, it is a compendium of the concerns of 1680. With the immediate danger passed (or dispelled), it was safe to laugh a bit. But the question of the shadow of the Pope over the tinkers and cooks of England was not a threat that was likely to vanish with the new decade. And who better than Elizabeth to offer both comfort and the promise of a safe future?

While we might suspect this play of containing at least the whiff of satire, there were many excruciatingly earnest accounts of Popish and Jesuitical plots against the life of the queen. The titles of these works are so detailed that they hardly require discussion; for example, the 1679: *The Instrument or Writing of Association: That the True Protestants of England Entered Into, in the Reign of Queen Elizabeth. While Her Life, and the Protestant Religion, by Hellish Popish Plots, was Attempted. Together with the Act of Parliament then for Confirmation, and several Observations thereupon. Usefully Accommodated to our present Day.* As comprehensive as that title seems, it appears vague next to one of the most detailed examples, this from 1680: *The Jesuites Ghostly Wayes To Draw other Persons over to their Damnable Principle, of the Meritoriousness of destroying Princes: Made clear in the two barbarous Attempts of William Parry, and Edward Squire on our late Gracious Soveraign Elizabeth Of ever blessed Memory.*[4] Setting out to tell the Parry story, the author then goes on to Squire's poison plot, introducing it by saying that had it not failed, it would have been called a miracle by Catholics: "And I do not question but if that enterprise had took effect as they had designed, it would have been Meritorious enough to be added to that Book of Miracles composed by ... [one] of the company of Jesus."[5]

> It was the last publick attempt that was made of taking away the Queens life; and it was by one Edward Squire a Scrivener living at Greenwich, who by Deputation was imployed as Purveyor in the Queen's Stable; but his wit being superiour to that of his calling, and not being content with the allowance of his Fortune, he put himself in the Year 1595 into the Fleet of Sir Francis Drake, who was taking his last Voyage to the Indies.[6]

Squire was captured by Spanish "Frigats," and taken as a prisoner to Spain where he was first "firm to his English Religion," but was brought before the Spanish Inquisition "and there being persons on purpose ordered to manage him as they saw fit, they knew so well how to work him, that they quickly got him to be a Catholick."[7]

After his forced conversion, he goes back to England and is soon charged with taking poison in a wine-skin and rubbing it on the pommel of the queen's saddle before she was to ride, doing the same for Essex. That way (as this amazingly detailed narrative goes), "The Queen must of necessity lay her hand on that, and then in all probability at one time or another bringing up her hand to her mouth, or to some part of her face, the poison would get such access to her, as most certainly to be her death."[8] (At least it was merely her hand that was supposed to touch the poisoned pommel.)

> But it pleased the Almighty, who had already delivered her from manifold dangers, to continue still his wonted and wonderful protection of her, keeping her in safety under the shadow of his wings; for although the season was then very hot, being in the month of July, and so consequently the veins more open and ready to receive any malignant influences, yet was she unhurt, and as God shut up the mouths of the Lyons that they should not touch Daniel the servant of the most high, so had to ordered that poison, and otherwise so strong and powerful, not to have the least vertue which was proper to it. She remained well as ever, and it had no more power over her, than Nebuchadnezzars [sic] fiery furnace had over the bodies of those three faithful and famous persons.[9]

As do all good villains, Squires gets up, dusts himself off, and tries it again, this time on Essex when he was at sea. Squires rubbed poison on the arms of his chair, but that failed too. Wallpool, the Englishman/Jesuit working for the Inquisition in Spain, hearing that the queen was still alive, began "to suspect that Squire had only abused him" and took revenge by sending over an Englishman who "pretending he had stole away from the Spanish Inquisition, by parcels and retail told them all the conspiracy, and that he had made his escape on purpose to give the Queen information of it."[10]

The authorities at first doubt this, but when Squires is brought in and questioned, after first denying it, "close circumstances being put to him, and his conscience withall working; he confesses the whole business, and how far he had gone in it." He was then sentenced at the Bar to death for treason and "accordingly executed in the year 1598 ... And if Richeome would take my counsel, he should put in this miracle too, to help fill up his Book."[11] That closing sentence bears more than a passing resemblance to any number of childhood exit lines. The whole tone of the work is child-like, although this may be as much to stress how credulous one must be to believe in miracles in the first place.

From the same year we also have William Miller's *A Pattern or President for Princes to Rule By, and for Subjects to Obey by. Together with the rare*

Example of Subjects tender and singular Care for the Life and Safety of their Soveraign; As Also for the continuance of fond and Orthodox Religion in the Church, and the well-grounded and tempered Government of the Common-wealth (London, Printed for William Miller at the guilded Acorn in St. Paul's Church-Yard. Where you may be furnished with most sorts of Bound or Stitched Books and Acts of Parliament, Proclamations, Speeches, Declarations, Letters, Orders, Commissions, Articles of War or Peace, As also Books of Divinity, Church-Government, Sermons on most occasions, and most sorts of Histories, Poetry, Playes, and such like etc. 1680). This text invites the reader "please to read the Character of this our English Deborah" written by "a Noble, and Learned Pen of one that was bred under her from his Youth, to her Death."

So in the 1679 book, God saves Elizabeth from the Jesuits, and in 1680 Elizabeth and her stouthearted Englishmen save Protestantism from evil Popes and preserve it for the "well-grounded and tempered Government of the Common-wealth." Having worked Elizabeth into the equation of the Popish Plot from almost every angle, these works may seem to us to be overkill. But both, albeit in different ways, suggest the level of anxiety of Londoners about both threats to the life of Charles from Rome and threats to the country from the soul of Charles, were he to follow his mother and his brother back to Rome. In both paradigms, the safest way to discuss these fears is by telling tales from the Golden Age of Queen Elizabeth.

*c.*1695: Gloriana and the Glorious Revolution

Mary Stuart – not, of course, to be confused with her great-great-grand-mother, the Queen of Scots – was the first queen regnant in the Stuart line to sit on the throne of England. She was only the third woman to do so. The unique solution of co-rule with her husband William III might seem to confuse the issue now, but at that time there was no normal pattern for a woman ruler. Mary Tudor had married the man who became King of Spain and who, had she lived, would have placed her attempt to rule England in an untenable position; Elizabeth married no one, but ended a dynasty; Mary, daughter of James II and Anne Hyde, also died childless, but her marriage gave England one of its most staunchly Protestant rulers and accomplished a bloodless revolution.

We should not, therefore, view as anything but inevitable her semi-apotheosis by comparison to Gloriana. Queen Mary II died of smallpox at the age of 32, having been married to William III for nearly 17 years. The next year, T. D'Urfey published a "Funeral Pindarique" in her honor, entitled simply *Gloriana*. By identifying Mary with Elizabeth, D'Urfey is able to highlight both her problematic relationship with her father (although James, for all his failings, never declared his daughter illegitimate) and her loyalty to her faith, both offered squarely on the altar of England. In the 14 stanzas, the poet moves from the Catholic England of Wolsey to the present day of mourning Mary II.

Gloriana
A Funeral Pindarique Poem:
Sacred to the Blessed Memory of that Ever-admir'd and most Excellent Princess,
Our late Gracious Soveraign Lady Queen Mary
[London: Printed for Samuel Briscoe, in Russel-street, in Covent Garden. 1695]

D'Urfey sets the beginning of his poem at Hampton Court (Mary died at Kensington), described as now "mouldering Flaws of craz'd Antiquity" once "that famed Palace, which to fix his Praise/ That Potent Prelate [Cardinal Wolsey] built in our VIII. Henry's days." By stanza XI, the poet's narrator is speaking openly about the Glorious Revolution:

> But Gloriana, when force'd to put on
> The weighty Trouble of a Crown,
> For the Peoples Satisfaction, not her own,
> In hot Ferment found the State
> Perplexed with Factions, Jarring and Debts;
> And with sad Heart submits to Heav'n's Decree,
> Torture'd between Her Country's Cause, and filial Piety.
> Yet still encouraged by celestial Aid,
> The Royall Shepherdess divinely sway'd,
> Held out her Crook, and the rude Herd obey'd.

The narrator goes on to call Mary a Hester, with the devout nature of Deborah, the chastity of Susanna, and the wisdom of the Queen of Sheba. We must doubt, however, D'Urfey's close knowledge of the actual narratives of biblical women, since his final compliment is to say Mary is "Like Michol kind and dutious to Her Lord" (stanza XIV). Fans of Second Samuel will recall that after Michal's initial rebellion against her father Saul, for the love of her husband David, she later undertook to chastise him about dancing before the common people in a manner that revealed the royal jewels. And thus Michal, the daughter of Saul, had no child for the rest of her life. Granted, some of this does apply to Mary –

choosing husband over a royal father, having no children – but the reason for the latter strikes a sour note here.

I'm inclined, however, to put this down to ignorance on the part of the poet, rather than to an intended slight, for the poem ends with an all-stops-out apotheosis of the queen. D'Urfey concludes by having "a radiant Cherub soaring through the Sky" proclaim the following at the end of stanza XIV:

> Let Women be no more defam'd,
> Nor ever henceforth for past Frailty blam'd;
> Th' unbounded Vertues of this ONE,
> Do amply for their Faults attone,
> With the Eternal Compensation make
> And all the rest of Female Kind are pardon'd for
> > Her Sake
> > Finis

This is a remarkably Catholic ending for a woman being praised as a Protestant. Her name, of course, carries the heaviest possible baggage, but to put her into the paradigm of a Second Eve, redeeming all woman-kind in the medieval Eva/Ave dichotomy, is either to put great faith in the theological soundness of his poetry or to make the assumption that poetic license transcends religious doctrine. Or perhaps D'Urfey simply feels that the weight of the nomination Gloriana speaks for itself.

*c.*1700: the generic secret life

In a time when so many people must have wondered what had really gone on during the Glorious Revolution and what was going on during the shift to the House of Hanover, the paradigm of the secret life must have carried particular force. Of course it's fair to ask when, if ever, the general public wasn't wondering what was really going on – a question of enormous relevance in the United States and Great Britain of 2003. But the plain fact is that, before the eighteenth century, most of any country's population would have lacked sufficient information or interest even to speculate. Not until the other end of the 1700s does the great age of newspapers begin, with John Walter founding the *Daily Universal Register* on the first day of 1785, a newspaper which was renamed *The Times* three years later. But the coffee-house culture of the late seventeenth century combined with the March 1702 founding of the *Daily Courant*[12] in Bishopsgate gave the citizens of London the ability to learn news (or versions of news) from private conversations and individual reading rather than from public proclamation or sermon. In addition to the more freely circulating written word, travel became easier, as the Turnpike Trusts, originally established in 1706, were extended in 1735; while many people protested the tolls, the result was indeed better roads. (Although – like the age of newspapers – the turnpikes didn't truly come into their own until the end of the century, when Palmer established the first mail-post service in 1784.) Nevertheless, with better roads, everything, including news and gossip, traveled faster.

If no one – or no one outside the immediate circle of power – knows anything that's going on, the concept of secret action does not exist. One either knows everything (or close to it) or one knows nothing. Rumor, of course, problematizes that simple statement, and gossip is a subject recently and fruitfully studied. While that topic is not as ephemeral as some of its detractors charge (for example, diaries and letters provide hard evidence of what was being said about what was being said), with the medium of print having become common, we find a different sort of rumor: the written word. For everyone takes a rumor for truth, at least fleetingly. Why else are people outraged when untruths or misapprehensions are printed? Because they fear that someone, somewhere will take those words as truth.

Even today, as cynical as we all have become about global politics and the media, the printed word still holds at least the illusion of verity for us. "I read it in the *Times*," or "the *Washington Post* uncovered the real story," are still words to conjure with, even in this age of eye-witness CNN-generated awareness. Ironically, with up-to-the-nanosecond coverage on every television screen, what Milton called "the cool element of prose" has taken on the patina of respected authority. Although there are still screaming broadsheets, serious newspapers have come to provide a considered and ordered evaluation of the jumble of images generated by daring photographers and glossed by breathlessly eager reporters, all concerned more with immediacy than accuracy or common sense. We have the ludicrous example of the American television personality "embedded" with the troops entering Iraq who, in his eagerness to be "the first-est with the most-est," failed to realize that he was also supplying the Iraqi military leaders with current plans for US troop movements. Yes, newspapers are still politically biased – whether a woman reads the *Guardian* or the *Telegraph* tells us much – but (with a few staggering exceptions) the general public tends to assume that they are all writing from the same fact sheet, as it were.

As the seventeenth century ended and the eighteenth century began, there was a flush of public interest in the "real" story of Queen Elizabeth's life. Like the myriad pseudo-news shows claiming to document "the story behind the story," the genre of the secret history offered the history-behind-the-history to a readership and audience just realizing that such a narrative might be possible. We have a number of examples of the genre, most notably: *The Secret HISTORY of the Most Renowned Q. Elizabeth and the Earl of Essex* By a Person of Quality (Cologne, Printed for Will with the Wisp at the Sign of the Moon in the Ecliptic, 1689). This two-part book was followed by another printing in 1689. It contains a very long-winded version of the Essex ring story, and is peppered with jealous fits from Leicester. According to the Person of Quality, Elizabeth had barely time to deal with the men she loved, let alone to run a country. Nor was Essex the only object of Elizabeth's secret attentions. In 1691 we have – by no author but from the same printer – *The Secret HISTORY of the Duke of Alancon and Q.Elizabeth. A True History* (London, Printed for Will with the Wisp at the Sign of the Moon in the Ecliptic). Of all the secret histories, this is perhaps the most fantastic. That the tale has little to do with Elizabeth herself is made clear by the opening lines: "There are few men, who have not heard speak of Catharine de Medicis. They all know, that this Princess, who was without doubt one of the most politick Women of the age, was also one of the most Ambitious. One of the things that she most heartily desired, was to put a Crown upon the head of every one of her Children."[13] Furthermore, the plot of the book is the tale of a disinherited heir – certainly a subject of some interest in 1691.

The author states that during Elizabeth's long reign, her main purpose had been to lure "all the Princes of Europe" to her, offering a marriage that she would never make, as she "too well loved" her own authority. "But whereas she was extremely Politick, and took delight in attracting courtship, which the knowledge of her design had made her lose, she was careful to keep it very secret, and it was not discovered until a long time after."[14] While using Alençon to make Leicester jealous and Leicester to work the same strategy on Alençon, she realizes she has gone too far and starts sending Alençon compliments. His response to her messenger is: "The Crown of England is not made for my head; 'tis too fast upon Elizabeth's for me to pretend unto it; and when it will please her to share it, I know very well that it will not be upon me whom she will cast her eyes."[15]

We then hear at some length of the virtues of the Duke: he "was then in the Flower of his Age, Handsome, Well-shaped, Gallant, and Magnificent: These Qualities were supported by that Behavior, and those charming Manners, which distinguish the Princes of France from all others."[16] Fearing that she was about to lose him, Elizabeth takes Alençon into her garden and makes the following speech.

It is so difficult for a Woman to maintain her self all alone upon a Throne, as that I have always regarded marriage as a thing absolutely necessary for the Establishment of my Authority. I have made to Secret of my Design: A Crown always communicates part of this Charm to those who wear it, and the splendor of mine hath concealed my imperfections from those who have been dazled with it. The Earl of Leicester appeared to me the most considerable: His Birth, which is from one of the most ancient Families of the Realm: His great Riches, and above all, the Support of the Parliament, which protects him, did flatter his hopes too much to be quite clean rejected. I did believe my self therefore obliged to hearken to him a little more favourably than to others, in order to prevent the mischievous Consequences, which a manifest Resistance would infallibly have drawn upon me.[17]

She goes on to tell Alençon that she only flirts with Leicester to keep the noble from making trouble. The narrator remarks: "Though there was some truth in the Queen's words, and that she did her utmost endeavours to put on the perswasive air of sincerity, yet the Duke of Alancon gave no great credit to them,"[18] and he tells her so, politely.

In order to stir the rivals up more, Elizabeth sends letters to both men, seeming to have mixed them up, so that Alençon thinks he gets Leicester's and the reverse. The letter sent to Leicester, supposedly written to Alençon:

Pardon me, Sir, if I could not have the Honour of seeing you in the Morning. 'Twas the greatest trouble that my present indisposition occasioned, but I am afraid that it will not be the only one, and that it may yet put off for some says the impatience I have of seeing you King of England, and Husband to

ELIZABETH.[19]

To Alençon she sends:

The Duke of Alancon presses me, and I no longer know how to colour my delays. I Counterfeit my self Sick on purpose, in Expectation that you invent some better pretense. I do not believe that I need intreat you to seek out one. You know well enough what Reasons oblige you to it.[20]

Leicester sees Alençon and waves the letter around, and says that he has more cause to be jealous than does the Duke. The Duke then shows the Earl his letter, "So that both seeing themselves equally deceived, they hardly knew whether they ought to laugh or grieve at this Adventure."[21] But the author turns the encounter into an episode of male bonding and Leicester tells the Duke what a "deceitful Woman" Elizabeth is, citing "how false she had been to the Queen of Scots" and "of the Cruelty with which she retained the Princess Marianna in Prison."[22]

The Marianna story is wild. According to Leicester, Catherine of Aragon was pregnant when Henry divorced her, and she had the baby in secret. On her deathbed she gives her loyal friend, Lady Norfolk, a "Sealed Letter" in "a Casket" and "A Table-book Set with Diamonds," both of which offered proof of Marianna's heritage. Lady Norfolk takes these and the little girl into her care. When she hears that Henry is dying, Lady N starts for court with the girl and the documents, but becomes ill along the way and by the time she recovers, Henry is dead. Lady Norfolk has always had Marianna pass as her kinswoman, and now the princess is a young lady "and even then gave hopes of the incomparable Beauty, which Time hath since brought to perfection." As she is dying herself, Lady Norfolk trusts her son with the truth of the girl's identity and the proofs. He, of course, promptly falls in love with Marianna, but recognizes the inequality of their positions.[23]

Meanwhile, Edward dies (time means nothing in this narrative) and Mary comes to the throne. "The Duke of Norfolk remembering the Order which his dying Mother had left him,"[24] starts for court to tell the queen she has a (full) sister. Mary opens the letter in the casket and reads what Catherine wrote to Henry:

> SIR
>
> I Die with Grief, since I die in your Disgrace; but I hope that the Present I make you after my Death, will restore to me that precious Friendship which you have deprived me of during my Life; and that the little Marianna, your Daughter and mine, whom you will receive from the Dutchess of Norfolk's hands, will make you remember, with some sentiments of tender ness, her Mother, and your Wife.
>
> Catharine.[25]

There is also a book and some pictures (pictures?) of Henry and Catherine and their two daughters. "All these Evidences were seconded by the Voice of Blood and Nature, which spoke in Mary's Heart. She without any great trouble acknowledged Marianna for her Sister."[26]

But Mary dies before she can change Henry's will, and when Elizabeth comes to the throne, she puts Marianna in prison and Norfolk in a dungeon. The Duke of Alençon, of course, also falls madly in love with Marianna. He carries her picture with him (where do all these pictures come from?) and drops it in an arbor where Elizabeth finds it and gets suspicious. He appeals to his countryman, du Lac, for help and advice, but that gentleman advises Alençon to give it up, for "He knew from the Queen of Scotland's Example, that there were no Laws, which Elizabeth would not put in Execution wheen her Authority was concerned."[27]

Alençon arranges to see Marianna: "Marianna was at that time in the Flower of her Age"[28] (figure up that age, please, if there were pictures of Henry with this daughter). Alençon speaks on behalf of Marianna; Elizabeth pretends to consider him as a "mediator" for the princess; Marianna is poisoned; the Duke waits by her bedside.

> But alas! his fears did not last long, and he soon saw himself in that unhappy state where fear is laid aside, because there is no longer room left for hope. Marianna was again relapsed into a Lethargy more dangerous than the first, and the poison either accomplishing its work, or those the Queens Physicians serving for new Ministers of their cruelty, this fair princess expired in a moment between their hands.[29]

Alençon goes home to France, after breaking with Elizabeth who expresses grief at his charges of cruelty: "Insult now over a miserable Woman (said Elizabeth, carrying on her dissimulation to the utmost) and if you seek only a pretense to break with me." He, "all in a rage in Fury," tells E to "enjoy in peace a Crown usurped. I do not envy you the fruit of your treachery, and perfidiousness."[30] He returns to France and dies "in the flower of his Age, esteemed and lamented by all the World, Elizabeth alone excepted, who was very glad to see her self delivered of so formidable an Enemy."[31]

While this is far from the only narrative of secret heirs (my favorite is the 1820 narrative of Rose Douglas, the daughter of Mary Stuart, who lived in Elizabeth's court), it's an interesting addition to the other sorts of secret lives of the eighteenth century. Rather than showing Elizabeth as a "real" (which is to say sexually active) woman, this shows her as a scheming monster willing to condone (if not to order) the death of her own half-sister. What this secret history does, in fact, is to cast Marianna in the role played by Elizabeth during her sister's reign, while turning Elizabeth into a more negative version of any Queen Mary extant in Protestant propaganda. Mary, after all, neither hid nor poisoned Elizabeth.

While few of these secret histories cast the queen in a very flattering light, this narrative makes her a true monster of ambition, as well as a creature of inappropriate appetite. Little wonder that, even in 1689, the work went unattributed.

In 1708 we find, not an author, but both an editor and a printer claiming responsibility for the *Secret Memoirs of Robert Dudley, Earl of Leicester, prime Minister and Favorite of Queen Elizabeth; containing an Instructive Account of his Ambition, Designs, Intrigues, excessive Power; his Engrossing the Queen, with the dangerous Consequences of that Practice &c.* Written during his Life, and now publish'd from an old Manuscript. The Second Edition. To which is added a Preface by Dr. Drake. Printed for Sam. Briscoe and Sold by B. Gragg, at the Blue-Ball in Ave-Mary-lane.

Nor does the genre die out with the changing of the century and the dynasty. In 1727 we find yet another text with no author (but attributed by the British Library to Samuel Jebb), *The Life of Robert Earl of Leicester, The Favorite of Queen Elizabeth: Drawn from original Writers and Records* (London: Printed for Woodman and Lyon, in Russel-Street Covent Garden, and C. Davis in Hatton-Garden). While the word "secret" does not appear in this title, the focus on Leicester as Elizabeth's favorite, rather than a man with other claims to fame, does suggest that we may find some personal moments detailed. Even as late as 1754 the genre continues, this time with both the author's name and his credentials on the title page:

Memoirs Of the Reign of Queen Elizabeth, from the Year 1581 til her Death. In which the Secret Intrigues of her Court, and the Conduct of her Favorite, Robert Earl of Essex, both at home and Abroad, are particularly illustrated.
From the original papers of his intimate Friend, Anthony Bacon ...,
and other manuscripts never before published
by Thomas Birch DD Rector of the United Parishs of St Margaret ...
and St Gabriel Fenchurch and Secretary of the Royal Society.
2 volumes
London: Printed for A. Millar in the Strand
MDCCLIV

The claim of access to private papers and unpublished manuscripts was a common one, but the titles of Dr. Birch give this work at least a speciously scholarly frame. In addition to books such as this, there were also pseudo-books, or books written in the eighteenth century claiming to be reprints of Elizabethan texts. These titles make much the same point as the secret histories, as we can see from the 1706 and 1708 printings of a book by a truly anonymous eighteenth-century author: *Sir William Cavendish's Memoirs of the Life of Cardinal Woolsey to which is added A Memorial against Favourites, Presented to Q. Elizabeth*, Written by the Lord-Treasurer Burleigh. London: Printed and are to be Sold by B. Bragg at the Raven in Pater-noster-row. How a text by Burleigh could have remained "secret" is never addressed in the text, which suggests that Elizabeth did not make the mistake that her father made with Wolsey. But it is hard to accept this at anything like face value, because, on the verso before that title page, there's the early-modern equivalent of a jacket blurb for:

BOOKS Printed for Sam. Briscoe
and Sold by B. Gragg, at the Blue-Ball in Ave-Mary-Lane.
Newly Published

These include the *Secret Memoirs of Robert Dudley, Earl of Leicester, prime Minister and Favorite of Queen Elizabeth* mentioned above, as well as for a book on Dr. Stanhope, Dean of Canterbury's, remarks on the word Moderation and *Two Campaigns in one Panegyrical Essay upon this grace the Duke of Marlborough Successes in the Years 1704 & 1705 ... To which is added, the fifth Ode of Horace's fourth Book, turn'd into English by way of imitation, and humbly address'd to his Grace, instead of Augustus, to whom tis dedicated in the Original.*

It's hard to know what, if any, the relationship between these three texts is supposed to be, beyond venturing the cautious conclusion that the printer must have thought that people reading one book might be interested in the others. It would be easy to say that the increasingly aware populace of the eighteenth century realized that the Gloriana of the portraits, of the Westminster tomb, and of the London church memorials, lacked both depth and any element of humanity. In *England's Elizabeth*, Dobson and Watson open their eighteenth-century chapter, "The Private Lives of the Virgin Queen," with this astute observation:

If one thing distinguishes the eighteenth century's many versions of Elizabeth from the uninflected Protestant nostalgia that characterized much of her mythos in the seventeenth, it is a growing consciousness that her status as a national idol might be at variance with her personal identity as a woman.[32]

As Dobson and Watson suggest, Elizabeth's status as an icon of Protestantism had been the most prominent element of her identity during the Restoration, where the question of religion was always and ever in the forefront of people's minds. The country entered a new century with a new identity – the Act of Union in 1707 made Great Britain a formal entity and no longer did the monarch have to be crowned in Edinburgh as well as London. In this new Britain, with its excesses of all sorts, its vision of the world as its own imperial treasure trove to be had for the taking, the idea of Elizabeth the Protestant, Elizabeth the almost-man as her Tilbury speech implied, became too one-dimensional to merit much attention. For once, no one wanted to talk about the Armada. The British Empire was using its control of the seas to gain control of staggering hunks of the world's landscape; if there was an aggressor on the high seas, it was Britain.

How, then, could English history be shaped to accommodate the growth of the British Empire? Lacking a Virgil to fashion a fictive dynastic inevitability, lacking, indeed, a dynasty as the Stuart line was clearly headed for extinction, it mattered not that Queen Anne dressed herself in gowns designed to recall the dresses of Elizabeth's portraits. The larger question was how to turn not one, but two short-lived dynasties into a history to rival that of the Romans. The answer, of course, was to invent more history – secret history. While a history can be both "Secret" and "True," as the 1691 Alençon history purports, the juxtaposition of these adjectives focuses attention on a crucial element of the genre. As the Stuart dynasty came to a close and the Hanoverian future looms, the newly British reader needs to find truth in the past. But if traditional truth – or the iconic truths passed down by history – are not enough, then secrets are required. Elizabeth was famed as a virgin. Anne ruined her health with 19 pregnancies. Neither woman was able to provide an heir who would continue her dynasty. Nor is this a situation which could be resolved by blaming women rulers. Henry VIII's famous quest for a male heir had found only weak and fleeting success, while the failure of Charles II to father any legitimate heirs was directly responsible for the whole problem of Stuart succession. Seen in this light, the Elizabeth of the Golden Speech, the Good Queen Bess who was married to her kingdom, appears in an almost mythic light. It is the idea of a monarch that can transcend the flesh and blood problems of the new eighteenth century. And the icon of Elizabeth offers both the truth of history and the secret of transcendence. If the life of a person is more than the sum of a set of specific actions, then there must be some space between the true and the secret, something that, even if unknown, is still somehow recognized. Beyond the struggle to reconcile private and public, woman and queen, the secret history moves the reader into the (perhaps imagined) reach of that part of the persona of Elizabeth that was neither shop-worn public knowledge nor unimaginable emotional satisfactions and longings. Gloriana never appears in the pages of Spenser's *Faerie Queene*. Even in allegory there are aspects of the Elizabeth icon that cannot be comprehended and represented. The generic secret history is not so much an attempt to know the unknowable as to acknowledge it.

*c.*1740: Britannia, Jacobites, and the Jews

While the conflict with Spain precipitated by the loss of Captain Jenkins' ear cannot claim a place of pride in the pantheon of British history, it did open the door for larger conflicts with France, conflicts destined to last for the rest of the century and beyond. As the War of Jenkins' Ear fizzled out in 1741, other issues of national identity took center stage, even as "Rule Britannia" was sung for the first time in 1740, during a masque written and performed for the disgruntled and disaffected Prince of Wales, Frederick. During this drama, the once-and-future King Alfred is advised by three royal visionaries: the Black Prince, Queen Elizabeth, and William III,[33] all giving what Simon Schama dubs "long, pull-yourself-together-for-Britannia homilies."[34] The subjects of the Prince's father (George II, who was fighting in Germany for non-British causes, under the flag of Hanover) certainly tried to obey those unheard injunctions by manning the eastern shores against the French. They were all saved, in truly masque-like fashion, by the "ever dependable Protestant wind," as Schama puts it. Like the storm (sent by God, forsooth) that drove the Spanish fleet north around the tip of Scotland, this evidence of God's national spirit was gratefully received.

> But both government and people knew that this was only a respite and not a victory. It did not take a strategic genius to predict that, sooner or later, the government of Luis XV would play the Jacobite card, in either Ireland or Scotland or both.[35]

In other words, the last chapter of the wayward Stuart heirs was about to be played out, costing the lives and homes of countless Scots and sowing seeds of an enmity still blooming today.

Elizabeth made a problematic Britannia, although metaphorically seeing her as the "Mother of her country, nursing mother to religion and all liberal sciences" from James' Latin Westminster epitaph was not a problem, as Dobson and Watson observe.[36] No, the biggest problem with making Elizabeth fit the icon of the moment (an interesting change from making the moment fit an Elizabeth icon) was her Englishness. Even her literal childless state did not raise the same anxieties that her execution of Mary Stuart foregrounded. Scotland was now, in theory, one with England. The mythology of the Mary Stuart and Elizabeth rivalry was more vividly fixed in the sphere of public memory than Elizabeth's giving the crown to James, Mary's son. How then, did a nation still struggling with an us/them mentality about the English/Scots dichotomy imagine Elizabeth as Britannia, mother of a united island?

Negative evidence would suggest that most of the nation didn't try. During the Jacobite uprisings, there were few invocations of the Tudor queen, at least in the form of an icon of Englishness. But what we can recover from the period is one of the oddest Elizabeth icons in this collection. The 1740 *The Chronicle of Kings of England* "Authored by Robert Dodsley under the pseudonymous title Nathan Ben Saddi, A Priest of the Jews," and written in, as the title page claims "the Manner of the ancient Jewish Historian," provides us with an Elizabeth icon of such force that it seemingly stops history.

The first question, of course, is how did the Jews get mixed up in all this? Exiled from England by Edward I, officially re-admitted by Cromwell, and allowed by the 1664 Order of Council to remain in England after the Restoration (provided that they "demean themselves peaceably and quietly"), the Jewish population of England was still in a precarious position. Having officially missed much of the history that defined Englishness, the one straw which an entire people could grasp was that Elizabeth famously allowed learned Jews in her court. While this didn't always work out well for the Jews in question, it nevertheless gave the re-admitted community a link with that fabled figure, Elizabeth. Still striving for equal status as English/British subjects (the Jewish Naturalization Act was passed in July of 1753, but repealed the next year and the "disabilities" reinstated in response to public protest), the Jews were in a precarious position within a country still sorting out its own national identity.

The author of *The Chronicle of Kings of England* manages to call both on Jewish tradition and English history during a time when the former would have been a liability and the latter a dubious prop. In the work's preface the author says he has "chosen to [write the history] in the Manner of our Forefathers, the ancient Jewish Historians, as being not only the most concise, but the most venerable Way of Writing."[37] And certainly the work is concise: from William the Conqueror to Elizabeth there are but 58 pages of large type. When he comes to the Tudors, Ben Saddi (to take the title page at face value) allots almost four pages to Henry VIII, less than a page to Edward VI, one page to Mary, and two pages to Elizabeth.

Wisdom and Strength were in her Right hand, and in her Left were Glory and Wealth.

She spake, and it was War; she waved her Hand, and the Nations dwelt in Peace.

Her Ministers were just, her Counsellors were sage, her Captains were bold, and her Maids of Honor ate Beef Stakes to Breakfast.

Now the rest of the Acts of Queen Elizabeth, and all the glorious things that she did, are they not written in the Chronicles of the Kings of England?

And Elizabeth slept with her Fathers, and James of Scotland reigned in her stead.[38]

This strange assortment of observations (I especially like the steak-eating Maids at breakfast) does not constitute the entirety of the commentary on Elizabeth. In a combination Medieval humility topos and homage to Boccaccio in *Concerning Famous Women,*[39] Ben Saddi offers a postscript:

And now, gentle Reader, peradventure thou wil ask me, why I have not proceeded further in this renowned History of the Reign of Queen Elizabeth?

... Perhaps, by coming too near our own Times, I might give Offense to some Persons who are now living; or perhaps it might tend to inflame the Parties which already too much divide the Land; or perhaps I might not be so impartial my self, in relating these Matters, as becometh the Character of a grave Historian.

But the best reason that I can give is this; [the deeds of Elizabeth's successors are so "glorious" and "wonderful], so sublime and exalted, that it is beyond the Flight of a Goose's Quill to reach them. This, I hope thou wilt believe, is the Truth.

Howbeit, if thou shouldst happen to be incredulous, and think that this was not my real Motive to desist, let it furthermore be known unto thee, that tho the Case was otherwise, yet it is the peculiar Privilege and Perogative of Kings, that they grow not wicked, neither do they wax foolish, til after they have been dead an hundred years.[40]

So is this an anti-Elizabeth icon? a satire? a slavish flattery? By concluding with Elizabeth, then appending these passages, Ben Saddi strongly suggests that she is the last monarch to be worthy of praise. But even such praise as he gives her is either wildly idiosyncratic or a poor attempt at apotheosis garnished with the comedy of diet. That being said, the current rulers of the realm could hardly complain at their exclusion.

The postscript is like Marc Antony's crocodile: "it is shaped like itself."

While it's just possible to argue that Ben Saddi stops short of the Stuarts because of the Jacobite troubles, we must remember that the Georgian claim to the throne derived from James I's daughter Elizabeth and her descendants. True, the current Stuarts were Catholic while Elizabeth Stuart's children and grandchildren were safely Protestant, but that's a fine hair to split in so brief a work. Could the author possibly have thought that this work would help the Jews gain freedom from restrictions? If the author's goal was the reverse (as the name Robert Dodsley rather does suggest), could he have believed that so literally light a piece of writing would have tipped the scales against the children of Israel? Without the postscript it's just possible that this recitation of English history could have been offered in the same cause as the apostle Stephen's recitation of Hebrew scripture in Acts: Stephen spoke to prove he was a good Jew; perhaps Ben Saddi wrote to prove he was a good Briton. But in a 58-page work, a two-page postscript cannot be lightly dismissed. Of course, the odds-on favorite for a good answer is that I'm taking this text far too seriously. With more question marks than full stops and the continual reiterations of "perhaps" in this paragraph, here may be a fitting stopping place for a section made up largely of odds and ends. As the Napoleonic wars begin, readings become much more straightforward, as there is once again an unproblematic occasion for an Elizabeth icon, both in the obvious paradigm of the Armada and as England's golden past.

*c.*1812: once more onto the beach ...

With the shores of England once more at risk of invasion by a European power, it would be unthinkable not to find Elizabeth and the Armada victory absent from the lexicon of public discourse. We find this, of course, in both art and literature. But in the days of conflict leading up to the formal hostilities with the French, we also find text framed as memories and songs – an as yet unexamined genre – summoning the spirit of Gloriana into the present age. In the 1785 *Memoirs of Sir James Melvil of Halhill* (subtitled with the lengthy addendum "Containing An impartial Account of the most remarkable Affairs of State during the Sixteenth Century, not mentioned by other Historians: More particularly relating to the Kingdoms of England and Scotland, under the Reigns of Queen Elizabeth, Mary Queen of Scots, and King James. In most of which Transactions the Author was Personally and Publickly concerned") we find elements of the secret history – "not mentioned by other Historians" – coupled with the claim of sixteenth-century authority, "Published from the Original Manuscript by GEORGE SCOTT, Gent." While the antipathy to both France and Spain would not be unbelievable in a Tudor manuscript, the recorded ages of Mary and Elizabeth suggest that George Scott, Gentleman, is indeed the author, with his eye firmly on the invasion-fearing, war-mongering reader of the late eighteenth century. Among the usual suspects in the gossip line-up we find this edifying tale. According to Scott/Melvil, after consulting "Diviners" and "Necromancers," Henry VIII was told that his son would die without issue, Mary would take the throne and marry a Spaniard; then Elizabeth would reign after her and marry either a Scotsman or a Frenchman.

> Whereupon the King caused to give Poison to both his Daughters: But because this had not the effect he desired, (for they finding themselves altered by vehement Vomitings and Purgings, having suspected Poison, and taken Remedies) he caused to proclaim them both Bastards.[41]

So the mere idea of an alliance with Spain, France, or even Scotland (not a surprising addition in a post-Jacobite text) was seen as cause for wholesale slaughter of daughters. The better-dead-than clause, however, may have ended with "Catholic," rather than "foreign-wed," since this text appeared only five years after the Gordon Riots in London where anti-Catholic mobs destroyed property and close to 850 people died.

In that text, Elizabeth is little more than a marker for the sacrifices necessary to preserve Protestant Englishness (although Mary's continued survival certainly owes more to history than to the sentiments of the author) from the taint of Papist blood. More substantive – in the sense that the narrative above does not present the queen as an icon – representations of Elizabeth are to be found in the songs of the period. In 1792–93, a chapbook contains the following dittie, of which the first and last of seven stanzas merit close reading:

> i   To my muse give attention, and deem it not a mystery,
> If we jumble together music, poetry, and history;
> The times to display in the days of Queen Bess, Sir,
> Whose name and whole memory posterity may bless, Sir,
>   [refrain:] Oh the golden days of good Queen Bess!

> vii   Thus renown'd as they liv'd all the days of their lives, Sir,
> Bright examples of glory to those who surviv'd, Sir;
> May we their descendants pursue the same way, Sir,
> And Kind George, like Queen Bess, have his golden days, Sir,
> And may a longer reign of glory and success,
> Make his name eclipse the fame of Good Queen Bess.[42]

In 1800 we find the same song in another chapbook, but with the addition of the following as the penultimate stanza:

> Then all great men were good, and all good men were great,
> And the props of the nation were the pillars of the State, Sir;
> For the sovereign and the subject one interest supported,
> And all our powerful alliance by all nations were courted.
>   Oh the golden days, &ec.

That chapbook also contains a set of lyrics using "Good Queen Bess" as a ruler with which to measure and praise King George.

> THE ALTERATION OF TIMES: or the Days of George the Third!
> [1st verse]
> Come listen my neighbours and hear a merry ditty,
> Of a strange alteration in every town and city,
> I'll tell you of the times when Queen Bess rul'd the nation,
> And take a view of things in their present situation.
> O what an alteration is now to be seen,
> Since the happy times when Elizabeth was Queen.

The middle lines are much the same as in the first song, but with better syntax, 25 lines, without stanza breaks, of then-and-now statements (with then definitely the winner); and the song concludes:

> But now everybody's business some people make their own,
> And if they see you rise, they'll strive to pull you down.
> Thus happy they did live, sir, as you may plainly see,
> And were a bright example for all their posterity,
> May we follow their steps til we happily attain,
> And the Lord restore the King to his royal throne again.
> And long may he reign with glory and success,
> And may he reign hereafter in heaven's happiness.[43]

The wish that the king might be restored to his royal throne is a reference to the power held by the Prince of Wales, who, by July of 1784, was shuttling regularly between Brighton and London. In 1788 George undeniably succumbed to his now-famous madness, and three months later Prime Minister Pitt introduced the Regency Bill to impose strictly limited authority on the Prince of Wales, a legislation that was dropped a few weeks later when George was said to have recovered. But a more likely reading renders this dittie as bald-faced satire. In late 1795 George III was stoned by an angry London crowd, and there had been bread riots for months in various cities. January of 1800 saw the opening of the first soup kitchen in London, an effort to relieve the acute food shortage. George III continued in uncertain mental and physical health until the issue could be no longer overlooked, and the Regency Act was passed in 1811. The king who made such a poor showing when compared with Good Queen Bess had brought the country to its 1800 "present situation," and the situation was soup kitchens and starvation. It's just as well that the author of this song did not read that 1740 "history" in which even Elizabeth's maids ate steaks.

As Prince Regent, the future George IV came to power over a nation that had lost a major colony in North America, had at one time or another in the past 20 years been at war with fully half of Western Europe, and was currently locked in a struggle with Napoleon's quest for empire. 1811 was almost the midpoint between the 1805 victory of Trafalgar and the 1815 Battle of Waterloo.

Clearly, some sort of intervention was needed. Even sentimental literature of the period cried out for the figure of Elizabeth. In 1809 Elizabeth Somerville's *Aurora and Maria: or The Advantages of Adversity, A Moral Tale, in which is Introduced a Juvenile Drama, Call'ed Queen Elizabeth or Old Times New Revived* appeared. The two little girls of the title – who have very odd mothers – give the three-act play's curtain speech, which purports to be Elizabeth's words upon hearing the news of the Armada victory.

Chance has bestowed on me an uncertain and an uncoveted crown; but clemency and justice are beyond the power of chance to bestow. They are the richest gifts of an higher and better governed world, whose slightest favor I would purchase could it be bought by the willing sacrifice of all my boasted greatness! Nor would I from the lowest state in nature, be one atom less a Christian, to be more than queen! This is a day of rejoicing; from this time may we anticipate the glad tidings of peace, and again trace the truant smile of content on the cheek of the childless and forlorn. From this day may every British son triumph in our victories, and proudly boast his scars, as fresh gained laurels in a mother's cause.[44]

At a time when the new French Armada had so recently been laid low by Nelson, the idea of little girls speaking sentimental lines of a bygone queen lies in an uneasy praxis between the culturally interesting and the openly maudlin. My point, however, mercifully does not require that I come to terms with the quality of the text. The words spoken by Somerville's little girls invoke the icon Elizabeth for whom all levels of British society seemingly cherished some nostalgia. That this nostalgia was mixed with genuine desire for a monarch capable of personally generating a victory makes both the Prince Regent and his father dubious candidates for uttering similar words in the current crisis. Small wonder then, that the collective memory of Elizabeth emerged from the sphere of the intangible and appeared, as it were, on every street corner.

The print of Elizabeth at Tilbury (Figure 5) is a detail after (but not from) an earlier print. This 1822 print by William Darton is copied after Thomas Stothard's 1805 larger print, which shows all of Elizabeth's horse, one bowing man in the foreground, soldiers before her and statesmen behind her. Dobson and Watson discuss that version of the print, making the important point that its vertical orientation speaks to the upright nature of the British as they saw themselves in comparison to the French.[45] This detail differs only a little from the Stothard print: Elizabeth's forehead is higher and the St. George Cross is more evident behind her than it is in the busier, larger work. While containing its own blooper – the hair of the man in Stothard's foreground is tangled here with the horse's mane – the larger problem with the Stothard print is here unnoticeable. In the large print the two flags in the background – the Royal Standard and the St. George Cross – are being blown from right to left, while the ends of the sash across Elizabeth's bodice stream from left to right.

These details, of course, are quibbles. The point is that we have an immediate and visual Elizabeth icon at just the time the island is once again threatened from abroad. Dobson and Watson argue that this print and much of the rhetoric of the times works to relocate the 1588 "broadly ... Protestant fiction" that "divine Providence had intervened to give the English victory," but that by the end of the eighteenth century, not only was the emphasis being changed to suggest that "God had intervened not so much on the side of Protestantism, but on the side of a nation's" liberty. "Indeed," they conclude, "God was fast being edged out of the story altogether."[46] To support their reading of the times, Dobson and Watson cite an impressive list of texts: Robert Southey's 1798 *Naucratia; or Naval Domination*; Robert Anderson's 1805 "Britons, United, the World May Defy"; and John Thelwall's 1805 *The Trident of Albion: an Epic Effusion*. These, along with Macauley's poem "The Armada," according to Dobson and Watson, collectively construct "a fantasy which again links national identity with the land rather than with religion."[47] There is nothing in these arguments with which anyone could seriously disagree, but there might be one point that needs to be appended to the Dobson/Watson

Figure 5   "Queen Elizabeth at Tilbury;" print by William Darton, 1822

analysis. The figure of Elizabeth herself the co-authors compare to the Cecil print of Elizabeth receiving a lance from Truth (see Figure 2); but – while such similarities as the queen mounted on a horse and wearing garb that suggests armor are indisputable – I would suggest that this Elizabeth icon (literally an icon in the detailed version) makes a very different statement. In the Cecil print, Elizabeth is perched in an unlikely, but effectively dominant pose upon the side of the horse; here she is realistically riding sidesaddle. Other than the central figures of Elizabeth and her horse, Cecil offers only Truth, the seven-headed beast beneath the horse's hooves, and the distant naval formation of the Armada. Elizabeth is the only human and one of only two personages in the frame. In the larger Stothard print, Elizabeth is surrounded by no fewer than ten men. Furthermore, the nineteenth-century print shows static men, but the queen apparently in motion, as witnessed by her flying scarf-like adornment. The action here is ongoing, with the battle yet to be won, but clearly to be won by Elizabeth, as the figures of the men defer to her motion and remain stationary. In the more iconic Darton print, the motion is even more pronounced. Queen Elizabeth is on her way, and with a firm sense of purpose, the George Cross of England (not Britain) waving behind her. Elizabeth in the Cecil print has already won her battle. Both the cognoscenti who knew of the Cecil print and the people who saw Elizabeth on a horse for the first time in Stothard's or Darton's prints would be left with no doubt that this was a woman on a mission. Even though Darton's 1822 print came seven years after Waterloo, he still pays homage to the spirit of the original print: a queen goes forth, paradoxically alone in a crowd, to face a task that will save her nation.

1837–1910:
The Shadow of a
Paternalistic Queenship

Elizabeth and Victoria – a power packaged by a title

The age of Victoria, especially in a book on a female monarch, has the potential to become that yet untraveled world whose margin fades forever and forever as one writes. Mercifully, the general outlines of both the history and the cultural climate of this period are essentially clear to the general public. My focus, therefore, is not upon the specifics of events that would parallel the Spanish Match, but rather upon characteristics of the era that gave rise to new venues for making and using images of Queen Elizabeth. Ironically, the most obvious point of comparison – two unmarried young women being crowned as queens regnant – is rendered largely unavailable by the circumstances of both the Hanoverian succession and Victoria's own background. The Protestant Reformation, the militant Catholicism of Mary Tudor, the threat of England becoming an annex of Spain through that queen's marriage to an heir to a foreign throne, even the undignified shadow cast over the House of Tudor by Henry VIII's infamous search for the womb that he could fill to his will – all these circumstances constitute serious affairs of state on the stage that the problematic heir, Elizabeth, must enter. Furthermore, before she could claim the crown, Elizabeth had had to survive more political intrigue and theological hair-splitting than Victoria ever had occasion to read about, let alone experience. Elizabeth's crowning was a triumph in itself; her survival was an even greater achievement. In further contrast, the excesses of the Regency, the bawdy court of William, the increasingly messy tangles with Parliament, all combine to provide a smutty background (literally smutty, too, with the amount of coal being burnt in London) for the undisputed and welcome entrance of a fresh, young, sheltered girl, arguably more German than English. And – despite suggestions by Parliament that Victoria rule as Elizabeth II – the nineteenth-century monarch actively rejected any comparison between herself and Queen Elizabeth.[1]

If Elizabeth had the heart and stomach of a king, Victoria had the heart and stomach of a pater familias. That she came equipped with a hyper-functional womb was a plus for the values she and her kinsman/consort set out to establish. Just about the only things the two women did share were the title and a strong sense of duty, for all that they would have defined the latter quite differently. It is perhaps only a slight over-simplification to say that Elizabeth was a woman grasping the opportunity of power by the title she inherited, while Victoria imparted a fresh significance – but quite another sort of power – to the title that she bore for so very long. Being a queen allowed Elizabeth scope to exercise her intellect, wit, and principles; being a woman of distinctly middle-class values allowed Victoria the scope to redefine the role of queen.

Of all the riches in the span of Victoria's reign, I've chosen two – the Pre-Raphaelites and their imitators for high art and the humble biscuit tin for low art. The literature of the period is, of course, rife with Elizabeth references (if not fully delineated icons), from Kipling's poem *Gloriana*, to the first wave of what would become a sea of biographies, to rollicking adventure novels, such as Lathom's 1806 *The Mysterious Freebooter; or The Days of Queen Bess*, and (to pick but one year) the 1897 pseudo-historical narrative by Robert Haynes Cave, *In the Days of Good Queen Bess: The Narrative of Sir Adrian Trafford, Knight, of Trafford Place in the County of Suffolk* (London: Burns & Oates, Limited), and its feminine counterparts of the same year: *The Honor of a Princess: A Romance of the Time of "Good Queen Bess"* by F. Kimball Scribner, published in both London and New York, and Lady Newdigate-Newdegate's *Gossip from a Muniment Room: Being passages in the Lives of Anne and Mary Fytton 1574–1618*. Despite all the rich opportunities afforded by the literature – both high and low – of the period, the visual arts are more fascinating. We are now getting to the age of the mass-produced image, and that phenomenon merits close scrutiny. While citizens of London or other large cities might have seen portraits (or, more likely, prints) of Elizabeth's image during the previous three centuries, the nineteenth-century Briton could fairly easily acquire either a print/engraving of a currently famous painting or a piece of kitsch elevated (or at least made more attractive) by a royal image. Owning an image is a tricky thing. One may be daily impressed and enlightened by it – the purpose of all those saints' icons littering the middle ages –

but one may also learn to take it for granted. Hamlet says that the greatness that was Alexander may have become loam with which to stop a beer barrel. But even that doesn't have the pedestrian immediacy of keeping one's pennies in a tin decorated with the face of a queen. Familiarity – here meaning cozy comfort – may not always breed contempt, but it generally does dispel awe.

And, for all its industrial, social, and cultural advances, a key phrase for the Victorian era would have to be "familiarity." Traced through Middle English and Old French to Latin, the word of course derives from the word for "family." Yes, in the big-picture sense, this was the time that Britons became familiar with the world. But literal family values, figured forth by the relentlessly middle-class royal family (surely one of the few examples in history of people aspiring to move *down* the social ladder) and by the family values we have now come to call, pejoratively, "Victorian," were a point of exchange for both national and individual identity. The public sphere of memory expunged such unpleasantnesses as the American Revolution, and instead celebrated tobacco as England's gift to the world; the problematic history of circumnavigation of the globe was revised over a reviving cup of tea, the new national drink. The Empire replaced – or expanded – the England of which the queen was a mother. The building of personal fortunes in trade, railways, or importing, established pseudo-dynasties of wealth and power. The venerated construct of the family may have been for some a reality or a realistic goal; but for most of Britain it was at once a charming façade masking many sorts of dark doings, and a century-long *son et lumière* of sufficient proportions to distract all but the most fanatical reformers from the many sores on the body politic. As an example of high art spectacle, the paintings of the Pre-Raphaelites rendered sadly pointless stories (Ophelia and Elaine, the maid of Shallot) as pretty tableaux (still, to the despair of faculty members, lovingly displayed on the walls of undergraduates' rooms) and real tragedies (Cordelia and Joan of Arc) as – yet again – tableaux in which the sensual beauty of a flower-strewn stream, a gown, a tapestry, a woman's hair, a rose, calls forth a stronger reaction than the allusion to a stupidly passive drowning or a death by flame, not flower petals.

At the other end of the family-culture spectrum, exemplifying the façade of the wholesome family, we find the biscuit tin. Occupying an awkward site between the utilitarian and the decorative, the biscuit tin and its cousins (tea, toffee, tobacco) could be found in every archetypally Victorian home. Gifted with the near-assurance of a utilitarian resurrection, the container went from its initial function on to any number of reincarnations. Indeed, the companies making the tins did so with an eye for yet another Victorian trait: collecting for the sake of collecting. Made in the shapes of books or baskets, decorated with English historical scenes or oriental fantasies, with flowers or faces, the boxes themselves became objects that generated the acquisitive instincts of those Victorians occupying houses filled with curio cases, elaborate display shelves, multiple decorative tables, all governed by the unspoken commandment: thou shalt leave no surface bare. As an inverse reaction to the vast swaths of land and sea ruled by Britannia, the Victorian home was allowed to have no empty spaces. More was more. (Or, as Mae West so wonderfully said in quite a different context: "too much of a good thing is wonderful.")

*c.*1867: a domestic empire – monarchy and the biscuit tin

The fashion for decorative tins sprang up in the second half of the nineteenth century. The English tin, popularly called a biscuit tin, is surely an exquisite example of bringing an exalted object to a humble subject. The object itself – the tin – is, of course, of very little value. But a tin with the face of Queen Victoria on it generates interest, amazement, or the desire to acquire it, depending upon the character of the customer. There were many types of decorated tins: mustard, cocoa, washing powder, tobacco, baking powder, and syrup are a few that spring immediately to mind. Tea tins are indeed called tea tins, but, "biscuit" remains a generic designation from Southebys to the Victoria & Albert to eBay, despite the rantings of experts such as M. J. Franklin:

> At present, *all* tin boxes seem to be given the misnomer of "biscuit tins". One of the major London salesrooms not long ago announced their first ever sale of tins as "A Collection of Biscuit Tins", when in fact about half of the items were tins that had never contained biscuits. A biscuit tin is a biscuit tin; a sweet in a tin that contained sweets, likewise tins for tea, mustard, etc. For some reason, tea and sweet manufacturers often did not put the name of the firm on the tin, so it is under-standable that this can only be guessed at and so can only be called "tins", but the author has yet to find a British *biscuit tin* which does not make mention somewhere on the tin of a biscuitmaker's name. Without such a mark it should not be called a *biscuit tin*.[2]

While respecting Mr. Franklin's expertise and apologizing to his sensi-bilities, I will continue to refer to almost all of the tins in this chapter as biscuit tins. The first tin, for example, is one of the earliest to be decorated with a royal image, and it is, in fact, a mustard tin. Moss Rimmington and Company sold this tin (Figure 6) around 1868. The subject of the

BOUDOIR OF THE PRINCESS.

SANDRINGHAM

Figure 6   Princess Alexandra in her boudoir at Sandringham. Moss Rimmington and Co., *c.*1868. Collection of the author

five pictures is the Princess Alexandra, wife of the Prince of Wales. As far as familiarity goes, this tin makes it from 0 to 60 in very short order. The lid is dignified enough, showing a head-and-shoulders portrait of the Princess of Wales wearing a coronet on her head and a high collar on her neck; two sides of the box show detailed pictures of Sandringham and Abergeldie Castle respectively; and a third side balances the royal residences with royal duties, showing Princess Alexandra visiting patients in a hospital ward. The fourth side, however, shows (carefully labeled) the "Boudoir of the Princess, Sandringham." While she is fully clothed and blamelessly reading a book, this still seems an odd choice. Quite alone in the picture, no servants and no husband (indeed Bertie is absent from all the pictures), Alexandra's private room is laid open to the public imagination on the side of a tin containing mustard powder and further abjuring the customer to "Try Our Anti-Rheumatic Mustard Oil for Rheumatism & Neuralgia." Control of royal images isn't what it once was. Whether or not Alexandra existed as an image in the public sphere of memory before this tin is a fascinating question. During her husband's long tenure as Prince of Wales, such images as there were of her are often misidentified as other members of the royal family, usually as one of Victoria's daughters.

The Alexandra tin, however, was either a trial run that failed or an unpopular subject to begin with, for on the tins with the images of both Elizabeth and Victoria, decorum is more in evidence. Huntley and Palmer, the most prolific producers of the genuine biscuit tin, made one of an elaborate early series into a pictorial history of Elizabeth's reign. The top of the tin is hinged in the center, so there are two lids. On the left is the raised relief of a traditional picture of Elizabeth entering London; on the right is the queen on her way to St. Paul's to give thanks for the victory over the Armada. On the back is Elizabeth's visit to Kenilworth, while on the left end is the knighting of Sir Francis Drake, with the surrender of Mary Stuart on the right end. The front panel (Figure 7) is an extremely detailed representation of Elizabeth at Tilbury, made to appear three-dimensional by the diminished size of the figures and battlements in the background. Even the cannon balls are clearly depicted – no flags blown by conflicting winds in this iconic rendering.

Rowntree and Co. of York also favored the decorated tin, although theirs usually contained chocolate or some other sweet. The tin shown in Figure 8 is undated, and could have been produced any time between 1910 and 1930. In collectors' guide books it's often used to show the deterioration in craftsmanship from the mid-nineteenth-century tins to those of the twentieth century. This tin is a particularly apt example of

Figure 7 Queen Elizabeth at Tilbury. Huntley and Palmer, 1878. Collection of the author

Figure 8 Queen Elizabeth's State Entry into London, Rowntree & Co. Ltd, c.1910–30. Collection of the author

that decline, since it also shows the state entry of Elizabeth into London, but with less careful detail (although in twice as large a space) as the same scene on the Huntley and Palmer tin.

The next two tins are sheer fun. While figures of women – real or imaginary – often decorate objects for or for the honor of men, on these Rowntree cocoa tins we see men decorating the margins of main panels featuring Elizabeth and Victoria (Figures 9(a) and 9(b), respectively). On the left side of the Elizabeth tin is Shakespeare, with Falstaff and Hamlet and the tragi-comic masks above him and the Globe beneath. On the right side is Sir Francis Drake, topped by two gentlemen playing at bowls. On the left side of the Victoria tin are (in descending order) her Prime Ministers: Disraeli, Peel, Palmerston, and Gladstone. On the right side is Prince Albert, looking serious below a rendering of the Crystal Palace. On the back of each tin we find brief biographical notes and a plug for Rowntree cocoa.

Carrs of Carlisle was second only to Huntley and Palmer in the biscuit tin business, and Figure 10 is a gorgeous example of the genre. The tin is octagonal, with Elizabeth's face on the cover, and (counter-clockwise from the left front) in framed oval medallions are Mary Stuart, Sir Walter Raleigh, Georgiana (Daughter of the Duke of Devonshire), Henry VIII, the Countess of Sunderland, Hans Holbein, Sir Thomas More, and Sir Philip Sidney. This is an astonishing group of people. Georgiana (1783–1858) is shown as a child; Sir Thomas More is shown without his chain of office. The order is not chronological, nor is it dinner party seating – boy/girl/boy/girl – although there are only three women besides Elizabeth. But why those women? Georgiana – or Little G, as she was called – was the daughter of the Duchess Georgiana who, with her husband the 5th Duke of Devonshire and Lady Elizabeth Foster, formed a famous and trend-setting Regency *ménage à trois*. Besides being the offspring of a famous couple (triple?) recently the subject of several books, and a collateral relation of the late Diana, Princess of Wales, Little G seems an odd choice for this, or any, biscuit tin. (And, in light of post-Andrew Morton royal history, any mention of Diana and a *ménage à trois*, would have been unfortunate, to say the least.) Dorothy Sidney (identified on the tin only as the Countess of Sunderland) was not only of Philip Sidney's family, but is also perched on the Spencer family tree. So, while the references to Lady Diana Spencer, late Princess of Wales, may explain these two women's presence, they still seem out of place with the likes of Thomas More and Hans Holbein – or the other way around. The blue of the tin is quite close to the famous blue of Holbein miniatures, which

Figure 9(a)　Queen Elizabeth with Shakespeare and Drake, Rowntree's Elect Cocoa. Collection of the author

Figure 9(b)　and Queen Victoria with her Prime Ministers, Rowntree's Elect Cocoa. Collection of the author

Figure 10   Carrs Biscuit Tin with Queen Elizabeth on cover, Mary Stuart, Francis Drake and others on sides. Collection of the author

the medallions themselves resemble. But where does that leave Thomas More? The fact that the tin is undated makes speculation even more frustrating. (Although, from my speculation above, I'd guess at the 1980s.) There was a traveling exhibition of Holbein's miniatures in the early 1980s, but he died in 1543 (as the tin helpfully tells us), so he could have painted only Henry VIII and Thomas More.

Or perhaps we have reached a point in time where a picture is just a picture, and figures from the sixteenth, seventeenth, and eighteenth centuries are all equally "historical." Since even Queen Elizabeth has her identity captioned, the question of public memory is deeply problematized by this mere biscuit tin. Is it an example of images for the sake of images, with no iconic value invested in their selection?[3]

The scarlet cake tin honoring Elizabeth II's coronation (Figure 11) is something of a rarity. Refusing to make the obvious leap back to the first Elizabeth (see the chapter "1953–2003"), the current monarch very seldom appears in tandem, or indeed in any configuration, with Elizabeth Tudor. Here the makers of the Lyons Dundee Fruit Cake tin have taken images of all the monarchs from the first Elizabeth to the second, with the counter-clockwise circle beginning and ending under the present queen's chin, pairing her father, George VI, with Elizabeth, newly the First. This is an iconic representation of a contemporary ideology – the New Elizabethans. Trivialized, perhaps, on a cake tin, the post-war attempt to

Figure 11   Coronation of Queen Elizabeth II with portraits of all monarchs from Elizabeth I to Elizabeth II; J. Lyons & Co. Ltd, 1953. Collection of the author

see the present monarch's reign as the dawning of a new Renaissance was a serious (if labored) effort for many public and academic figures.

Next to biscuit tins and tea tins and toffee tins, tobacco tins are common currency in iconic folk-culture. Even more prevalent in the United States, tobacco tins make a fascinating cultural byway down which the curious may wander. A brief digression into the life of the tobacco tin gives us a number of interesting examples of attempts to make icons that could be both recognized by virtually uneducated people and still draw upon some cultural notion of Englishness.

A brief digression on tobacco

Sir Walter Raleigh has become perhaps the best-known of Queen Elizabeth's courtiers, not as the author of *The History of the World* nor even as the mythical gallant who sacrificed his cloak to save the queen's shoes (a narrative with little support beyond the cloak on his coat of arms and in his National Portrait Gallery likeness); instead, Raleigh's popular fame grows from the tobacco plant. Raleigh's association with tobacco is a fine example of memory as a public sphere, spanning as it does time, nationality, and the Atlantic Ocean. Raleigh's name graces the capitol of the state most associated with tobacco, North Carolina, as well as one of the most popular brands of early cigarettes and current brand of pipe tobacco. Raleigh's name and image have become a icon – not of colonial exploitation, but rather of the apotheosis of a native American product becoming one with canonical English history. Sir Walter Raleigh's name evokes the perceived glamour of the English Renaissance and the court of Good Queen Bess, bestowing on this American plant in American packaging a sense of history that is quite reversed.

In addition to ignoring history and geography, the elision of Raleigh and tobacco is factually inaccurate. John Hawkins, of course, introduced tobacco into England in 1565, but the name "Hawkins" has few, if any associations with the plant and its products, while Raleigh – who never set foot in North America – continued to be associated with the product's growing popularity, even to the point that King James I banned tobacco because of his extreme dislike of Raleigh – who supposedly smoked a pipefull just before his execution. Although, after James lifted his ban in favor of raising taxes, and tobacco was grown in Britain during the sixteenth century (mainly in Gloucestershire), the public demanded the imported tobacco from the Elizabethan colony of Virginia. The plant was denounced by clergy even as its smoking was embraced as a preventative measure against the plague, with Eton boys being required to smoke every morning.

According to "The Tobacco Story," the website of the Imperial Tobacco Group PLC, "over a period of seven years from 1702 to 1709 the aggregate consumption in England and Wales was 11,260,659 pounds a year, or just over two pounds per head of the population."[4] Although the icon of the Indian Princess – sometimes specifically Pocahontas, sometimes merely a generic "La Belle Sauvage" – became popular outside of shops selling tobacco products, the problematic display of the female body was soon replaced by a male. The Blackamoor was more prominent than the clichéd cigar store Indian, and the former was sometimes re-figured as a Turk or a Saracen. The element shared by all of these figures is, of course, their status as foreigners. In England, tobacco was associated with the exotic, with the other. The same principle generates the American choice of Sir Walter Raleigh. While the English tobacco symbols figure the source of tobacco as exotic and adventurously daring in Britain, the American use of English titles – Prince Albert, Sir Walter Raleigh – pushes the image of tobacco use in the other direction, toward the established and the establishment. Snuff was brought from France and made fashionable by Charles II after his restoration to the throne.

Unlike ships and storms, tobacco and cigarette brands have not traditionally been named after women. Philip Morris and the Benson and Hedges Company, originally British, have offered a selection of brands with English place names – Cambridge, Bond Street, Bristol, Bucks – with names taken from English family names and culture – Parliament, Marlboro, Chesterfield, Commander, English Oval. Smaller British companies followed this trend, with Kenilworth by Cope Bros & Co., with M.F.H. by H. Archer & Co., Guinea Golds by Ogden Ltd, Empress by Burstein Isaacs & Co., with Gainsborough Cigarettes by Cohen Weenen & Co., and St. Dunstan's by Carreras Ltd, West End by Teofani & Co.

The US companies also strove for the ambience of English tradition, with offerings such as Pall Mall, Barclay, Carlton, Viceroy, and Raleigh, all cigarettes processed by Brown and Williamson, originally of North Carolina. Their loose tobacco, Big Ben, along with R. J. Reynolds' popular Prince Albert, is still overshadowed by the best-selling Sir Walter Raleigh. The American Tobacco Company (paying extensive tribute to the English) offered blends called Buckingham Bright, Old English, Oxford, Piccadilly, Royal Bengals, Sovereign, and Twelfth Night, while Phillip Morris went for the horse and hound crowd with Barking Dog, Field and Stream, and Country Doctor. The United States Tobacco Company marketed more international choices, with the native Dixie Queen and Central Union (and the ironically mirrored Idle Hour) balanced by Battle Royal, North Pole, and Sphinx. The American Tobacco Company produced an entire series of exotic nominations: Egyptienne Luxury, Hassan, Hindu, Mecca, and Sultan.

The British Empire's connections with Mother England can be seen in a number of brand names: from Canada, King George's Navy Chewing Tobacco, British Consuls, and Big Ben by the patriotically named Imperial Tobacco Company of Canada; both Coronet and Peter Pan by Sniders & Abraham of Australia; as well as Rugger and Scots from South Africa. But the Empire/Commonwealth also acknowledged the place of the former colony in the tobacco equation, with names such as Old Virginia Choice by D. Ritchie & Company and Dominion Tobacco's Uncle Sam Smoking Tobacco, with the British Australasian Tobacco Company's Yankee Doodle, and the wonderfully multivalent Baron's Honest Virginia, by Carreras of Canada; R. J. Reynolds' most patriotic brand was George Washington Cut Plug. Red Man, the only popular tobacco product named for the Native Americans, has become synonymous with chewing tobacco, at least in the US. Other US brands with Native Peoples' nomenclature were Ojibwa by Scotten-Dillon Co., Red Indian Cut Plug by the American Tobacco Co., and Arrow Snuff by A. Soderberg Co. and Hiawatha (although arguably literary more than racial) by Daniel Scotten and Co., Detroit.

And finally, we do find a clear reference to Elizabeth. The Surburg Company, a late nineteenth-century American enterprise, offered Golden Sceptre and – the one brand named for a female monarch – Gloriana Mixture (Figure 12). Although Philip Morris' brand Virginia Slims is marketed to target women, its name is ambiguous. The only two contemporary brands named unambiguously for women are RJR's two cigarettes, Eve and Diana.[5] The Gloriana Mixture flourished only for the period of its immediate manufacture, the Chicago Exposition of 1893. As an icon, it was a failure. Not only does it lack the queen's image – whereas Walter Raleigh's is fixed in the mind of half the over-40 population of the US – but the title Gloriana may have been (especially without the image) too literate a jump for mid-western tobacco buyers to make. On the Chicago side of the Atlantic, evidently, Elizabeth holds only the most limited sort of space in the sphere of public memory.

A personal epilogue on tins

Tins are made to contain things. They are manufactured as packaging for small items that must be kept together – tea leaves, biscuits, loose tobacco, mustard powder – or for large, solid substances that require sturdy packing – fruitcakes, lard. Tins have a long half-life as containers for odds and ends, change, personal treasures. Therefore, unlike more ephemeral packaging, the image on a tin may make a lasting impression

Figure 12 Gloriana Mixture Tobacco Tin; Surburg Tobacco Co., 1893. Collection of the author

on its owner. Why, then, do we have tins – such as the early biscuit tins – on which the product's name appears only (and often not completely) on the bottom? Because we think in images, not words. To make a tin with an actual image is to give its purchaser/owner a tangible piece of the history – of the moment, of the personality that is displayed. Even if a person does not understand the image, the impression is there, fixed in memory, ready to tap into factual public knowledge offered at school, through entertainment, from friends, or found by chance. My own interest in British royal families began at the moment my mother told me to tidy up my hair clips and gave me a toffee tin with a picture of the newly crowned George VI, Queen Elizabeth, and the little princesses. They were not dressed as royalty on the tin, nor was the picture current in the late 1950s, but, my mother told me, this was because they were real, not in a storybook. How that toffee tin found its way into the southern Appalachian Mountains is a mystery to me, but that image gave me an idea of monarchy, a link to the sphere of public memory in which I would soon find the first Elizabeth and various other figures who did look like the books I'd been reading. But their reality, for me, grew from the reality of the image on the tin, not the other way around. Had the local A & P carried toffee tins, I would have bought every one, collecting the many versions of the young royal family that I now know exist in that series. People think in pictures. If we can't have pictures, then we need pictorial words – Red Man, Bond Street, Pall Mall. The closer the word is to the image, the more likely we are to make it our own and to link our personal memories with that modern sphere of public space. Ironically, when I wrote of the early icons, it was to make the point that people needed to be pulled together by a collectively recognizable image. Today, as bombarded by the visual as we are, we need a particular piece of that public space to call our own, to mine out our own versions of an image and take it home in our heads. The icons we take with us – home in our heads or out into the world – contain elements of shared history and individual perception. Did I share a knowledge of the picture on that toffee tin with any number of eight-year-old girls in England? Definitely. Did I perceive the Royal Family in the same way as an average English girl of my age? Definitely not.

The split in this book is between the icons which are tied directly from history to history – from the Armada to the Battle of Trafalgar – and the icons which we need to serve two purposes: making that link with history, but also speaking to our own experiences. As we have become collectively more educated, we have become individually more isolated. In both paradigms, the early-modern and the post-modern, the icon is a point of transformation.

*c.*1885: the Pre-Raphaelites colonize Elizabeth

The 1885 I use here is an arbitrary date, taking *circa* in its most useful sense. The prints and engravings from the years 1875 to 1896 are not necessarily in the chronological order of the paintings from which most of them were made, but neither does chronology play as important a role in my argument as it did for the art linked to the Spanish Match. Once again, we need to recognize the differences between the reign of Elizabeth and the reign of Victoria. Elizabeth wielded real life-and-death political power; Victoria's role in the governing of her people was not without power – she could urge that attention be paid or put a royal stick in the spokes of programs she disliked – but she was not the divinely empowered monarch of the Renaissance, nor could she ever be, for all that she had the title of Empress. Celebrating Elizabeth's power, glory, or conquests was thus an exercise in distinctly bad taste. We have no grand paintings of Gloriana from the Victorian period. But we do have scenes from English history; if these scenes have a unifying topic, it may be that of putting Elizabeth in her place: the past.

As a number of scholars have observed, conflating Elizabeth with Shakespeare was an effective way both to define an age and to canonize a playwright. Shakespeare was extremely popular during the Victorian era, and making Elizabeth part of Shakespeare's England was an acceptable way to represent the mature queen without flaunting her royal powers. There are so many pictures of Shakespeare reading to Queen Elizabeth that they almost constitute a genre in Victorian painting.[6] Eduard Ender's painting of Shakespeare reading *Macbeth* to Queen Elizabeth and her court, reproduced *c.*1880 as an engraving (Figure 13), is an excellent example of this limited and limiting sort of Elizabeth icon. Very much in the school of Ford Madox Brown's 1851 painting (generally on display in the British Tate) *Geoffrey Chaucer Reading the "Legend of Custance" to Edward III and his Court, at the Palace of Sheen, on the Anniversary of the Black Prince's Forty-fifth Birthday*, the work is much more about Shakespeare than it is about Queen Elizabeth. At the center of a circle formed by the gowns of the seated women and the elaborate over-mantle, the dark-clad, upright male figure stands out on the pale field of the curving forms of women, dresses, and the effeminately (in comparison) clad men. Shakespeare looks out of the frame, with only a slight turn of his torso indicating any acknowledgment of the queen's presence. Elizabeth herself is the most dramatically (and sentimentally) inclined of all the figures

SHAKESPEARE AT THE COURT OF ELIZABETH.

Ed. Ender, pinxt.

Figure 13 Shakespeare at the Court of Queen Elizabeth, engraving after the painting by Eduard Ender, c.1880

focused on Shakespeare, and – although her dress takes up a dispropor-
tionate amount of space, she is clearly in the margin of the painting. For
in addition to the central circle he fills, Shakespeare is at the apex of a
triangle formed by the two dark figures in the foreground – the draped
footstool on the right and the dress of the seated woman on the left.
Finally, there is the queen's besotted expression. Some women of her
court also gaze with awe and fascination, but most of the men are paying
only partial attention or – as is the man with the pointed beard at the
foot of the large pillar on the right – are in the act of turning disdain-
fully away.

Creating a relationship that did not exist between Elizabeth and
Shakespeare, this engraving, the painting it reproduces, and the collection
of paintings and engravings and prints that it represents all strive to
suggest that Elizabeth's relationship with writers (or at least with this
writer) was one in which the power was vested in the writer, not the
monarch. Elizabeth gets marginal credit for having the good sense to
foster Shakespeare's talent (more so than she did in reality or in *Shakespeare
in Love*) and for appreciating his genius, but this iconic Elizabeth is nearly
as powerless as the dead Elizabeth of the Gheeraerts painting. She has,
in fact, come close to being the devoted wife/mother figure of Victorian
narrative painting, every atom of her being focused on the accomplished
and dominant male. Here Elizabeth's court is a stage worthy of
Shakespeare; we are not being told that Shakespeare was worthy of
Elizabeth's golden age.

This historical misrepresentation did not go unnoticed or unremarked,
as is evidenced by the 1896 cartoon sketch from *Punch* (Figure 14). Titled
"Unrecorded History. V," the cartoon shows a caricature of Queen
Elizabeth in the dress from the Ditchley portrait, seated on an elevated
throne, under a canopy bearing her initials (which would, incidentally,
block Shakespeare's view of the enormous portrait of Henry VIII) reading
from an extremely long scroll. As the subtitle tells us with vast understatement, she "just runs through a little thing of her own composition."
No one – certainly not Elizabeth or Shakespeare – looks good here. The
queen's courtiers, soldiers, and ladies in waiting are all inattentive, busy
talking or rolling their eyes or in the process of falling asleep. Shakespeare
himself – a dumpy little figure – is indeed on the edge of his seat, but
we are in doubt as to the cause of this posture. Is he really interested,
really polite, really afraid to seem uninterested, or actually afraid of being
shaken back into attention by the courtier poking at his back? But the
real target of satire here is the group of paintings discussed above. The
Victorian desire to locate the genesis of Bardolatry back in the age of

Elizabeth, to show the queen as a frame for the accomplishments of one of her subjects, to shift the emphasis from Shakespeare in the Age of Elizabeth to Elizabeth in the Age of Shakespeare – all these take a beating in the *Punch* cartoon. Furthermore, the comic mode of representation itself takes dead aim at the elaborate Victorian set-pieces. The silly dog, the ever-unrolling "little thing," the huge but unseen portrait of Henry, the queen's pointed head, the Bard's plump rump, the neglected state papers on a table in the foreground, and the exaggerated suits of armor hanging on the wall all parody the anachronistic and busy Victorian detail of paintings such as Ender's.

Shakespeare's audience, however, was not the only role in which the Victorians endeavored to cast Elizabeth. Another favorite version of her life was the five worst years from her span of 70 – Elizabeth as a prisoner. Here she could be brave (as in the Millais engraving) or dejected (as in the Sherratt engraving), but in either case, the queen – or more accurately, the princess – is quite without power over others. This plays to two cultural preferences of the Victorian era – the reluctance to make Elizabeth obviously more powerful than Victoria, and the desire to sentimentalize any story involving a famous woman.

The more bathetic of the two, T. Sherratt's engraving from R. Hillingford's painting (Figure 15), show Elizabeth huddled on a bare stone bench, clutching an outsized handkerchief, glumly refusing to look in the direction of the head jailer's gesture – likely toward some amenities, or at least an unblocked window, judging from the light. Here Elizabeth is almost literally spineless, the reversed S curve of her body, when continued, follows the curve of the arch above her, making her physically at one with her cell, even as her face expresses nothing of the stubbornness and spirit and sheer political acumen that got the real Elizabeth through these years. Here, stubbornness has become a bad case of the sulks. While the men seem to pity her, their expressions are free from any sort of admiration, and even the dog seems to want out the door as quickly as possible. The only positive note in the frame is that the left side of the image is darker than the right, with the jumbled figures in the doorway further emphasizing Elizabeth's isolation or singularity. But whether this increased lighting is meant to symbolize Elizabeth's coming triumph and present virtue or is merely to show her despair in sharper relief is impossible to guess.

We are literally less in the dark with John Everett Millais' engraving after his own painting, "Elizabeth in Prison" (Figure 16). This prison, while possibly in the royal apartments in the Tower, could be set at any time during Elizabeth's life, for her main activity seems to be study and

Figure 14 Unrecorded History V; Queen Elizabeth ... William Shakespeare. From *Punch's Almanack for 1896*

Figure 15 "The Princess Elizabeth in the Tower"; engraving by T. Sherratt after the painting by R. Hillingford, c.1875

writing. Not knowing what else to do with her, and because of the enlightened views of her last step-mother, Catherine Parr, first Henry, then Edward's advisors, gave her a superlative education. If not for the title of the picture, there's little here to suggest a prison other than the plainness of the room. Even that could pass for historical accuracy if Elizabeth's dress were more clearly of her own period. The princess has paper on the desk/table, two open books on the floor, and holds a quill in her right hand while she looks up toward the source of the light. She is resting her cheek on her left hand, but the attitude is far from the head-propping gesture of the dead queen in "Elizabeth with Time and Death" (see Figure 3). And her expression, especially with those eyes directed upward and to her right, is thoughtful, but not gloomy. In the act of writing, in the midst of study, thought is both natural and positive. The expression on the face and the angle of the head could be read as pensive, but pensive is a long way from either despair or gloom. We know that Millais was concerned about the reproduction of her expression. In a letter to Mrs. Hunt on 18 November 1880, the artist writes: "I will attend to all you say about the proof of Elizabeth & see how it may be made much more effective but the head is charming which [is] a great matter."[7] Millais' concern about the head as "a great matter" and his declaration that it is "charming" suggest that he knew that the posture was ambiguous, but was striving for the triumph of the positive over the negative, while still showing that this was a struggle and thus a true triumph.

The final example of Victorian icons of Elizabeth is representative of yet another popular sub-genre of the period: the Elizabeth and Mary Stuart story. "Elizabeth and Mary Stuart" (Figure 17) shows a pastoral confrontation between the two queens. Originally an illustration from a book about Mary, the image requires attentive reading. As Dobson and Watson quip, "In reality Elizabeth and Mary, Queen of Scots, never met, but on the stage they have been doing so ever since John Banks composed *The Island Queen* (1684)."[8] Not only is this image interesting in its own right, but it is a radical revision of any early portrait of the queen.

In the Victorian print we see the two queens standing on level ground, with Elizabeth, in white, in the right foreground, with Mary (darker in both dress and expression) on the left, but only a step or two in the background. The picture divides evenly between the two women, with Elizabeth's right glove and riding crop thrown on the ground between them, presumably as a challenge. If so, it's a challenge Mary seems more than prepared to meet, as her left hand claws toward Elizabeth's face. Mary is restrained by one lady in waiting, while Elizabeth is backed up, but not touched, by two gentlemen. Given that the source of this picture

PRINCESS ELIZABETH IN PRISON.

Figure 16   "Princess Elizabeth in Prison." Millais, engraving, after his own painting, *c*.1880. Collection of the author

ELIZABETH AND MARY STUART.

Figure 17   "Elizabeth and Mary Stuart," print, W. Kalbach, *c*.1896. Collection of the author

Figure 18 Elizabeth I and the Three Goddesses, attributed to Hans Eworth, painting *c*.1569. Reproduced with permission from Queen's Gallery

is a book about Mary Stuart, the expressions of Elizabeth's men are interesting. They don't appear all that loyal or ready to defend their queen. The man on the right appears concerned, but seems to be looking at Mary; the man on the left seems frankly embarrassed and is looking at the ground.

The two women's postures mimic, rather than mirror, each other. Mary's right arm, raised toward her heart (or restrained by that lady in waiting), has a crucifix dangling from it. Elizabeth's right arm is held staunchly in front of her waist, with the hand angled up toward the heart, with her decorative string of pearls incidentally clasped against her torso. Mary's left arm and hand are fully extended, as if to scratch the English queen's face. Elizabeth stands unflinching, her left hand clutching a (rather out of place) rose bush. Her left glove, presumably, is still on her hand. Her face shown in stark profile, Elizabeth's figure fills more of the space, while Mary's two-thirds face disappears into shadow on the ominous left side. In the background behind Mary is the tower of a castle, whether one of her places of imprisonment or a visual allusion to Edinburgh is unclear without the context of the book in which the illustration first appeared. On the ground before Elizabeth is a hooded falcon or hawk. Again, this can be read as an allusion to the fabled "sport of kings," or as the artist's association between Elizabeth and a bird of prey.

In the context of this study, however, the most interesting thing about the print is that it is a remake of *Elizabeth I and the Three Goddesses* (*c*.1569), one of the first allegorical paintings of the queen (Figure 18). In that work, the scene is itself a remake of the Choice of Paris, but with Elizabeth as a fourth female figure. She stands, elevated by three steps, on the left of the canvas, holding the symbolic apple, her orb. Hera is in the act of turning away from an angry confrontation, turning so quickly that she loses a slipper. Elizabeth is attended by two women, making the body-count equal on both sides (unlike the nineteenth-century version), but both of Hera's companions are famous in their own right. Athena, wearing her armor with the Medusa head, holds up her palm in a conventional gesture of amazement. The only still member of the classical trio is Aphrodite, the original winner of the Choice of Paris. She sits casually at her ease, son Cupid by her side, and her eyes locked with those of Elizabeth, the new winner, forming a strong diagonal across the canvas. Behind Hera's swan-chariot is the Round Tower of Windsor Castle, marking the very landscape as English.

The visual allusions to the sixteenth-century work could – I suppose, in a stretch – be a coincidence. All the better. The clear power struggle, also clearly victorious in the immediate moment, but ultimately ambiguous (as figured by the relaxed posture of Aphrodite), when transferred to the nineteenth-century picture makes much the same statement. In Victoria's time, Elizabeth may have won the battle, but Mary is going to win the war. The castle behind her head is most emphatically not Windsor, so the very land upon which Elizabeth stands is in the process of shifting. In this light, the rose bush can be read as the bramble of Jotham's Parable in the Book of Judges. The olive tree, the fig tree, and the vine all refused the title of king on the grounds that their fruit was a greater glory than any title. Only the lowly bramble, that bore no fruit, agreed to become king, providing all the other trees would bow low before him. Mary may be undignified, under-attended, and more in the dark in this picture, but the fruit she has already borne will out-last Elizabeth's barren Tudor Rose.

Like the Henry VII Chapel in Westminster Abbey, this picture argues for the ultimate judgment that women who are mothers (like Victoria, of course) will achieve more lasting good and greater fame than the flashy brambles, however rampant. It's a sobering view of history, and a depressing testimony to the reality that Victoria's view of the role of the female monarch was closer to that of James I than to that of Elizabeth.

1910–1953: The Shadow of History

Elizabeth and the Suffrage Campaign

Between the early 1860s and 1918 various groups of variously dedicated people worked to bring women the right to vote in Great Britain. Although branches of the Suffrage Movement were active in villages, towns, and cities across the UK, my attention – like that of the contemporary media – is focused on activities in London. The relationship between the English political movements advocating voting rights for women and the image and history of Queen Elizabeth is not straightforward. While we might expect that Elizabeth would have provided a template or at least an exemplum of the astute and accomplished political woman, and thus so much grist to the suffrage mills, two major figures problematized that seemingly logical connection: Queen Victoria and Joan of Arc. Moreover, the chronology of these two figures in relation to Gloriana is ahistorical, with the culturally massive figure of Victoria blocking the early suffragists' view of Elizabeth, while the gleam of Joan's fabled armor partially blinded many suffragette speakers and writers to the image of the queen who was closer to them in both centuries and national identity. But, once again, the icon of the late queen of glorious memory was simply too vividly present in the public sphere of memory not to become a major touchstone for the rhetoric and spectacle of the Movement.

For clarity of discussion, I would employ the distinction between "suffragist" and "suffragette" set forth by Martin Pugh, who speaks of Victorian suffragists and Edwardian suffragettes – the former adhering to constitutional models of behavior in their quest for enfranchisement, the latter taking a more radical stance.[1] Pugh, however, warns against dismissing the earlier group as less committed or daring, simply because they stayed with the law, justly admonishing us that "in the late 1860s one should remember, the suffragists who mounted public platforms were *militants*."[2] These Victorian suffragists, he continues, employed a tactic "described disparagingly as 'mixed speaking,' since men were also present, and was thought to be rather shocking."[3] "Rather shocking" may seem a quaint Victorian hyperbole to us now, but there was nothing quaint about the views expressed by Victoria herself and those in her circle. Lady Amberly, one of these "rather shocking" public speakers, exclaimed at the public's response: "'people expressed surprise to me afterwards to see that a woman could lecture and still look like a lady!'"[4] Queen Victoria's (in)famous response to reports of the spectacle was less complimentary, writing to Sir Theodore Martin on 20 May 1870, referring in general to women participating in "mixed speaking" and to Lady Amberly in particular:

> The Queen is most anxious to enlist every one who can speak or write to join in checking this mad, wicked folly of "Women's Right," with all its attendant horrors, on which her poor feeble sex is bent, forgetting every sense of womanly feeling and propriety. Lady — ought to get a GOOD WHIPPING.[5]

Constance Rover's assessment of this is that, despite the "Queen's attitude, it was at least obvious that there was a certain contradiction in [the state of the government] ... As may be imagined, the suffragists were not slow to point out this anomaly."[6] Interestingly, as much attention as Queen Victoria's remark garnered when Sir Theodore published it in 1908, the general public was largely unaware of her feelings at the time. Thus we see that the image of Victoria as a woman ruler had more power than the actual sentiments of Victoria the person, for during the late 1890s, when the nation's imagination was most taken with the queen's long reign, "Sir Wilfred Lawson and others suggested [in 1897] that it would be appropriate to mark her diamond jubilee by enacting a women's suffrage bill."[7] Needless to say, that never happened. But, in these days when tabloids purport to bring us every thought that flits through a royal head, it's salutary to be reminded that a century ago, a Member of Parliament could be so unaware of the monarch's long-standing (17 years, at least) and strongly (if semi-privately) expressed sentiments, so unaware as to propose a bill entirely at odds with the views of the queen he was trying to honor. Insofar as is possible, we should cling to this distinction between then and now.

But 1897 was actually well over 50 years into the Parliamentary debates on the topic of women and the vote. We have no less than the words of one of the nineteenth century's most famous politicians on the subject:

I say to you that in a country governed by a woman – where you allow women to form part of the other estate of the realm – peeresses in their own right for example – where you allow a woman not only to hold land but to be a lady of the Manor and hold legal courts – where a woman by law may be churchwarden – I do not see, where she has so much to do with the State and Church, on what reasons ... she has not a right to vote. All this proves that right has nothing to do with the matter.

Benjamin Disraeli,
in a debate in the House of Commons
on 20 June 1848.[8]

That Disraeli began his series of parallel clauses with a reference to Queen Victoria is hardly surprising, given the inarguable fact that she was a queen regnant. That he speaks, in Parliament itself, of the country being "governed by a woman" is hyperbole in the service of a political agenda. Victoria, of course, did not govern as did Elizabeth Tudor. Nevertheless, the language of monarchy still flourished in the mid-nineteenth century, just as it does today, when circumstances – such as the Golden Jubilee of Elizabeth II – elicit it. Separating the images of the queen who would symbolize the Empire from the images of the queen who first fostered empire-building proved a difficult task for supporters of the suffrage movement. From our vantage-point, using the examples in tandem might seem both logical and effective. And, to some extent, it was.

Millicent Fawcett's 1895 *Life of Her Majesty Queen Victoria*,[9] makes this point in a number of ways. Illustrating the awareness of Victoria's father, the Duke of Kent, of the place of importance held by his new-born daughter, Fawcett tells us that he "wanted the baby to be called Elizabeth, because it was the name of the greatest of England's Queens, and therefore a popular name with the English people"; his German relatives, however, insisted on Alexandrina Georgiana. But the Prince Regent objected to his name coming second, so she was to be christened simply Alexandrina, when the Duke added, at the last moment, his wife's name, Victoria, a name "then almost unknown in England."[10] (Surely it would have been one of history's most ironic jokes if three of the four longest-reigning monarchs of England were named Elizabeth.[11])

Framing her argument by remarking acidly on the fact that the birth of a prince is celebrated because it saves a nation "from all the perils and evils supposed to be associated with the reign of a female Sovereign," Fawcett goes on to make a jest of that sentiment by cataloging successful queens regnant.

[I]t is not a little curious that the popular opinion to which these articles and speeches give expression, namely, that the chances are that any man will make a better Sovereign than any woman, is wholly contrary to experience; it is hardly going too far to say that in every country in which the succession to the Crown has been open to women, some of the greatest, most capable, and most patriotic Sovereigns have been queens. The names of Isabella of Spain, of Maria Theresa of Austria, will rise in this connection to every mind; and, little as she is to be admired as a woman, Catherine II of Russia showed that she thoroughly understood the art of ruling. Her vices would have excited little remark had she been a king instead of a queen. It is an unconscious tribute to the higher standard of conduct queens have taught the world to expect from them, that while the historic muse stands aghast at the private life of the Russian Empress, she is only very mildly scandalized by a Charles V or a Henry IV, thinking, with much justice, that their great qualities as rulers serve to cover their multitude of sins as private individuals.[12]

Her nail in the coffin, as it were, is delivered with succinct aplomb: "The Salic Law did not, to say the least, save the French monarchy from ruin."[13] Indeed, this is an exquisite understatement, as the French obsession with crowning only male heads led directly to the dynastic disaster of the Hundred Years War and failed to save the royal necks during the French Revolution.

Reminding her readers that in the five (at that time) queens regnant of England "we have had three of eminent distinction as compared with our other Sovereigns; and of these three, one ranks with the very greatest of the statesmen who deserve to be remembered as the Makers of England."[14] And here she speaks of Elizabeth. Although a bit florid, Fawcett's judgment is unequivocal: "when the feeble flame of Edward VI's life was extinguished … England acquired at the most critical moment of her history, in the person of Elizabeth, perhaps the greatest Sovereign who has ever occupied the throne of this country."[15] Here Fawcett is carefully trying to thread a critical needle. Elizabeth, she argues, is simply and absolutely (perhaps) the best monarch England has ever had. But (and here's the hard part) if Elizabeth is an exceptional monarch, she is, de facto, an exceptional woman. Never mind that outstanding male rulers are also exceptional men; men are the gold-standard. It does not diminish the ranks of men in general for there to be exceptional men. For women, on the other hand, "exceptional" resonates with the clearly heard, even if unarticulated, echo "for a woman." Far worse, to call Elizabeth an exceptional ruler – rather than an exceptional "woman ruler" – sets her so entirely apart from all her sisters that she becomes something "more" than a woman.

And this argument can cut both ways. Partly in response to Cicely Hamilton's 1909 *Pageant of Great Women*[16] – a debate between two abstractions, Woman and Prejudice, mediated by a third, Justice – Ford Madox Ford published (yet another) pamphlet called *This Monstrous Regiment of Women*, in 1913. In the *Pageant of Great Women*, Woman brings categories of extraordinary women in Western civilization: Learned, Saintly, and Heroic Women, as well as Artists, Rulers, and Warriors. As Barbara Green recounts, "forty-four exemplary Edwardian women (suffragettes, suffragists, and actresses like Ellen Terry and Edith Craig) represented forty-four exemplary women from history (like Jane Austen, Sappho, Elizabeth, Joan of Arc, and Florence Nightingale) through a grand spectacle."[17] Ford zeros in on one of the weak points of using exceptional women, already a matter of some debate within the Suffrage Movement: such women are, he argues, by definition, not the norm. While the women in the Movement worried primarily about ordinary women feeling shut out or failing to identify with any of the great women of history, there is another side to the problem. Ford's rendering of this issue is more an *ad hominem* attack than an intellectual response. After this, in the spirit of Boccaccio's *Concerning Famous Women*, Ford professes to acknowledge the connection between national success and women on the throne. But he continues, introducing the argument that Elizabeth and Victoria were successful precisely because they embodied un-womanly qualities.

> As so Elizabeth paid nobody, cheated everybody, and was mean in a manner in which no man could have been mean. Had she been a fine lady living today she would have been the sort of person who would have underpaid her cabman, docked half the wages of her footman, ridden first-class with a third–class ticket – and at the cabman, at the footman, at the ticket collectors she would have made such eyes that not one of them but would have protested that she was the most charming lady in the world.[18]

Barbara Green takes on the other weakness of the exceptional woman, although more fairly, saying that the Movement itself owed more to the celebrity of women such as Christabel Pankhurst than to the needs of the disenfranchised. She points out the fundamental "incompatibility of celebrity (the exception) and citizenship (the dream of equal participation)," remarking that the WSPU's willingness to agree to limited enfranchisement constituted "seeming indifference to the demands of working-class women."[19] Needless to say, Green does not cite any examples from the life of Queen Elizabeth. Nice to mice she may have been, but Elizabeth was markedly not nice to other women; certainly she did little or nothing to improve the lot of her gender within her kingdom, except insofar as she made the lives of all her people safer and more prosperous. In this regard, Elizabeth is strikingly unhelpful as an icon for the Suffrage Movement's goal of citizenship.

But, to paraphrase one of the brothers in Milton's Mask: "peace, [sister], be not over-exquisite." The most general goal of the Suffrage Movement was to better the lot of women, politically and socially. Not that they were content to take what they could get, but – within the context of the British class system in which the activists lived and moved and had their meetings – Elizabeth's elite status was no reason to cast her image aside.

The problem of Joan of Arc is only a problem for this book. For the women in the Suffrage Movement, she must have seemed literally heaven-sent, regardless of their varied theologies. An active phenomenon in 1429 – and surely seeming to Christine de Pizan, the author of the first French poem about her, to be the living proof of the arguments in that author's 1405 *The Book of the City of Ladies* – Joan did indeed literally lead an army to victory on not one, but numerous occasions, and crown a King of France. Burned at the stake after a rigged trial in 1431, re-tried and vindicated in a process that lasted from 1452 until 1456, declared Venerable in 1903, Beatified by Pius X in 1909, and Canonized in 1920, Joan was also a present-tense phenomenon for the women of the Suffrage Movement. Although her official Canonization[20] came after British women (and even American women) had been partially enfranchised, Joan was still the de facto secular saint of the moment and the Movement.

> Joan of Arc is the militant women's ideal. They feel the closest kinship with her and in every word and every act of hers they recognize the same spirit as that which strengthens them to risk their liberty and endure torture for the sake of freedom.
>
> *The Suffragette*, 9 May 1913

Like Christine de Pizan, the Pankhursts and their supporters must have had trouble believing their eyes. There was a figure of Joan, almost always on a white horse, at every Suffrage spectacle. Pamphlets, posters, banners – all of the media at the Movement's disposal figured forth, at one time or other, Joan. In a 1910 biography of Joan, Grace James writes a clever analysis, not of Joan, but of the king she crowned, Charles VII.

The most casual student of the life of King Charles VII of France cannot fail to be impressed by a very remarkable factor in the working out of his destiny. This is the feminine influence, both for good and for evil, to which he was subjected throughout his career.

Of course, almost all men are influenced by women. During their early years, life is for them what their mothers make it to be. Later, they have more or less to do with their sisters, their wives, and their mothers-in-law. A body of feminine thought, ideas, sympathies, and instincts mingles with the sum of influences, impulses, and emotions which go to make up a man's existence.

The feminine element in Charles VII's history has nothing of this vague and general character. It is strong, constant, peculiarly distinct, and very important, something almost unique. It is scarcely any exaggeration to say that every decisive action undertaken or accomplished by Charles VII was prompted by a woman. Isabel of Bavaria, his mother; Yolande of Aragone, his mother-in-law; Marie of Anjou, his gentle wife; Joan of Arc, his military leader and his saint; Agnes Sorel, the lady whom he loved – all these had their day of power over him, as well as other women, whose names and reputations are less well known to history. All Charles's efforts and aspirations in the direction of self-respect, strength, sense, sanity, and kingliness were the result of women's labours.[21]

She goes on to ask what it was about Charles that generated this, since he was "not beautiful," his personality "not engaging" and his character "as it has come down to posterity, is by no means delightful."[22] I have quoted James at such length, because this passage comes from the first pages of her biography. Why would she be talking at such length about Charles, when her topic is Joan? King Edward VII, he of the long-reigning mother and the many mistresses, died the same year her book was published. Grace James makes no criticism out of the fact that Charles' life could be sub-titled (as the Moses story can be renamed "How the Brave, Strong Women Saved the Baby Boy") "the man whose life was ordained by women." Some of both sets of women were good for each man, and some were bad. Perhaps the most striking similarity was that each king's mother kept him waiting years for the throne – Victoria making Bertie the longest-running Prince of Wales until the present day, and Isabel doing her very best to keep Charles from the throne at all, by marrying her daughter to England's Henry V with the understanding that their child would be the next King of France. James' parallel not only between Joan and the suffragettes, but between Charles VII and

Edward VII was both clever and apt. But we must remember that she was living, not in the time of absolute monarchy, but in a day when the real enemies of the current versions of Joan were housed in faux medieval glory at Westminster.

With the coming of World War I, or the Great War, the image of Joan became an even stronger symbol for the Movement, just as it became a talisman for the French. After German bombs damaged the cathedral where Joan had crowned Charles, Christabel Pankhurst's editorial in *The Suffragette* in April 1915 was accompanied by a front cover reproduction of "a French cartoon of Joan of Arc in full military armour, hovering as an angel above Rheims Cathedral, which had been badly damaged in September 1914. The headline screams: 'That which the Fire and Sword of the Germans Can Never Destroy'."[23]

So it was not that Elizabeth was judged unsuitable for public display – far otherwise, as I will discuss in the next two sections – but that Joan herself was so perfectly suited to the historical moment of the Suffrage Movement that (even though she was a royalist, a Roman Catholic, and French) Joan's icon present in the sphere of public memory was powerful enough to urge the claims of immediacy over those of English history.

*c.*1880: Gloriana, the Suffragists' utopia

Gloriana; or The Revolution of 1900 was written by Lady Florence Dixie and published by Henry and Company of London in 1880. To speak about Lady Florence Dixie is itself a struggle with the gendered language of stereotype and polite cliché. I found myself telling a friend that she was "one of those intrepid nineteenth-century lady-travelers who traipsed to the ends of the earth and back again, coming to no harm and doing God knows what." What a way to dismiss a life. That sounds as though these women came by the dozen, all cut from the same cloth, when, in fact, the most outstanding mark of each woman was her singularity.

Since so little has been written on Lady Florence (really, I cannot refer to her as "Dixie"), I am balked of the usual canonical prose to cite and dismiss, so I have cited and dismissed myself.

Born Lady Florence Caroline Douglas in 1857, she was the daughter of the 7th Marquess of Queensberry, and thus the sister of Lord Alfred Douglas, famous to fans of Oscar Wilde. Holidays at home must have been gruesome. Perhaps she traveled out of self-defense. But travel she did, going in 1878–79 to Patagonia, where there are still a number of hotels named for her. After working as the London *Morning Post*'s field correspondent during the 1879 Zulu War, she continued her writing in a number of genres, notably the travelogue; *Across Patagonia*, first published in 1880, is still in print. Less popular, to state it mildly, is *Gloriana*. Although Lady Florence was involved in Anglo-Irish politics in London at the turn of the century, she seems not to have been visibly active in the Suffragists' Movement – unless, of course, one counts writing the book. She died in 1905, just as the more militant philosophies of the Pankhursts were being put into practice, but before even the first step toward her feminist Utopia had been taken. Indeed, we must wonder, as we do of Christine de Pizan, if she would find the status of women in today's world all that fundamentally changed. She sets forth her agenda very clearly in the book's dedication.

ALL WOMEN

and

Such Honourable, Upright, and Courageous

MEN

As, regardless of Custom and Prejudice, Narrow-mindedness and Long–Established Wrong, will bravely assert and uphold the Laws of Justice, of Nature, and of Right; I dedicated the following pages, with the hope that a straightforward inspection of the evils afflicting Society, will lead to their demolition in the only way possible – namely, by giving to Women equal rights with men. Not till then will Society be purified, wrongdoing punished, or man start forward along that road which shall lead to Perfection.[24]

Because the work is so little-known and seldom cited[25] I want to present a long passage from this Suffragist Elizabeth icon. Like the *Romance of the Rose* and other canonical works, the book opens with a dream-vision poem. The dreamer is called Maremna, described as a "Noble's child, rear'd amidst Nature's scenes," whose hope is for a life of rest after a "world-wide pilgrimage" to "learn the ways and woeful deeds of men."[26] The novel itself begins in an Italian garden, where the young Gloriana, "or as we shall prefer to call her," Gloria de Lara and her mother, Speranza de Lara, speak to each other of dreams and imagination.[27] Gloria de Lara will go on to become Prime Minister of England and bring about the realization of the utopian vision described in the book's last chapter. But first, let us read the Preface.

> "Thus we were told in words Divine
> That there were truths men could not bear
> E'en from the lips of Christ to hear.
> These have not slowly been unfurled,
> But still to a reluctant world.

"Prophets will yet arise to teach
Truths which the schoolmen fail to reach,
Which priestly doctrine still would hide,
And worldly votaries deride,
And statesmen fain would set aside."

I make no apology for this preface. It may be unusual but then the book it deals with is unusual. There is but one object in "Gloriana." It is to speak of evils which DO exist, to study facts which it is a crime to neglect, to sketch an artificial position – the creation of laws false to nature – unparalleled for injustice and hardship. Many critics, like the rest of humanity, are apt to be unfair. They take up a book, and when they find that it does not accord with their sentiments, they attempt to wreck it by ridicule and petty, spiteful criticism. They forget to ask themselves, "Why is this book written?" They altogether omit to go to the root of the Author's purpose; and the result is, that false testimony is often borne against principles which, though drastic, are pure, which, though sharp as the surgeon's knife, are yet humane; for it is genuine sympathy with humanity that arouses them.

There is no romance worth reading, which has not the solid foundation of truth to support it. There is no excuse for the existence of romance, unless it fixes thought on that truth which underlies it. Gloriana may be a romance, a dream; but in the first instance, it is inextricably interwoven with truth, in the second instance, dreams, the work of the brain are species of thought, and thought is an attribute of God. Therefore it is God's creation.

There may be some, who reading "Gloriana," will feel shocked, and be apt to misjudge the author. There are others who will understand, appreciate, and sympathize. There are yet others, who hating truth, will receive it with gibes and sneers; there are many, who delighting in the evil which it fain would banish, will resent it as an unpardonable attempt against their liberties. An onslaught on public opinion is very like leading a Forlorn Hope. The leader knows full well that death lies in the breach, yet that leader knows also that great results may spring from the death which is therefore readily sought and faced. "Gloriana" pleads woman's cause, pleads for her freedom, for the just acknowledgment of her rights. It pleads that her equal humanity with man shall be recognized, and therefore that her claim to share what he has arrogated to himself, shall be considered. "Gloriana," pleads that in woman's degradation man shall no longer be debased, that in her elevation he shall be upraised and ennobled. The reader of its pages will observe the Author's conviction, everywhere expressed, that Nature ordains the close companionship not division of the sexes, and that it is opposition to Nature which produces jealousy, intrigue, and unhealthy rivalry.

"Gloriana" is written with no antagonism to man. Just the contrary. The Author's best and truest friends, with few exceptions, have been and are men. But the Author will never recognize man's glory and welfare in woman's degradation.

> "And hark! a voice with accents clear
> Is raised, which all are forced to hear.
> 'Tis woman's voice, for ages hushed,
> Pleading the cause of woman crushed;
> Pleading the cause of purity,
> Of freedom, honour, equity,
> Of all the lost and the forlorn,
> Of all for whom the Christ was born."

If, therefore, the following story should help men to be generous and just, should waken the sluggards amongst women to a sense of their Position, and should thus lead to a rapid Revolution it will not have been written in vain.

THE AUTHOR[28]

Divided into three books the plot of the novel has all of the genre's usual adventures, with the single difference being that they are experienced by women. There are voyages, storms, captures, escapes, bonds of friendship, rivalry, love lost, dirty doings, betrayal, marriage, acts of heroic self-sacrifice, and a final grand procession from St. Paul's to Westminster for the inauguration of the new government of enlightened women and men. Chapter X of Book III is set in 1999, when a stranger in a balloon passes over London, seeing no dirt or poverty. He asks questions of his guide who tells him of "the great Duchess of Ravensdale, of noble memory," Gloria de Lara who was Prime Minister, followed by Lady Flora Desmond, who was the next Prime Minister and "carried on her noble works of reform."[29] Gloria and her husband spent all their money on the poor, and by their example, so did others, and "There is no poverty in this country now, sir."[30] The Imperial Parliament is, according to the guide:

"where the representatives of our Federated Empire watch over its welfare. To Gloria of Ravensdale we owe the triumph of Imperial

Federation. She lived long enough to see England, Ireland, Scotland, and Wales peacefully attending to their private affairs in their Local Parliaments, while sending delegates to represent them in the Imperial Assembly. Ah, sir! That Imperial Assembly is a wonderful sight. Therein we see gathered together representative men and women from all parts of our glorious Empire, working hand in hand to spread its influence amongst the nations of the world, with all of whom we are at peace."[31]

And the narrative ends as it began, in the dream of Maremna, when by the light of "a blood-red sunset" her vision comes. She arises to:

> "... buckle on her mail
> Far off she hears the busy din of war,
> And knows that duty calls her to the fray.
> In that brief hour Maremna's vow is made.
> Low sinks the sun, and gloom o'erspreads the earth,
> As down the rugged mountain side she wends
> Her way. Maremna's high resolve is ta'en –
> Faithful till Death to be, unto her vow."[32]

It is not, I think, insignificant that imaginative literature played little, if any, role in the Suffragette Movement. Yes, they wrote poems and pageants, but these were turned into spectacle of one sort or another. Reading the 350-page book is a private undertaking (pace the orators who read Dante's *Commedia* aloud each summer in Florence or those in Dublin who similarly share *Ulysses* in Bloomsday). For all that they had trouble remembering to include working-class women in their goal of universal suffrage (a small, but significant, evidence of this lack of thought was the choice of purple, green, and white – very expensive colors on a hard-to-keep-clean background – as the colors of the Movement), the Pankhursts and others of their circle could not be accused of title-hunting. If women of title chose to join the Movement, they were welcome, as were the increasing number of university women. But the inner circle wrote and read largely for didactic purposes, and Emmeline Pankhurst famously urged the argument of a broken window pane, not of an allegorical dream-vision.

Indeed, high art fared poorly in the hands of the suffragettes. In protest against Mrs. Pankhurst being arrested yet again, one Mary Richardson attacked the National Gallery's Rokeby Venus (by Velasquez) with a small ax on 4 March, 1914; this and other attacks on canonical works of high art, especially works with female subjects, caused many museums and galleries to close across the nation. Sometimes the closures were total, but in other museums only women were denied entrance. Diane Atkinson recounts:

> At places of historical interest the rule of "No muffs, writs-bags, or sticks" was widespread. Later, in May 1914, the Royal Academy and the Tate Gallery closed to the public. The British Museum was more flexible, opening to women accompanied by men who would accept responsibility for them. Unaccompanied women were only allowed in if they had a letter of recommendation from a gentleman who would vouch for their good conduct and take responsibility for their actions.[33]

The London *Morning Chronicle*, quoted in *The Suffragette*, 18 July 1914, recounts:

> Another picture outrage was committed at the National Portrait Gallery at about half past 11 yesterday morning by a Suffragist. A young woman of refined appearance and very respectably dressed attacked Millais's unfinished portrait of Carlyle with a butcher's cleaver which she carried concealed beneath her blouse, and before she could be restrained made three large cuts on the face and head of the portrait … [elipses sic]
>
> The blows were delivered with lightning-like rapidity, and then an attendant sprang forward, and, grasping her round the waist, swung her away from the picture. On the way to Vine Street Police Station, she offered a string of energetic protests against Mrs Pankhurst's re-arrest. At the station she gave her name as Annie Hunt, but refused her address.[34]

Making the direct attacks on high art – and on any number of windows – foregrounded the point that women could do damage; moreover, women could be banned from public places, not simply because they were women (that age-old reason), but because they could do real damage in support of their campaign. They were waging war. Here is yet another reason that the image of Elizabeth did not appear more often. Elizabeth had become – and perhaps always had been – the property of the patriarchy. Her wars were against foreign enemies and domestic foes of "right" religion. Carried too far, the Elizabeth icon could lead to an unpleasant transmogrification strongly resembling Margaret Thatcher.

As an Elizabeth icon, Gloriana may seem a bit of a stretch. Elizabeth, after all, did not desire to empower either Parliament or other women. But, as the Preface makes clear, Lady Florence is writing instructively.

While it would be fanciful to say she was instructing the Elizabeth of the past, she is surely making a strong case for serious revisions in the Elizabeth icon as it currently existed in the sphere of public memory. Yes, print icons are always more problematic than visual icons, but as works realized – at least in part – on the level of imagination, they can claim even broader scope. And the written word, along with the spectacle, was becoming a skillfully used tool of the Suffrage Movement. The Virago Press, which the twentieth-century suffragists founded, had as the Virago logo an apple with a bite taken out of it, and on the recto page before the title:

VIRAGO is a feminist publishing company: "It is only when women start to organize in large numbers that we become a political force and begin to move towards the possibility of a truly democratic society in which every human being can be brave, responsible, thinking and diligent in the struggle to live at once freely and unselfishly."

While Elizabeth Tudor would not have contemplated women organizing "in large numbers" with any degree of approval, she was equitable in that she felt the same way about large groups of men trying to effect social change. Balanced as she was, relying both on the traditional power of the monarch and the relatively untainted exercise of that power by a woman, Elizabeth must have had all the social change she could handle. In Lady Florence's Elizabeth icon, we recognize the idea, not the reality of Gloriana. While this was just what people were meant to do with the Pre-Raphaelite art and the eighteenth-century icons, the difference is that the crafters of those icons did not want their public to recognize change; they were playing a continuity card to bring about change almost (or ideally) without the public noticing it. Lady Florence Dixie shows us that such change is not only necessary, it is imperative. Furthermore, it is crucial that we realize just how great the need is for such change. Rather than completely constructing an Elizabeth icon to suit her agenda, Lady Florence has forced her readers to do that work for themselves.

But, more than any of the philosophical reasons above, the obscure fate of *Gloriana* may have been sealed by its date. Like the queen whose epithet it bears, it was born before its time. In 1880 it was still a brave act for a woman to speak in public. The notion, even in a dream-vision, of a woman as a Prime Minister is an idea whose time had not yet come – and, some might argue that time is yet before us.

*c.*1908: one banner in the history of the world

On the 13th day of June in 1908, over 13,000 suffragists, "members of various societies," came together on the Embankment and began the march to the Albert Hall. According to the account given in the pamphlet *Woman's Effort: A Chronicle of British Women's Fifty Years' Struggle for Citizenship, 1856–1914* (1917), it was "a picturesque and striking pageant which ... opened a new phase in the history of the movement ... Many Gorgeous banners were carried ... Some of the banners bore simple devices, other recorded deeds of heroism [sic] done by women, or referred to the achievements of women whose names have become household words."[35] Twenty-three of those "gorgeous" banners, along with photographs of ten leaders, were displayed on a page in the *Illustrated London News* of 20 June 1908 under the heading "The Woman Militant: Leadership of the Suffragist Procession and the Symbolic Banners Commemorating Great Women of All Ages." There the banner for Queen Victoria is in the center, just beneath the first photograph, that of Mrs. Despard, Leader of the Women's Freedom League. On the banner are the words "VICTORIA, QUEEN AND MOTHER." There is no image of the queen. To the right of the Victoria banner is the Elizabeth banner (of which more, later), and to the left is the banner of Boadicea (Boudicca), forming a trio of queens regnant.

The banners were one of the chief devices of the Suffrage spectacles, and were carefully researched and designed by the Artists' Suffrage League. As Lisa Tickner observes in *The Spectacle of Women*: "As women, the suffragists were subject to the alienating effects of serving as the raw material for allegory and myth;[36] but as artists, perhaps for the first time, they were peculiarly placed to exploit it."[37] Tickner continues:

> Banners celebrated a "women's history" in their iconography, their inscriptions and their collective workmanship; they focused a sense of shared identity and imbued it with political significance. In so far as they made reference to the past it was as part of a political strategy for the present; and in so far as they mobilized women's traditional needlework skills – so much a part of the contemporary feminine stereotype as to be almost a secondary sexual characteristic – it was to challenge the terms of that femininity in a collective political enterprise.[38]

Three years after this procession came the Women's Coronation Procession, on 17 June 1911. These suffragettes, dressed as notable women from the past, joined in the march and the rally in the Royal Albert Hall. "These characters included: Jenny Lind (1820–87), the most celebrated soprano of her day; Grace Darling (1815–42), a heroine who rescued survivors from a boat wrecked off the Farne Islands; and Mrs Somerville (1780–1872), a science writer and advocate of higher education for women and women's suffrage, after whom Somerville College, Oxford, is named,"[39] and, of course, Queen Elizabeth. (There is but one dark and partially obscured photograph of the Elizabeth figure in the archives of the Women's Library.) Once again, the traditional woman's task of needlework could be turned to political ends, as the costumes were both elaborate and historically appropriate.

In 1889, Millicent Fawcett wrote *Some Eminent Women of our Times: Short Biographical Sketches*,[40] to which she attaches two epigraphs on the fly leaf, one from Dante and the other from George Eliot. The former is more than a bit daunting, as it is what Virgil says to Dante the Pilgrim as they approach the entrance to Purgatory.

> "Non aver tema," disse il mio segnore:
> "fatti sicur, ché noi semo a buon punto:
> non stringer, ma rallarga ogni vigore."
> *Purgatorio* Canto 9, v 46–48

["Have no fear," said my lord; "take confidence, for all is well with us; but put forth all your strength."] Looking at this more positively, they have just climbed out of hell and are finally heading in the right direction. Evidently Fawcett thought that this tercet spoke to the historical moment at hand. In these brief sketches Fawcett includes the lives of Elizabeth Fry, Mary Carpenter, Caroline Hershel, Sarah Martin, Mary Somerville, Queen Victoria, Harriet Martineau, Florence Nightingale, Mary Lamb, Agnes Elizabeth Jones, Charlotte and Emily Brontë, Lady Sale and Her Fellow-Hostages in Afghanistan, Elizabeth Gilbert, Jane Austen, Maria Edgeworth, Queen Louisa of Prussia, Dorothy Wordsworth, Sister Dora, Mrs. Barbauld, Joanna Baillie, Hannah More, and the American Abolitionists – Prudence Crandall and Lucretia Mott. In 1905, she published *Five Famous French Women*, chronicling Joan of Arc; Lousie of Savoy and her daughter, Margaret of Angouleme, Duchess of Alençon and Queen of Navarre; Jeanne D'Albret, Queen of Navarre; and Renée of France, Duchess of Ferrara.[41]

Here we see the beginning of what was to become a necessary device for the Suffrage Movement: the list. The long list. Copia, as the medieval rhetoricians called the piling on of example after example, was used literally and figuratively to weight one's argument. If three examples are good, then 30 are even better. Christine de Pizan exemplifies the use of this trope in *The Book of the City of Ladies*, and we see poetic versions of it as early as Homer's epics, where the catalog – in the *Iliad*, a virtually endless list of ships and those who arrived in them – is used to impart a sense of historical reality and accuracy. This is the print version of the 13,000-person procession. For such occasions – in print or in action – more is definitely more.

Taking this device to perhaps its most extreme use in the period, Margaret Wynne Nevinson compiles a 1913 work entitled *Ancient Suffragettes*[42] and gives us an almost overwhelming catalog of women. Her argument is that "the race of Suffragettes is of very ancient lineage,"[43] and she disputes the claim that "the enfranchisement of women is unscriptural," calling Leah "one of the earliest martyrs to the 'mariage de convenance'!" saying that even "the Jewish Jehovah had compassion upon her and gave her a son."[44] Heading her list are Deborah and Jael as "militant women," and Ruth, who was praised by "both women (who said she was better to Naomi than seven sons)" and Boaz, who calls her "a virtuous woman."[45] She allows that the Queen of Sheba had much wealth and power and that her subjects, "like Englishmen seem to have had no objection to the rule of a woman, though with strange want of logic the enfranchisement of the sex seems so repugnant to them." Ignoring Esther, she pronounces:

> In those days of the Oriental subjection of women it is cheering to read of the spirited action of Queen Vashti, who very properly refused to make a spectacle of herself at the command of a drunken husband."[46]

Judith, we are told, joins Boadicea and Joan of Arc as heroic women who save both their countries and their "sex for ever from the charge of weakness and cowardice."[47]

Digressing a bit over the topic of divorce, she picks up the thread of her argument within the classics. Saying that Homer's times were short of suffragettes, she labels as

> contemptible to a modern house-wife ... the supineness of the faithful Penelope, who suffered so dejectedly the enormous appetites of the suitors and their havoc in the wine-cellar! Not once does it occur to this doubtfully virtuous woman to assume the keys of the cupboards, to turn out the wooers, and to assert her inalienable right to make her own rules in her own house.[48]

She continues to lay waste to the classical examples of the feminine, calling Helen of Troy a typical bad example of "'the protected women' beguiling and ruling men through their lowest nature"; but she nevertheless objects to Helen and the Greeks and Trojans putting blame on "'the god' in a resigned Calvinist spirit, [appearing] to have had little or no consciousness of Free Will." Remarking scornfully that Aphrodite "would never have gone to prison for her opinions, nor headed a raid on the House of Commons" Nevinson goes on to list "Athene, goddess of wisdom, defender of the state" as one who "still leads women in their revolt against injustice; and with her is Hera, wife of Zeus," who is "no Griselda; she stands up boldly to Zeus for the equality of the sexes and the rights of women." She then adds to "these immortals ... the race of Amazons and the two queens Hippolyte and Penthesilea ... In Sophocles, AEschylus, and Euripides, we find women of character and high courage – Antigone, Clytemnestra, Alcestis, Medea," saying that Medea's speech on the subjugation of women is great and "might be given to-day from the Suffragist platform without anyone in the audience suspecting its antiquity."[49]

All that wit and erudition in a mere seven pages. One marvels at her existence in 1913, even as one mourns the lack of opportunity to meet her. But all this is a long way round the mulberry bush to the banner of Elizabeth. Or not so long. For the first time we are seeing an iconic representation of Elizabeth as one figure in a crowd. Just as Lady Florence Dixie forces us to realize we are revising the icon held in our memories, so do these processing, list-making, banner-sewing women fighting for the vote force us to acknowledge that Elizabeth is not as singular as we have been persuaded to believe. These lists and parades of banners place the queen in a progression of women, but the progression is not one of chronology or degree. As Nevinson reminds us that Medea's speech would not be out of place in the twentieth century, she also implicitly makes the point that Euripides' character had a bolder view of her own worth as a woman than Elizabeth allowed herself to express. As we are invited to recall the bravery in combat of Penthesilea, Judith, Boadicea, and Joan, we must realize that making a speech before a battle in which she has no plans to participate is not the same as Henry V's invitation – however disingenuous – to be one of "we few, we happy few, we band of brothers." No, Elizabeth might not make the cut for Margaret Wynne Nevinson (Mrs. H. W.). But she is there, caught in her historical moment, serving as a feminist critique to the more modern Victoria, even as the ancient Boadicea puts Elizabeth to shame in some respects.

And the banner itself (Figure 19, see also front cover) is very beautiful. The once-orange background has faded a bit to a sort of golden rose, but

Figure 19   Queen Elizabeth Suffragette Banner, *c.*1908. Reproduced with the permission of the Women's Library

it is picked up in Elizabeth's gown and does contrast with her famous hair and the blue of the English Channel. She is depicted as a queen associated with war. The ships of the Armada battle are ranged behind her just as they are in the Armada portrait and "Truth Presents the Queen with a Lance." Furthermore, unlike the warrior queen Boadicea, the other bracket to "Victoria, Queen and Mother," Elizabeth exists in real time, as it were; she is of early modern history, in the period where the visual image of an individual leader first could lodge in the memories of a significant number of subjects. And, most importantly, Elizabeth's face is the only face on any of those 23 banners. Not only has the work of the artists reached an extraordinarily high degree of detail and realism, but the complexity of the banner itself sets it apart from all of the others. Both the women lost in the mists of time – Boadicea, St. Teresa – and the women whose photographs were readily available – George Eliot, Angelica Kaufmann, Fanny Byrney – are represented, as are Victoria and Joan of Arc, simply by their written names. Elizbeth's face, itself an icon of a powerful English woman, adorns her banner above her name. She doesn't require the title "Queen." She simply is. Elizabeth.

An icon for the Great War and the second Armada

c.1915: ships, spies, cabbages, and queens

The BBC History website gives us the headline stories from the *Daily Mirror*, 24 April 1915,[50] including the story "Shells that Gave Queen Elizabeth Her Baptism of Fire at Dardanelles," from a Special Correspondent. Here are some highlights from the story:

Eastern Mediterranean, April.
… We left Malta on Friday, April 2 … Many of our merchant captains and their crews have never traversed the waters of the Mediterranean: its currents, changing weather conditions, its lights and the innumerable islands of the archipelago are a new field of discovery to them. Amazing as it may seem the charts are also old and very inaccurate, all of which adds to the difficulty of correct navigation.
But we are a Fleet messenger, under orders to arrive at our destination without delay; the same blood and spirit of enterprise of the Elizabethan era courses through the veins of the officers and men, and we press on, groping our way blindly and risking bumps with the archipelago …
[As the ship enters the Dardanelles, the correspondent describes what he sees.] The first sight which greets our eyes are the fighting-tops of

the mighty *Queen Elizabeth*, the most powerful warship afloat in any waters. Her huge body is hidden by some low-lying land ...
A pinnace takes me across to the *Queen Elizabeth* to visit the admiral. This, the latest of our super Dreadnoughts, is a revelation. She only carries eight great 15-inch guns, and a secondary armament of six-inches. But those eight make every other gun you have ever seen look ridiculous and contemptible.
The gunners say they can almost land on a penny at 15,000 yards even with three-quarter charges.
The great ship has in turn received her baptism of fire, and has been struck by three shells, one of which came through the gun-team, but fortunately all the midshipmen were at their stations, and no one was hurt.

Certainly the image of HMS *Queen Elizabeth* – also known as "Big Bessie" – in the Dardanelles is one of the most famously reproduced naval images of the Great War. So pronounced was the patriotic fervor generated by descriptions, photographs, and narratives about the ship, that the famous cartoon in *Punch* (Figure 20) is both easy to read and seemingly inevitable. It is an Elizabeth icon of great wit, lampooning not the memory of the queen herself, but the nationalistic image constructed in the popular imagination. In the *Punch* icon we see an image of the queen, formally clad in a dress very like the one she wears in the Armada portrait, with a scepter in her right hand (that which rested on the globe in the 1688 portrait), while her left hand daintily, but practically, plucks up her skirts to keep them dry. She seems to be flying upright over the disputed waves, with suitable outcroppings of foreign lands in the background.

The combination of a great naval battle and the tradition of christening ships with feminine names was certain to produce a concrete allusion to Elizabeth and the Armada. The *Mirror's* Special Correspondent also speaks of the "same blood and spirit of enterprise of the Elizabethan era" coursing "through the veins of the officers and men, and we press on, groping our way blindly and risking bumps with the archipelago," combining both the Elizabethan spirit of adventure and the enchantment of discovery. They are sailing blind, with bad maps, but they sail literally for – as in the direction of – Queen Elizabeth.

If this icon is easily read, the next is not. One can, indeed, hardly bring oneself to take it at face value. The 1915 text by Augusta Cook, *Queen Elizabeth: or Spies and Plots in the Sixteenth Century With an Introduction: History Repeating Itself in the Events of Today,*[51] has on its title page the obscure biblical quotation: "Thou shalt remember all the way the Lord

PUNCH, OR THE LONDON CHARIVARI.—March 17, 1915.

QUEEN ELIZABETH ENTERS THE DARDANELLES.

Figure 20   Queen Elizabeth enters the Dardanelles, from *Punch*, 17 March 1915. Collection of the author

thy God led thee" (Deut. VIII. 2). If ever a text needed to be read in context, this little epigraph cries out most loudly. Even the immediate context of Deuteronomy VIII is a testimony to an Empire's faith in God as an Englishman. Verse 1 reads: "All the commandments which I command thee this day shall ye observe to do, that ye may live, and multiply, and go in and possess the land which the LORD sware unto your fathers." The wording of the King James translation lends this justification of Empire additional authority, although that is rendered redundant by the larger context of the passage.

When we look at the whole of Deuteronomy VII, the chapter that provides the true context for Cook's epigraphy, the verse's significance becomes clear, if horrifically apocalyptic and breath-takingly fascist.

1   When the LORD thy God shall bring thee into the land whither thou goest to possess it, and hath cast out many nations before thee, the Hittites, and the Girgashites, and the Amorites, and the Canaanites, and the Perizzites, and the Hivites, and the Jebusites, seven nations greater and mightier than thou;

2   And when the LORD thy God shall deliver them before thee; thou shalt smite them, and utterly destroy them; thou shalt make no covenant with them, nor shew mercy unto them:

3   Neither shalt thou make marriages with them; thy daughter thou shalt not give unto his son, nor his daughter shalt thou take unto thy son ...

5   But thus shall ye deal with them; ye shall destroy their altars, and break down their images, and cut down their groves, and burn their graven images with fire.

6   For thou art an holy people unto the LORD thy God: the LORD thy God hath chosen thee to be a special people unto himself, above all people that are upon the face of the earth.

7   The LORD did not set his love upon you, nor choose you, because ye were more in number than any people; for ye were the fewest of all people:

8   But ... the LORD loved ...

16   And thou shalt consume all the people which the LORD thy God shall deliver thee; thine eye shall have no pity upon them: neither shalt thou serve their gods; for that will be a snare unto thee.

17   If thou shalt say in thine heart, These nations are more than I; how can I dispossess them?

18   Thou shalt not be afraid of them ...

20   Moreover the LORD thy God will send the hornet among them,
until they that are left, and hide themselves from thee, be destroyed.

Ok, so the British "we few, we few, we happy few," with their new Queen
Elizabeth, constitute God's chosen people, while their foes are the —ites
de jour. The book's sub-title, *History Repeating Itself in the Events of Today*,
gives us the parallel between the Armada and the Battle of the Dardanelles,
and the Bible passage citation on the title page gives us the moral context:
all enemies of the chosen people will be destroyed by and/or at the
pleasure of God.

As unambiguous as this seems, the book itself still sends mixed signals
to the reader. Its large, thin, almost quarto-sized format, horizontal orientation, its brevity (56 pages), and illustrations make it look, at first
blush, like a children's book. On the cover and frontispiece is the *Punch*
cartoon, clearly captioned "Queen Elizabeth Entering the Dardanelles"
and credited: "Reproduced by kind permission of the Proprietors of
'Punch.'" On the verso before the first page of text is an illustration of
the ship itself, with the following sub-text:

> "The Queen Elizabeth" – called after the Great Queen of the Sixteenth
> Century – is the mightiest War Vessel in existence. Her four turrets
> contain each a pair of 96 ton 15-inch guns. She burns only oil in her
> furnaces, and is the fastest battleship in the world.[52]

If the rendering of the ship came first and the cartoon after, we might
conclude that Cook is stressing the reality and approving even of the
hyperbole. To put the hyperbolically floating, fully-dressed queen first,
making a secondary reference out of the battleship, is to privilege
chronology over, it would seem, common sense, as well as fancy over fact.
Nor does Cook provide the reader with great enlightenment in her
Introduction:

> History Repeating Itself in the Events of Today
> The following pages on "Queen Elizabeth" were written before the
> present War broke out. The publication thereof was postponed until
> a suitable opportunity. That seems to have now arrived; for History is
> repeating itself. Prophecy also is rapidly finding accomplishment. To
> this twofold aspect, in the light of present happening, I would direct
> the reader's attention.[53]

Cook continues, pointing out that Revelation is the "sacred Book dealing pre-eminently" with "Divine Prophecy," a "Programme – foretold in heiroglyphs – of the most salient points in the history of the Christian Church, of Israel, and the World."[54] Whether, as does the *c.*1625 print "Truth Presents the Queen with a Lance," Cook means to allude literally to the book of Revelation or to the prophetic nature of the cited passage from Deuteronomy is not entirely clear. I would, however, argue for the latter, considering that she took the trouble to put the passage on the title page, and that its specific context of the killing of earthly enemies is better suited to the conflict at hand.

This "Programme," she argues, is chronologically ordered, revealing as it progresses, the purpose and goal of God's actions. "That goal is the return of all creation to the obedience of God ... To achieve that goal, counterforces have to be subdued, and hostile agencies must be overthrown."[55] She calls the Devil the "invisible instigator" of opposition to this divinely ordained progress, saying that his "Satanic operations" against God's people (read "Englishmen") and against God take on multiple forms. But, the rant continues, "two systems are specially the agencies through which he has laboured in this dispensation, and through which he still works in opposition to the kingdom of Christ. Those two hostile systems are ROMANISM AND MOHAMMEDANISM."[56]

Well, we might certainly have seen the bogey of Roman Catholicism coming, as Elizabeth's Armada victory was perceived to be as much religious as geo-political. That Islam is here included, however, brings up both aspects of the Turkish setting of the Dardanelles and the theme of an Empire that would bring the godless infidels either to their knees or to their deaths. (And, writing this in the post-9/11 US, I must say that this last social construction of evil has a chilling familiarity.)

Cook's theology would seem to owe more to jingoism than to careful study – surprising in an author with over a dozen biblically-based books and published lectures to her credit[57] – as she states that the two systems "one in their origin, similar in their characteristics and wide dominion – the one dominating chiefly the West, the other the east – and united in their final doom at the coming of Christ."[58] Well, yes, Islam and Catholicism do have the same source – Abraham in the Genesis narrative – but so do Judaism and the rest of Christianity, not that Cook considered Rome to be Christian. Nor should we be surprised to find an author who denies that Catholics are Christians discounting any connection between Christianity and Islam; again, we have only to pick up any of today's papers to read that rhetoric. Sweeping theology aside for "my volumes on the Apocalypse," Cook goes on to what she perceives as the heart of the matter: "while the warlike person of Queen Elizabeth was the means in the sixteenth century to oppose the Western system, the war-vessel called after her – 'The Queen Elizabeth' – is the one employed in our days to shatter the strongholds of the Eastern Evil."[59]

After reminding the reader of this, Cook pronounces: "Here is not coincidence only." She goes on to conclude her Foreword with the invitation to the reader to enter into her conspiracy theory: "those who know Divine Prophecy will realize there is a Providence behind this interesting fact, working out the fore-ordained counsel of Jehovah."[60]

After a discussion covering the inevitability of empire, the virtue of queens who founded and crowned it (Elizabeth and Victoria), and all manner of plots to subvert this most admirable of world orders, Cook takes the strands of fanatic Protestantism, blind nationalism, and the sort of feminism that has justly become a bad joke and combines them to tie up the end of her venture into this prophetic re-reading of history.

> Queen Elizabeth is the strongest, as well as the most interesting monarch that ever graced the throne of England ... But she was by no means perfect ... she exercised [tyranny] against the Puritans, who were more Protestant than she was herself. Apart from this blemish, Elizabeth's reign is one of the grandest in the annals of English history; it marked the beginning of Imperial prosperity, the first dawn of world-wide sovereignty destined by Providence for this Empire, and which, foretold by the Druid-bard in the reign of Boadicea, had its genesis in the reign of Queen Elizabeth and found its consummation in that of another Queen – Victoria!
>
> Each Queen was suited to the age in which she flourished, and both Elizabeth and Victoria constitute the greatest monarchs in English history.[61]

And where, we might well ask, does this leave the Elizabeth icon? Obviously, the answer is "at sea."

*c.*1940: iterations of "Armada"

We have seen the Elizabeth icon brought into play for the various and sundry wars of Albion up through the centuries, wars ranging in significance from Jenkins and his ear to Napoleon and his ambitions for empire (wisely, Elizabeth and her icon took a pass on the American Revolution, unless there's some buried text playing on the theme of "easy come, easy go"). But when a twentieth- or twenty-first-century person thinks of Britain at war, the first image is always the Hitler War – World War II.

The Battle of Britain, the Blitz, the national and personal bravery we learn from history books, novels, films, documentaries, and – decreasingly – those who participated in and survived it, this is the war by which we define our immediate sense of the England that will be always there. Modern warfare, unlike the battles of the Hundred Years War or even the Napoleonic wars, happens with shattering immediacy. The long debates, the weeks or even months of waiting for the outcome of a distant battle, these are all collapsed into hours, minutes, even seconds. We should, therefore, hardly be surprised that there is little time for imagery among the various tasks of national readiness. Not only is there too little time, but there is too much at stake. Any politician would hesitate to place the weight of a national identity on the outcome of a battle which can be won or lost in the blink of an eye and reported to the world at large almost as quickly.

And yet that is exactly what Winston Churchill undertook to do. In one of his most famous speeches to the House of Commons, on 18 June 1940, Churchill plays the Armada card, and with it the whole treasure-trove of England's past. Covering first the many difficulties of modern warfare, the Prime Minister turns his attention, and that of the world, to the old issue of England's island status. The danger will come, he tells them even in that age of air wars, from across the sea. And that danger will come as an Armada. Below is part of the eighth paragraph of the famous oration and all of its last paragraph.

> The efficacy of sea power, especially under modern conditions, depends upon the invading force being of large size; It has to be of large size, in view of our military strength, to be of any use. If it is of large size, then the Navy have something they can find and meet and, as it were, bite on. Now, we must remember that even five divisions, however lightly equipped, would require 200 to 250 ships, and with modern air reconnaissance and photography it would not be easy to collect such an armada, marshal it, and conduct it across the sea without any powerful naval forces to escort it; and there would be very great possibilities, to put it mildly, that this armada would be intercepted long before it reached the coast, and all the men drowned in the sea or, at the worst blown to pieces with their equipment while they were trying to land. We also have a great system of minefields, recently strongly reinforced, through which we alone know the channels. If the enemy tries to sweep passages through these minefields, it will be the task of the Navy to destroy the mine-sweepers and any other forces employed

to protect them. There should be no difficulty in this, owing to our great superiority at sea.

What General Weygand called the Battle of France is over. I expect that the Battle of Britain is about to begin. Upon this battle depends the survival of Christian civilization. Upon it depends our own British life, and the long continuity of our institutions and our Empire. The whole fury and might of the enemy must very soon be turned on us. Hitler knows that he will have to break us in this Island or lose the war. If we can stand up to him, all Europe may be free and the life of the world may move forward into broad, sunlit uplands. But if we fail, then the whole world, including the United States, including all that we have known and cared for, will sink into the abyss of a new Dark Age made more sinister, and perhaps more protracted, by the lights of perverted science. Let us therefore brace ourselves to our duties, and so bear ourselves that, if the British Empire and its Commonwealth last for a thousand years, men will still say, "This was their finest hour."[62]

In his final lines, Churchill summons the essence of what it means to be an island nation, the perpetual importance of a strong navy, and he does so after using the word ineluctably linked to Elizabeth's own sea battle: Armada. It is not one battle that is at stake; it is a way of life, the threat of a return to the time before Elizabeth, "a new Dark Age."

War, in 1940, was no longer a matter for kings. Even as recently as the Great War, the personalities, and even the blood ties, of the monarchs had their place in the paradigm of war. Even if that were not banished by the absence of a conventional ruler in Germany, the late unpleasantness of Edward VIII's abdication and the substitution of a man who would not have been king, rendered any invocation of the present-tense monarchy inappropriate, especially by a Prime Minister speaking to the House of Commons. Interestingly, George VII and his two Elizabeths, wife and heir, would rapidly grow into their roles under the pressure of German bombs. But that was a happy outcome that, by its nature, had to be manifested over time. In June of 1940, Churchill tells the Commons that they have no time. Only two weeks before this, after the disaster at Dunkirk, the Prime Minister had delivered what were to become his most famous lines: "We shall go on to the end, we shall fight in France, we shall fight on the seas and oceans, we shall fight with growing confidence and growing strength in the air, we shall defend our Island, whatever the cost may be, we shall fight on the beaches, we shall fight on the landing grounds, we shall fight in the fields and in the streets, we shall fight in the hills; we shall never surrender ..." But that was not the curtain line of that speech. After the famous parallel clauses, the definitive uses of "we shall," Churchill once more turns to the sea, this time to the west. Realism and history combine as he closes with: "even if, which I do not for a moment believe, this Island or a large part of it were subjugated and starving, then our Empire beyond the seas, armed and guarded by the British Fleet, would carry on the struggle, until, in God's good time, the New World, with all its power and might, steps forth to the rescue and the liberation of the old." Once again the Royal Navy is cited as the ultimate salvation of the culture, now with the help of those lands colonized first during the reign of Elizabeth. Three and a-half centuries may have gone by since her captains sailed out to lay claim to that Empire. But even now, that is the "new" world, and the work and care which England invested (from England's point of view) in that new world can now be repaid to the old.

True, this is an allusion to an allusion. Queen Elizabeth may have been more distant from Churchill's mind than the fate of Antarctica. But her image is bound too tightly to the national identity of a sea-going nation to be completely absent. The Elizabeth icon here is the ruler of Spenser's New Jerusalem, of the idea of England. Even Winston Churchill, who has himself become an icon of Englishness, cannot deliver his most serious addresses without somehow raising the image of Elizabeth in the minds of his audience. And, indeed, why should he wish to?

The other Elizabaeth icon I'm taking from World War II is greatly at odds with the might and significance of Churchill's political eloquence. This Elizabeth is the girl in the 1944 biography *Young Bess*. In a scene as willfully meaningful as any episode of the *Faerie Queene*, Margaret Irwin gives us the unlikely vision of the young princess accompanying her father and his last wife, Elizabeth's only true step-mother, Catherine Parr, on a voyage aboard the ship named *Great Harry*. The precocious princess suddenly screams, supposedly to interrupt an argument between the king and queen, then – literally casting about for an explanation for her inter-ruption of the royal exchange – pretends to have seen the French fleet on the horizon. Since the argument was about degrees of Protestantism (see also Churchill's reference to a Christian Western Europe in the speech of 18 June), we have almost the entire Elizabeth story rolled into a ball and snatched through the iron gates of reality by Irwin. Warned by sooth-sayers that there would be a sea battle in her future, Young Bess is taken aback by the seeming power of her own speech, for indeed, a French fleet does appear. Easily dispatched, the departure of the French leaves the unlikely outing of royals in a rather crude parallel with the royal family of 1944. King George became famous for staying in London during the Blitz; his Queen Elizabeth became famous for staying with him, even after Buckingham Palace was damaged by a bomb; the princesses, Elizabeth and Margaret, of course became famous for staying in England, rather than seeking safety in the New World. So in their immediate future, readers of Irwin's book, written in the year of the Normandy invasion, could look forward to yet another young Bess coming to the throne and continuing to save her people.

Dobson and Watson also discuss this book (albeit a bit more positively), and offer their usual acute analysis: "In the year of D-Day, the Armada is shuffled away as something the reader already knows is won by 'an old, old woman' [a phrase from Irwin's book], in favour of a different story, a fiction of a young England embodied by a young woman."[63]

This "fiction" of which they speak will lead us straight into the fantasy of the New Elizabethans, the only total failure of those who manipulate cultural agendas to fashion an Elizabeth icon for all seasons.

1953–2003: The Shadows of Modern Imagination

A second Elizabeth ascends the throne

c.1977: *The Virgin in the Garden*

"She happened and she continued to happen."

This line, from Charles Williams' 1936 biography of Elizabeth, reprinted for the post-coronation market in 1953, could be the epigraph for A. S. Byatt's 1978 novel.[1] Written during the year of Elizabeth II's Silver Jubilee, and set in the year of her coronation, the novel's observer character is Alexander Wedderburn. We meet him in the National Portrait Gallery, at a 1968 exhibition entitled "People, Past and Present," the poster for which features the Darnley portrait of Elizabeth. As he wanders toward the Tudor gallery looking for the Darnley portrait itself (his favorite), his absent-mindedness or uncharacteristic lack of familiarity with the elements of public spectacle (he is a playwright) causes him to overlook the obvious: the portrait had been taken down for the performance about to begin. He is thus "left to sit on a bench contemplating an alternative Gloriana, raddled, white-leaded, bestriding the counties of England ... painted an inch thick, horse-hair topped and hennaed, heavy with quilted silk, propped and constricted by whalebone."[2]

He then looks for Frederica, described as Britomart, "her hair itself cut into a kind of bronze helmet, more space-age, maybe, than Renaissance,"[3] amid a crowd of literati, including Lady Antonia Frazer's "modern Belphoebe," of "urban elegance."[4] Failing to catch the attention of Frederica, Alexander gazes at his favorite Elizabeth portrait.

There she stood, a clear powerful image, in her airy dress of creamy stiff silk, embroidered with the golden fronds, laced with coral tassels, lightly looped with pearls. She stood and stared with the stillness and energy of a young girl. The frozen lassitude of the long white hands exhibited their fineness. They dangled, or gripped, it was hard to tell which, a circular feathery fan whose harsh whirl of darker colors suggested a passion, a fury of movement suppressed in the figure. There were other ambiguities in the portrait, the longer one stared, doubleness that went beyond the obvious one of woman and ruler. The bright-blanched face was young and arrogant. Or it was chalky, bleak, bony, any age at all, the black eyes under heavy lids knowing and distant.

Her portraits had been treated as icons and as witches' dolls; men had died for meddling with them in various ways, such as stabbing, burning, piercing with hog's bristles, embedding in poison. She herself had been afraid, but had not lost her head.[5]

After such a beginning, the reader begins to see Elizabeth icons under every rock and bush. There are plenty of them, and, as the line from Williams' biography suggests, they continue to happen.

The main plot centers around a Yorkshire family consisting of a self-referential control-freak of a father, Bill Potter; his nearly invisible wife, Winifred; his brilliant daughter Stephanie, who works very hard to make the worst of her Cambridge education and feels that she should aspire to be ordinary; a twitchy, edgy red-haired daughter, the ambitious Frederica, who wants desperately to be brilliant at something, and thus gives her all to everything; and Marcus, the sickly youngest child and only son.

Yes, that family does sound familiar, and not because their name is Potter. Bill is a schoolmaster at a minor boarding school, and the literature program is his personal kingdom. Stephanie has a religious crisis when she accidentally falls in love with a Roman (oops, not quite that literal) Anglican clergyman. After much yelling and with uncharacteristically spirited help from her mother, she marries him and becomes pregnant. Frederica is unexpectedly cast as the virginal young Elizabeth for the Seymour scene of Alexander's play, written to celebrate the coronation of Elizabeth II. Marcus mixes with all kinds of forces and goes quite mad – yes, a symbolic death.

There are three literal virgins in the garden of this novel: Frederica (from lack of opportunity to be otherwise), Alexander (from lack of conviction), and Marcus (from any number of lacks). There is much talk of the Festival of Britain and of the New Elizabethans – in which at least

Alexander and Frederica fervently believe, in the face of all odds, because they each want to become one of them.

Of all the continually happening Elizabeth icons in the novel, the most interesting appears when all the major characters gather before a television to watch the coronation of Elizabeth II. The narrator and some of the characters are dreadfully hard on the BBC commentator, but fascinated by his repetitions of the word "tiny" and its synonyms. The queen, young and slight, is dwarfed by the Abbey, by the male clergy, and by her own robes of state. In order to capture this entire spectacle on the small screen of an early box, the camera's image of the queen herself is tiny indeed.[6] The point is strongly made that the queen is tiny visually because the monarchy's significance – even to those dedicated viewers who have, respectively, written a play, learned a part, sewn costumes and made scenery – is actually of minute importance. Why, then, is there all the fuss?

We come close to an answer to the question as the narrator remarks on the media's simultaneous attempt to cover the historic Everest climb. Speaking of the *News Chronicle*'s attempt to do both, the narrator judges: "It was not quite prepared, although it flirted cloudily with the concept, to say that the Coronation and conquest of Everest indicated the coming of the new Imperium, Heaven on Earth, Golden Age, Cleopolis or any such conjunction of temporal imperfection and eternal satisfaction."[7] And, of course, the BBC compares the Second Elizabeth with the First, at considerable length.[8]

There were times when this novel reminded me of a Donne poem. It is ambitious without being substantially satisfying, but too intriguing to walk away from. Byatt fills it with the sorts of odd juxtapositions Donne references when he speaks of meeting at "the round earth's imagined corners." Although the plot resolves, after a fashion, nothing quite works out. At times mocking, at times despairing, the narrator tries to make sense out of an England and an idea of monarchy that no longer exists. Reading this novel, then looking at the ephemera generated by the coronation, left me with nothing so much as a sense of outrage, outrage that Elizabeth Tudor's singularity should be turned into a sequence by a young woman whose avowed monarch of choice was Queen Victoria. In fact, Elizabeth II did not welcome any of the allusions to a New Age of Elizabeth. She had often said that she disliked the first Elizabeth because she had executed her ancestor, Mary Stuart. For the amount of Stuart blood that flows through Elizabeth II's veins, she might as well take against Herod for slaughtering the Innocents.

And yet, during her 1953 Christmas Speech, broadcast to the country and the Commonwealth, she states:

Some people have expressed the hope that my reign may mark a new Elizabethan age. Frankly I do not myself feel at all like my great Tudor forbear, who was blessed neither with husband nor children, who ruled as a despot and was never able to leave her native shores.[9]

Rendered metaphorically speechless with fury at this ill-considered statement, I shall, of necessity, hold my fire until this study's closing lines.

Elizabeth in film: a celluloid canon

As this topic merits books in its own right, this chapter must be, therefore, either very long or very short. It will be very short. For excellent and virtually encyclopedic discussions of Queen Elizabeth on the screen, I refer the reader to "Romancing the Queen" in *The Shakespeare Trade*,[10] by Barbara Hodgdon, and (yet once more) to the work of Michael Dobson and Nicola J. Watson in *England's Elizabeth*. Having said that, I'm left to address the medium of film as perhaps the one venue where pointing out the iconic would be redundant. That, of course, is why there are so many films about Elizabeth, so many films made over such a relatively long period of time that the collective whole earns the designation "canon."

The film industry, it hardly needs be said, is in the business of making icons, having created yet another sort of entrance into the public sphere of memory. Not only are these icons visual, as we might expect, but arguably verbal as well. Phrases such as "Frankly, my dear, I don't give a damn," "Fasten your seatbelts; it's going to be a bumpy ride," and "Play it Sam" (the latter separating the true iconographer from the faux by the necessary omission of "again" in the same way one can tell an Anglican from a Roman by where one stops, or not, in the Lord's Prayer) have become verbal icons, triggering our responses almost as effectively as the visual. When a pillar of my community, in his early sixties, recently confessed to having just seen *Casablanca* for the first time, a village wit shot back: "which means that you must have missed roughly half the cocktail-party jokes of the last forty years." Her point is well taken. When we expand our definition of cultural literacy to include popular culture, film is an important category. Indeed, here is yet another example of an arena in which the distinction between high art and art of the people becomes difficult to make.

But can there be an icon of words? Earlier I argued that there could be, but that was before the visual electronic media existed, when the choice was between the printed page and the painted canvas. Films, television, the World Wide Web (the latter making the definition of "icon" redundant) have given us a visual language that needs no alphabet. Certainly words can be art, in reference to the discussion above, but isn't an icon inherently visual? Yes. And even as those tag lines are cultural currency, when we exchange them, it's not the words themselves we see in our minds' eyes. We see Clark Gable smirk or Bette Davis swing her hair back, or Bogart hunched over his own bar. That's why Donne's sermon, using such a visual story as the death of Sisera (for who can read/hear that narrative act without picturing it?) can be said to have constructed an Elizabeth icon. We think in pictures, so moving pictures are halfway to becoming icons when we first view them.

Hollywood – used here as metonymy for the Western film industry – has been more fascinated by Queen Elizabeth than by any historic figure. The list of women who have acted her part (as well as at least one man) is itself a history of leading ladies. The gilded and lengthy – even though incomplete – list of the famous names that have played Elizabeth on the large and small screen includes: Judith Anderson (*Elizabeth the Queen*, 1968), Helen Baxendale (*In Suspicious Circumstances*, 1996), Sarah Bernhardt (first in *Elisabeth, Reine d'Angleterre*, then in the 1922 *Loves of Queen Elizabeth*, the only of Bernhardt's films currently available on VCR), Cate Blanchett (*Elizabeth*, 1998), Ellen Compton (*Mary of Scotland*, 1936), Quentin Crisp (*Orlando*, 1992), Bette Davis (*The Private Lives of Elizabeth and Essex*, 1939; *The Virgin Queen*, 1955), Dame Judi Dench (*Shakespeare in Love*, 1999), Florence Eldridge (*Mary of Scotland*, 1936), Glenda Jackson (the BBC production *Elizabeth R*, 1971; *Mary Queen of Scots*, 1971), Miranda Richardson (the series *Blackadder*, 1986), Flora Robson (*Fire over England*, 1937; *The Sea Hawk*, 1940), Athene Seyler (*Drake of England*, 1935), Jean Simmons (*Young Bess*, 1953), Imogen Slaughter (Channel Four *Elizabeth*, 2000), Sarah Walker (the opera *Gloriana*, 1984), Irene Worth (*Seven Seas to Calais*, 1962).

Even when Elizabeth is not nominally the focus of a production, she is very much the axis around which the characters turn. Katharine Hepburn's virtually saintly rise to her execution in the 1936 *Mary of Scotland* is prefaced by a pairing with Elizabeth (with an inaccurate preface saying that they lie "side by side" in Westminster), is packaged, in VCR format, by prose that describes her first in relation to Elizabeth ("Loathed and feared by the less beautiful English Queen, Elizabeth [Florence Eldridge], Mary lived a tragic, but heroic life of political and social intrigue"[11]), and is dramatically punctuated by yet another of those secret visits. Florence Eldridge's queen, resolutely stocky and middle-aged from the first scene, bears a striking resemblance to Elizabeth's effigy on the tomb that James commissioned. With a ruff that connects her bosom to her chin and her ears to her shoulders, this Elizabeth appears to be a penguin in a bejeweled skirt, an obvious foil to the ethereal Hepburn's Mary. For all that John Ford directed this film, the secret confrontation (the night before Mary's execution, no less) sounds more like a nursery spat combined with a cat-fight than an exchange between monarchs.

> Mary: "… you're not even a woman."
> Elizabeth: "I'm a queen; you're a woman; see where it's brought you."
> [then]
> Elizabeth: "What do you know of my life?"
> Mary: "It's been a failure, a magnificent failure."
> [Elizabeth departs, with Mary shouting in reference to James as heir to the throne.]
> "I win!"

Mary would have been an intriguing figure for song, story, and film even without an heir. But with James to play as her trump-card, she can continue eternally, in the stones of the Abbey as well as the celluloid of the screen, the debate over whether a woman can have both a career and a family.

In the 1971 *Mary Queen of Scots*, besides not one but two secret visits and a narrative in which Elizabeth's Southern plotting gets almost as much screen time as Mary's Scottish histrionics. (Not that Vanessa Redgrave corners the market there, since Jackson gives a furiously inward-directed explosion of the apocryphal line "The Queen of Scotland is lighter of a fair son, while I am but barren stock!") The last scene on the film lingers over the lonely Elizabeth, surrounded by shadows, holding the dead Mary's rosary and prayer book. While Redgrave's voice echoes the French lament which opens the first gorgeous scenes of the film, the prose rolls down the screen, making pretty much the same point that Hepburn's Mary makes: Mary will ultimately "win," because Mary's son – here, it is implied, both because Elizabeth feels guilty and because there are no other claimants (not true) – will sit on the throne of England.

The frequent frame of contrast between the childless Elizabeth and the heir-producing Mary is an important element of many Elizabeth films, yet not because of politics. Historically, of course, the two women, both queens regnant, provide perhaps the earliest set of examples in the argument about women in the workforce. And, as we can see from the clothing of the two queens, Mary is always subliminally more fluid, more pliant, more naturally attired, while Elizabeth is encased in the virtual armor of her profession. And yet, how many children did Mary have? We are not discussing Queen Victoria. But one child, especially one son, seems to be the line of demarcation beyond which Mary has to do nothing to prove her femininity, while Elizabeth – for all her jewels and ruffs and elaborate frocks – is seen to be trying too hard to make a point already lost.

c.1998: Cate as *Elizabeth* first, icon last

Cate Blanchett is, for 99.44% of the 1998 film by Shekhar Kapur,[12] most emphatically *not* Elizabeth. Or rather, she is a woman named Elizabeth who comes to the throne of England in 1558. She is not the Elizabeth icon. Even playing a royal woman in her mid-twenties – mature for 1558 – Cate[13] slouches and crouches, slumps, jumps, glides, strides, hops, flops, and generally moves and looks like a real and vital and strikingly modern woman. Even when her streams of hair are put up in more formal styles, Cate's gait and mien convey more the informal realism we see when she practices her first speech to the bishops than the decorum stereotypically associated with any adult monarch. Surrounded by courtiers and ladies-in-waiting who strike traditional poses in conventional postures, Cate's flexible, whimsical, sometimes awkward movements are all the more striking and make her the icon of nothing – nothing except a desirable young woman. And this, I would suggest, is the most successful contribution that the film makes to the canon of Elizabeth screenings.

The most frequently used publicity poster (also the VCR and DVD cover) for the film shows Cate against a hot red background, red-gold hair flowing over a glowing golden dress, looking as though she had just flung herself into a regal armchair and were about to announce – not "I have the weak and feeble body of a woman," but – "don't mess with me." Unlike the island-straddling farthingales and lethal ruffs encasing Bette Davis or the BBC's rigid gowns worn by Glenda Jackson (each painstakingly referential to a portrait dress), Cate's clothes flow and droop and glitter. Even when, like her hair, they are tidied up, they still have a style and flair that reminds us of the impact that Elizabeth's real dresses – now clichés (those that were not actual fictions[14]) – must have had on those around her.

Yes, the film does have iconic moments, for all its famed historical inaccuracies.[15] Elizabeth learns of her sister's death under an oak tree, if not actually an oak on the grounds of Hatfield House; the coronation – for all that it's in York Minster rather than Westminster Abbey – provides us with the flesh-and-blood version of the lost coronation portrait. (And, considering the marble junk-yard that the nineteenth century made of the nave and crossing of the Abbey, this was a brilliant location choice, for all that they do cheat with the crossing windows.[16]) And then there is the ending.

But before we see Cate become the Elizabeth icon, we get a very post-modern use of both historical space and historical narrative. Most of the interior scenes were shot in various parts of Durham Cathedral. The ahistorical presence of the massive Norman pillars and arches dwarfs the characters and prevents even the most imaginative viewer from investing the scenes with high Gothic, let alone Renaissance, gilt and detail. This gives us the occasional, but not comfortably sustainable, sense that we are watching a stage play with an impressionist set designer. The lighting, pronounced "too dark" by hosts of movie-goers, gives us both the obvious metaphor of dark doings in dark days and an evocation of the limits of candlelight. More practically, it fills those large spaces with chiaroscuro and a sense that anything might come next, anything, that is, but a summer-stock courtier speaking faux Shakespeare. This sensory deprivation forces us to concentrate on the dialogue and the situations at hand, seeing the characters and hearing the words as they are presented in that theatrical moment, not as we were ready to see or hear them when we walked in to our seats. As for the sequence of events, Kapur picks and chooses episodes – real, adapted, and fictive – from the traditional Elizabeth narratives and condenses nearly 40 years of her reign into a fast first five. Even before that reign begins he cuts, sparing us both the distraction of the Seymour episode and the traditionally rain-drenched scene at the gates of the Tower. Robert Dudley's first wife – living or murdered – never appears, although his future second (and supposedly secret) bride is briefly and cleverly and, yes, ahistorically introduced. On the other hand, there's no Raleigh, let alone a cloak over a puddle. The Armada is never hinted at, for all the fast-forwarding of events such as the French marriage negotiations, while the problem of Mary Stuart becomes the drama of her "warrior queen" mother. The film simply won't let us turn it into a late-twentieth-century Elizabeth icon.

But why should it? Do the people who fill the seats of the gratifyingly large theaters in which this film was screened care about the difference between the Babington Plot and the Ridolfi Plot and between either and the plot presented in the film? about the subtle distinction between a Pope (even one played by John Gielgud) excommunicating a monarch and directly ordering Roman Catholics to kill her? Certainly I did not care at the time, for all that my companion kept hissing in my ear "did this really happen?" What Kapur does is to sacrifice historical veracity for cultural and political verity. The people of Elizabeth's England were as unprepared for an unmarried female monarch as contemporary audiences are for a screen Elizabeth who looks nothing like Bette Davis or Dame Judi Dench in *Shakespeare in Love*. The necessary sense of otherness comes forcefully across exactly because our expectations are violated rather than met. The essence of what the historical Elizabeth accomplishes – changing herself from a woman, expected to marry and produce an heir, into an icon of monarchy, both bride and mother to her nation – is captured in Kapur's film; it's just condensed into five years instead of being paced out over 45.

Two fictive scenes in the film give us a clear sense of history's need to be transformed so as to disengage us from a public sphere of memory so layered with Elizabeths that the icon has all but lost its power. The first example is Cecil ordering that he be shown the queen's sheets every day. Sir Richard Attenborough's William Cecil is old, orotund, and relentlessly patriarchal. The actual Cecil was much younger and was Elizabeth's cherished advisor until the day of his death in 1598. By making the Cecil he gives us, Kapur personifies the patriarchal view of the queen as natural by placing it in the person of so famously loyal a courtier. But it is still a world-view with which both Elizabeths must break. As the audience recoils from the idea of his bed-checks, Cate's Elizabeth coldly dismisses Cecil, making even his elevation to the title Lord Burghley seem an insult. Turning Cecil into a metaphor for the old courts of Europe, the passing age of debates over whether or not women possessed souls let alone minds, allows the film's Elizabeth to show, in one tidy stroke, a bit of the forward-looking and forcefully adroit policy-making for which the real queen was famed. Nor does Kapur quite make the mistake of slotting Francis Walsingham (always and correctly referred to as "a shadowy figure" in popular histories) into a substitute for a father substitute. By making him sexually ambiguous, coldly murderous, and almost supernaturally clever, Kapur prevents Walsingham (Geoffrey Rush) from filling any emotional void in the film or the hearts of the audience. He is a shrewd politician who teaches as much by example as by exposition, but his screen persona is set clearly in the bounds of the political, not the personal, allowing Cate's Elizabeth to learn from him without becoming a surrogate daughter. He helps her empower herself, but leaves her, in almost every way, quite alone.

The scene between Cate's Elizabeth and Walsingham at the foot of a statue of the Virgin Mary is both the film's most unlikely moment and its most logical. Something must be offered to the audience to make

Elizabeth's transformation, still a work in progress even in the early 1590s, seem believable in 1563. For all its political and theological absurdity, the scene has tremendous power and conveys in mere seconds the assessment, decision, struggle, and commitment that it took Elizabeth Tudor a life-time to achieve. Cate's Elizabeth looks at the statue as an icon of power, not as the Mother of God. She speaks of the power that Mary "had" over men's hearts. Walsingham murmurs his only disingenuous line in the film when he states the obvious: "they have found nothing to replace her." We see the realization of the power of virginity take Cate's Elizabeth as a concept, not a conversion. And just as coldly as the second-millennium theologians set out to craft the cult of Mary and the doctrine of that virgin's own immaculate conception, Cate's Elizabeth conceives the political strategy of virgin queenship. Clasping shards of her hair in her lap, she sets out to "become" a virgin. That the film's sex scenes make it crystal clear for the audience that social construction is the only way to go on this epithet simply highlights, rather than negates, the deliberation with which the real Elizabeth charted her course to stay married to her kingdom.

And then we get the icon (Figure 21), lead-painted, bewigged, clad in a version of the Ditchley portrait dress. In the last long and nearly silent moments of the film, we see with fresh eyes the stock image appearing in our minds' eyes when we heard there was to be a new film on Queen Elizabeth. But Cate and Kapur have spent 120 minutes pushing that image to the side, so that we now may see it, finally, as a newly, painfully, and deliberately minted identity, the image that will become the icon of Elizabeth I.

Not surprisingly, the film garnered strongly worded reviews, saying, as reviews so often do, more about the critics themselves than about the film. Leaving this reader somewhat befuddled, Peter Travers of *Rolling Stone* speaks of its "annoying" self-absorption with "campy, post-feminist cleverness," even as he calls it "revisionist history" (as a seeming compliment) and abjures the reader to think of Elizabeth, like Princess Diana, as "a girl forced into womanhood by the duties of royalty."[17] Also alluding to feminist rhetoric, in a review sub-titled "Amour and High Dudgeon in a Castle of One's Own," Janet Maslin shows a lack of famil-iarity with Elizabeth Tudor's more famous lines when she announces that Cate Blanchett "sounds an awful lot like Tootsie when she declares: 'I may be a woman, Sir William. But if I choose, I have the heart of a man!'" Writing in the *New York Times*, Maslin finds that the film "is indeed historical drama for anyone whose idea of history is back issues of *Vogue*." Providing ironic evidence that we all lay claim to Elizabeth's history

Figure 21   "I have become a virgin" – Cate Blanchett as Elizabeth, from *Elizabeth*
(d. Kapur, 1998) © The Roland Grant Picture Archive

because her icon exists vividly in our collective memory, Maslin slams the film's use of history even as she fails to recognize the words decontextualized from Elizabeth's speech at Tilbury. Roger Ebert's succinct contribution to the debate crowns a positive review: "It didn't happen like that in history, but it should have." Blanchett herself, quoted in a CNN review of the film, parallels late twentieth-century culture with Elizabeth's:

> "When we were in England last week, people were making parallels between Elizabeth's situation with Elizabethan paparazzi, I guess, and Diana," Blanchett says. "And now we're in the States, where people are talking about Clinton, how his personal life is up for grabs rather than his political platforms, which is kind of I guess a similar situation that Elizabeth found herself in."[18]

Weighing in from the British side of the pond with another sort of political immediacy, Matt Ford, writing for the BBC, declares it an "intelligent period drama [that] skillfully avoids the swamp of nostalgic fantasy," but he spends nearly as much time bashing Bloody Mary as examining this representation of Elizabeth. In that sense, the drama of the film continues in real time. Insofar as the reviews of Cate's Elizabeth were critical, their bite could be measured in direct correlation to the reviewers' expectation of yet another manifestation of the icon. Looking forward to my next chapter, it seems that the waning of the power of that icon might be no bad or sad thing.

The selling of Gloriana in the agora and the arcade

The Industrial Revolution was not a felicitous development for the dignity of the first Elizabeth. Mass production of an image can be a tasteful process, if done with quality as the controlling principle. When quantity becomes the issue, however, both the image and that for which it stands generally suffer. So it is with the Elizabeth icon. There's nothing essentially Luddite about the reproduction of the queen's image. In her own time portraits were copied by making pin-holes along key lines – jaw, eye socket, hairline, piercing both the original and a blank canvas beneath it. Then the blank canvas could serve as a pattern, with chalk being rubbed over it so as to make another outline, this time in dots, on yet another blank canvas beneath the pattern. Want another image? Flip the pattern-canvas on a vertical axis. Thus does the face of the Siena Sieve portrait differ from the face of the Darnley portrait.

But that sort of reproduction is not what we mean when we now say "mass-produced." No. Now counted in hundreds-per-minute, images of the queen who saved England from Spain and the clutches of Rome can appear on tea towels and playing cards, and tea cards (to be collected with each new box of tea, the goal being a complete set); images of the queen with the face of a cat adorn the lids of sweets tins in the gift shop of the National Portrait Gallery. There are Elizabeth rulers, pencils, fans, paper dolls, collectable dolls, even – I grieve to say it – Barbie dolls. Eight-sided teapots offer scenes from the queen's life. There are miniature action figures called Gloriana. And, as if there were not enough items handy on which to affix the royal image, there are also inventions. Harmony Ball Pot Belly are small figurines made of resin, "detailed and whimsical representations" of animals, people, and thematic objects. "These delightful box figurines portray the round and humorous side of life," says company president and co-founder Noel Wiggins. "Each is named in homage to celebrities known for living larger than life, both in character and in stature." The dimensions for each of these pieces is 1¼" × 1¼" all around. Used to store small treasures in a decorative fashion (Figures 22 and 23),[19] the main function is decorative, since the actual storage space is very small. In addition to Elizabeth and many, many little animals, the following figures are also available: Winston Churchill, Abraham Lincoln, Henry VIII, Chairman Mao Tse-Tung, William Shakespeare, Franklin Delano Roosevelt, Mikhail Gorbachev, the Queen of Sheba, Queen Victoria, George Washington, Napoleon Bonaparte, King Louis XIV, Ulysses S. Grant, Dr. Martin Luther King, Jr., Queen Catherine the Great, Empress Woo, Thomas Jefferson, John F. Kennedy, Ronald Reagan, General Robert E. Lee, Queen Nefertiti, and (naturally) Marie-Antoinette.

And then there is the Celebriduck. Yes, Elizabeth I is manifest as a rubber bath duck (Figure 24). In a happy exchange of e-mails with Craig Wolfe, of Celebriducks, I learned that the Elizabeth duck was one of the second set their company made (the first were Groucho and Betty Boop). Paired with the Shakespeare duck, Elizabeth came out the same year as *Shakespeare in Love* in a run of 5000 that sold out quickly. There's now a new Elizabeth model, "smaller, softer, squeak and float great ... also new packaging ... a real upgrade," according to Mr. Wolfe. They have also "ducked" Chaplin, Babe Ruth, Santa Claus, and Mae West. Saying that his daughter and wife, who design the ducks, are always pushing for more female ducks, Wolfe promises his customers the dream of equal opportunity. After branching out into sports figures, Wolfe's sales rose to "around a half million ducks sold this year [2002]" and still rising. When the Elizabeth duck was new, Wolfe writes, "we even sent one to the

Figure 22 Queen Elizabeth with head; Harmony Ball Historical Pot Belly, © Harmony Ball Inc., 2003

Figure 23 Queen Elizabeth without head; Harmony Ball Historical Pot Belly, © Harmony Ball Inc., 2003

current Queen Elizabeth, and it made it to Buckingham Palace as we knew the Queen actually had rubber ducks; but her assistant sent it back with a letter since the Queen didn't know us personally."

Although my tone may have been snide when I described the Eliza-cats and the teapot, there's something so genuinely unpretentious about the duck that I confess, I love it entirely. And just *try* to forget it. Try.

Figure 24   Queen Elizabeth Celebriduck, *c.*1999. Reproduced with the kind permission of Craig Wolfe, president of Celebriducks Inc.

*c.*2003: the Celebriduck and the eBay scholar

It's a cliché that the world is a smaller place since the invention/invasion of the World Wide Web. But clichés, we must remember, become clichés through the process of being produced as heartfelt iterations and reiterations. They are stored in the public sphere of memory because we all have recognized and continue to recognize the situations that generate them.

Never have I been so forcefully struck by the "smaller place" cliché than one Spring Break morning in 2001, sitting in a cyber café in the oldest section of Bologna. I opened my e-mail to find a message from a class of Australian secondary school students. The student who had tapped out the message sent fairly conventional greetings, told me that their class had chosen to study Elizabeth I as their senior history project, and that each group within the class was to study the life and work of a famous historian of the queen. "And we," she cheerfully informed me, "are studying you!"

Yes, I did think it was a joke. In fact, I literally fell off my only-slightly-post-Renaissance rickety chair. But since several days of e-mails had piled up, I was able to read through a series of follow-up messages, and the young woman seemed to be sincere. I dashed off a couple of lines of "so flattered" and "in Italy until" and then wrote for the first time what was to become the refrain of this lengthy exchange: "But I'm not an historian."

Out then, into the high arcades and blooming fruit trees of Bologna, to find my dear house party pals and lay myself open to their gleefully unrestrained derision.

How had this happened to me?

The World Wide Web.

The sequence must have gone something like this: teacher makes class assignment; Commonwealth students chose that very English subject, Elizabeth I, she who was famously "nice to mice"; students divide into groups and adjourn to their computer screens where various library databases or Amazon.com will help them generate a bibliography; helpful Boolean searches allow them to arrive at a list of histories of Elizabeth with living authors; Duke University Press' decision to market *Dissing Elizabeth* on their history list rises up to haunt me and to confuse antipodean teenagers; they like the title; click.

The mouse stopped here.

Yes, this is absurd. But a glance at the listing of figures within this book will show the web has great and serious resources for scholars. I can now sit in my red chair in my little study in my tiny village and buy toffee tins from Australia and engravings from dealers in Vancouver. Had I been able to find a print of the tombs of Elizabeth and Mary Stuart side by side for sale on eBay, I am sure that it would have cost less than the permission fee I paid to reproduce the image kindly (and very promptly) provided by the Bridgeman Art Library. Without breaking it down, I will say that it took over $800 for the permissions to reproduce images for this book. I spent less than $150 on the items that I purchased, mostly on eBay. Nor is this a statement only about money. The question of access is an enormous one. Yes, the world is smaller, but for scholars working far from rare book libraries or constrained by obligations from traveling abroad, simply learning of the existence of such a wonderful thing as the *Punch* cartoon of Elizabeth reading to Shakespeare (or the dear Celebriduck) is both a pleasure and a great help. Even the transactions for the images I had to pay fees for were (with one exception) done on-line.

We will never, of course, or at least never in my lifetime, replace the riches of archival work with a click of the thumb-pad. But this is changing the face of scholarship.

The Internet is also changing the space of public memory. With this unfathomable cyberspace available to us for learning and communicating about new ideas, we are given more to store than most of us think we need. But never fear; we can save it on the hard drive. The decision to download and save is generally a minor one, unless a high-definition image is tying up a phone line. But that decision, however quickly taken, gives us a usefully specific example of the generally unconscious decision to remember something.

Much of this book has been about the memory of Queen Elizabeth Tudor. How she was remembered, to what ends those memories were used or reshaped, recalled or suppressed, is linked to the history of the last 400 years. Elizabeth herself is simply an example. She is a fascinating and complex example of an icon stored in memory, but that complexity is what has given her such a long afterlife. We can decide to recall and we can decide to remember, of course. But more often than not, we are unaware of making those decisions or at least unaware of what prompts us to make those decisions. Our leaders are more than willing to prompt or delete memories for us. Even as I write this, I can watch Bush and Blair try to account for those "weapons of mass destruction" that were threatening us so gravely a mere four months ago. Did not Operation Shock and Awe knock those awkward questions from our heads? Can we not remember the last time the United States sent uninvited troops to a country that did not ask for our help or our way of life? Does the constant stream of new ideas and information obviate that which we were hearing yesterday? The public sphere is both larger and increasingly crowded. As we are urged to live from news-cycle to news-cycle today, let us not neglect the public space we both share and possess alone: memory. For perhaps as much as do our words and deeds, our memories define us.

Conclusion:
The Shadow of an Icon –
the BBC's Most-admired Britons

In 2001, the BBC solicited nominations for the Top Ten Great Britons. Certainly the World Wide Web gives us an example par excellence of a new sphere of public space in which memories can be both recalled and constructed, and this grand, or even great-grandchild of the various Millennium lists gives us a fascinating view into the making of public icons. The BBC list allows for an interestingly nationalistic elision of the public sphere and memory, of high and low culture, of traditional and popular history. According the BBC website,[1] 30,000 people each named a Greatest Briton: "the definition of a 'Great Briton' for the purposes of the nominations was [being] anyone who was born in the British Isles, including Ireland; or anyone who lived in the British Isles, including Ireland, and who has played a significant part in the life of the British Isles." (One wonders if the BBC consulted the Irish on this, or if a desire to claim Bono ruled the day.) Over 1.5 million votes were cast in the final countdown following a series of one-hour presentations on the top 10 in the fall of 2002. The BBC Top Ten is accompanied by an ordered list of 90 also-rans, and the whole site makes fascinating reading. The most popularly remembered Brits are:

1	Churchill	456,498 (28.1%)
2	Brunel	398,526 (24.6%)
3	Diana	225,584 (13.9%)
4	Darwin	112,496 (6.9%)
5	Shakespeare	109,919 (6.8%)
6	Newton	84,628 (5.2%)
7	Elizabeth I	71,928 (4.4%)

8	Lennon	68,445 (4.2%)
9	Nelson	49,171 (3%)
10	Cromwell	45,053 (2.8%)

Surely no one would be surprised to find Winston Churchill at number 1, although the mere 28.1% of the vote he garnered should take WWII vets/survivors and history buffs aback.

For non-Britons, the second choice is a distinct shock; it might have prompted a stampede for the encyclopedia had not the site provided a thorough and illustrated link to the life and times of the man most responsible for the British railway system. In the US, this spot might be filled by Henry Ford, but that would be the choice of a new country, one that went almost directly from one form of individual travel – the horse – to another. While the limited rail system in the US and Canada certainly changed significant elements of the economy, it never did and never will have the hold that the village-encompassing rail system had and has on the British imagination. The geographic isolation of North America from the culture of Western Europe and ancient land-routes east and south is also an obvious factor in this disassociation. A person may leave tiny Ravenglass on the north-west coast of Cumbria, travel to London, to Victoria, "the mother of all journeys," then take the traditional route east across continents via the Orient Express; or one may go to Waterloo – so historically appropriate – and triumphantly arrive in Paris in less than 180 minutes. Isolated by the Atlantic and Pacific, the psychological connection provided by rail travel, the everyday nature of the village station, is lost on the inhabitants of the Americas.

The somewhat deliberately florid prose of the last paragraph can be read as a memorial wreath to those who crash and burn during flights of e-research. It might even be true, at least in part. What needs also to be said, however, is that scores of students from Brunel University – a collection of technical schools at the end of London's Piccadilly Line – logged on multiple votes to ensure their founder's immortality.[2] Similarly, we must ponder the place of Ernest Shackleton at number 11. Would he be so very "Great" had not Kenneth Branagh's frozen face appeared on UK television screens in January of 2002? The most expensive production ever undertaken by Channel 4,[3] this two-night drama aired after the voting was over, but the publicity blitz started in the last two months of 2001, just as the list was being generated.

The professional demographics of the top 100 are both fascinating and a bit shattering. The headings below are my own, with some Britons falling under two or more headings – Sir Thomas More, for example, is under politics, writers, and religion. Some decisions are arguably editorial, but if I put Cromwell under politics, religion, and war heroes, surely Emmeline Pankhurst belongs under two of those headings as well. Those with multiple listings are noted by asterisks. The exception to this is "women," all of whom are listed more than once. For other Britons it was hard to find a category; Lord Robert Baden-Powell, founder of the Boy Scouts, falls into this lacunae. I am unspeakably grateful for the heroic efforts of De'Von Re'Shad McRavion, my son and a future historian, whose screen-time in tracking down the accomplishments of Great Britons unknown to American college professors was considerable.

women		science/technology/medicine	
3	Diana, Princess of Wales	2	IK Brunel
7	Elizabeth I	4	Charles Darwin**
16	Margaret Thatcher	6	Isaac Newton
18	Queen Victoria	20	Sir Alexander Fleming
24	Queen Elizabeth II	21	Alan Turing OBE
27	Emmeline Pankhurst	22	Michael Faraday
35	Boudicca	25	Professor Stephen Hawking
52	Florence Nightingale	39	John Harrison
59	Dame Julie Andrews	42	Sir Frank Whittle
61	Queen Elizabeth, the QM	44	John Logie Baird
70	Jane Austen	52	Florence Nightingale
83	JK Rowling OBE	57	Sir Alexander Graham Bell
100	Marie Stopes	65	George Stephenson
		68	William Caxton
		78	Edward Jenner
		80	Charles Babbage
		84	James Watt
		91	James Clerk Maxwell
		95	Sir Barnes Neville Wallis
		99	Professor Tim Berners-Lee
		100	Marie Stopes

sports		art	
33	David Beckham		
36	Sir Steve Redgrave		
69	Bobby Moore		

politics		stage and screen	
1	Winston Churchill**	17	Michael Crawford
10	Oliver Cromwell**	32	Eric Morecambe

16   Margaret Thatcher
27   Emmeline Pankhurst**
28   William Wilberforce
30   Guy Fawkes
34   Thomas Paine
37   Sir Thomas More***
45   Aneurin Bevan
55   Enoch Powell
64   James Connolly
67   Tony Blair
79   David Lloyd George
97   Tony Benn

66   Sir Charles (Charlie) Chaplin
96   Richard Burton

literature

5   William Shakespeare
26   William Tyndale**
37   Sir Thomas More***
38   William Blake
41   Charles Dickens
70   Jane Austen
81   Geoffrey Chaucer
83   JK Rowling OBE
92   JRR Tolkien

music

8   John Lennon
19   Sir Paul McCartney
29   David Bowie
46   Boy George
56   Sir Cliff Richard
58   Freddie Mercury
59   Dame Julie Andrews
60   Edward Elgar
62   George Harrison
75   Bob Geldof KBE
77   Robbie Williams
86   Bono
87   John Lydon (Johnny Rotten)

monarchs/royals

3   Diana, Princess of Wales
7   Queen Elizabeth I
14   King Alfred the Great
18   Queen Victoria
23   Owain Glyndwr
24   Queen Elizabeth II
35   Boudicca
40   King Henry VIII
51   King Arthur
61   Queen Elizabeth, the QM
72   King Henry V
74   King Robert the Bruce

war heroes

1   Winston Churchill**
9   Lord Nelson
10   Oliver Cromwell**
15   Duke of Wellington
27   Emmeline Pankhurst**
31   Leonard Cheshire
47   Sir Douglas Bader
48   William Wallace
53   TE Lawrence
76   The Unknown Warrior
88   Field Marshal Montgomery

82   King Richard III
90   King Henry II
94   King Edward I

explorers
  4   Charles Darwin**
11   Ernest Shackleton
12   Captain James Cook
49   Sir Francis Drake
54   Captain Robert Falcon Scott
93   Sir Walter Raleigh
98   David Livingstone

business/media/other
13   Lord Baden-Powell
43   John Peel
63   Sir David Attenborough
71   William Booth
73   Aleister Crowley
85   Sir Richard Branson
89   Donald Campbell

religion
26   William Tyndale**
37   Sir Thomas More***
50   John Wesley

After this breakdown, one positively welcomes the snarky insights of media experts on this media-generated survey of the public sphere of memory.

22 August 2002

MediaGuardian
While the BBC is being coy about the order in which the 100 appear, preferring to keep the revelation for a BBC2 programme in the autumn, it is understood that Churchill topped the poll, followed by Shakespeare and Nelson.[4]

BBC News
The series begins in the autumn by revealing the British public's top 100 nominations and the top 10 will then feature in a series of one-hour programmes.

Viewers will be asked to choose a single winner after seeing the shows fronted by people such as Jeremy Clarkson, former editor of *The Independent* and *The Daily Express* newspapers Rosie Boycott and the BBC's political editor Andrew Marr.[5]

But veteran radio DJ John Peel, who features on the list, disagrees. "If this list is genuine and not an elaborate Mickey-take, there is something very strange going on in our lovely country," he told BBC News.[6] BBC 2 controller Jane Root said: "This series will arouse enthusiastic debate in offices and homes all around the country." And executive producer Tom Archer said: "It will be a real insight into what people think this country means and what they think greatness is. It is much more varied and interesting than just an A-list of celebrities and goes against the idea that Britain is dumbing down." Helen Haste, an expert on cultural icons who is based at Bath University, agrees the absence of celebrities proves Britain is not as superficial or transient as many believe.[7]

On the other hand, not having a monarchy has hardly stopped generations of US citizens from actively engaging in the romance of the royal. That Diana, Princess of Wales, is number 3 on the list probably shocks no one. Even as we must lament that the current population of Great Britain places her personality, activities, and antics above the work of Jane Austen, Florence Nightingale and Emmeline Pankhurst, to say nothing of Newton, Chaucer, Caxton, Francis Drake, Thomas More and Bobby Moore, Stephen Hawking and Bono, we must nevertheless acknowledge that this pop culture icon fills the space of public memory more clearly and more universally than those figures cluttered by more tangible accomplishments. Diana, of course, is pop royalty, with her famously televised wish to be "queen of hearts." Crowned monarchs and their consorts have fared far less well with the Great British Public, with only one in the top 10 and only four others in the top 33%. Again, the imagination of the non-Briton might have worked to fill that space with more crowns than not. Overall, the Plantagenets, with both Lancastrian and York roses, are the best-represented dynasty – also, of course, the most numerous – with Edward "Longshanks" I (94), Henry II (90), Henry V (72), and Richard III (82) representing this longest unbroken line (and greatest collection of recent box-office successes). Three pre-Norman monarchs also make the top 100 – Queen Boudicca (35) and Kings Arthur (51) and Alfred the Great (14). Scotland is represented by Robert the Bruce (74), now in the cinematic shadow of William Wallace (48).[8] No Stuarts or Hanovers are in evidence (except in the genes of number 18, Queen Victoria), and the House of Windsor is represented by the current Queen Elizabeth, in 24th place, and her mother, Queen Elizabeth, the Queen Mother, at 61st, the latter the only consort on the list, proving, perhaps, that secondary husbands have yet to find a place in the public sphere of popular memory. On par with the size of the House of Windsor (even though it lasted only three generations) is the Tudor dynasty, also represented by two names, both ruling monarchs: Henry VIII in 40th place, and Elizabeth I at number 7.

This brings me back to the Elizabeths of A. S. Byatt's *The Virgin in the Garden*. No neat icons there, but a fist-full of shattered illusions, flung across a field as barren and poisoned and bizarrely powerful as the ground across which Marcus must walk on his way home from school. But the problem is not with the image of the first Elizabeth. It's the tiny figure on the box that generates the dissonance. The mirror opposite of the monstrously large Ditchley portrait, at which Alexander is forced to gaze, the tiny Elizabeth does not fit into the world of her people any more than does the exaggerated figure in white, with little ships sailing under her skirts. It's the Elizabeth of the Darnley portrait who is real. A life-sized woman in a realistic dress, Elizabeth actually sat for this painting. She fits into the frame in a way that her figure refuses to do in most of the other portraits. Complicated by allegory or geography or military history, other images of the queen seem larger than the canvas on which they are painted, always in danger of falling out of or escaping from the frames.

But the image of Elizabeth II stays tiny. Small, stiff, tidy, and very diligent, she rewards her subjects with a fixed smile and a stiff wave of her hand. For all that she has traveled widely, both within her realm and the greater world, she is less a fellow-creature to her subjects than was the original Elizabeth. Even on the eve of war, even in a speech so important to constructing her gender and her title, Elizabeth takes time at Tilbury to assure all the men that she guarantees their pay. The present Elizabeth is so isolated that she was genuinely (I hope) shocked when the nation expressed outrage that she (at the time, the richest woman in Britain) thought they should bear the cost of repairs after the fire at Windsor Castle. The Queen Mother had a place in the public sphere of memory, but that place is ineluctably linked to one of England's greatest trials: the Blitz. Picking her way through rubble, the ever-beaming queen offered comfort, good cheer, genuinely expressed sympathy, and that oldest of royal myths: the magic touch. The magic, of course, comes from the person who receives the touch, not from the monarch. In the bathos that was the time of national mourning for Diana, Princess of Wales, one genuine sentiment filtered out through the media blitz. A child had written on a card attached to some flowers: "You touched my face when I was a baby."

And that story would have been that child's defining memory, even if she or he was too young actually to recall it. The memory of being told about the Princess' touch would, itself, become a memory, and the power of that touch resides in the care with which the moment is preserved by the individual. When that was made public, it touched more people – or, at any rate, more cynical American academics – than any other aspect of the orgy of grief. As flawed (or as simply real) as she may have been, Diana had the royal touch. The people gave it to her.

We have only to look back at the Venetian Ambassador's report about James' lack of popularity to realize how much Elizabeth Tudor's people missed that touch. Old, geographically confined, and hedged about by courtiers, she could still touch the common people. The tiny queen on the box, she of whom Byatt writes does not have that power. Her ranking of 24th is part hype for the millennium and the Golden Jubilee, and part sheer politeness. The inclusion of Diana in the top 10 highlights both the iconic (or extra-historical, if you will) status of the two women on this, or, indeed, any such list. Indeed, the BBC webpage offering the Top Ten Great Britons as a screensaver[9] features two pictures: Diana, barely in black, immediately juxtaposed with Elizabeth, covered with puffs and pearls from the Armada portrait. The two images – the two icons – are thus the selling points for the whole project.

That these two women stand for greatness in the minds of the third millennium British public says more than any prose could about the nature of icons. Icons exist in the imagination, and the imagination – even when public – is selective. The most conventional use of the word icon, before computers, was in the context of religion. Saints and biblical figures are identified iconically: St. Michael is the dragon-slayer with wings; St. George kills his dragon without benefit of wings, but often on horseback. The list goes on, and is often multivalent. David with a harp is making a different statement than is David with a rock and sling. St. Peter with a rock emphasizes his role as the rock upon which Christ planned to build the Church, but St. Peter with keys abandons the earthly reference and makes him the gatekeeper of heaven. St. Catherine of Alexandria is usually depicted with both her books, the icon that makes her the patron of scholars, and the instrument of her torture, her wheel. The reader of the icon is thus free to concentrate on her learned life or her gruesome death, both experienced for her faith.

Unlike the relatively pristine public canvas of Diana, Princess of Wales, Elizabeth's multitude of accomplishments, from her learning to her political acumen, has allowed popularizers a myriad of choices for packaging her icon. The flip side is that, just as everyone has his or her own Diana, everyone has her or his own Elizabeth icon.

In Plato's *Republic*, Socrates tries to explain to Glacon and the guys the cognition of the fourth level of the divided line, the level of intellection. On that level, to demean Plato's thinking, there exists an idea of Elizabeth that encompasses all possible manifestations of her, apprehended or as yet unapprehended. The only way to end this book is with a gesture toward the Elizabeth of the intellect, for whatever fragments of her we store as icons in our memory – private then public now closely guarded again – is there, somewhere in that at once multivalent and abstract idea. The idea of Elizabeth has been shared for 400 years. What idea, what image of our own time will fill a similar space? By existing and surviving she made possible countless arguments about the equality of men and women, for all that she made none herself. By existing she gives English-speaking peoples a visual fix on the Renaissance that is unparalleled. By existing in the newly public space of her own time's visual memory, she offers a texture, an accent to statements made in later years, seeming to have nothing to do with England or its Renaissance. By existing, she proves Faulkner's problematic declaration that

"memory believes before knowing remembers."

Notes

Introduction

1. *The Book of Common Prayer 1599: The Elizabethan Prayer Book*, edited by John E. Booty (Washington, D.C.: Folger Shakespeare Library, 1982) 310.

1603–1620: The Shadow of the Rainbow

1. Jürgen Habermas, *The Structural Transformation of the Public Sphere: An Inquire into a Category of Bourgeois Society*, translated by Thomas Burger with the assistance of Frederick Lawrence (Cambridge: MIT Press, 2000) 14.
2. E. M. W. Tillyard, *The Elizabethan World Picture: A Study of the Idea of Order in the Age of Shakespeare, Donne, and Milton* (New York: Random House, 1959). More striking than the definite article in the title of this once-required study is its length: 114 pages.
3. Habermas, 15.
4. *Westminster Abbey Official Guide* (London: 1988) 69.
5. Edward Carpenter, *A House of Kings: The Official History of Westminster Abbey* (New York: 1966) 142.
6. Arthur P. Stanley, Dean of Westminster, *Historical Monuments of Westminster Abbey* (London: 1876) 163.
7. WAM 41095. I am greatly in the debt of Miss Christine Reynolds, librarian of the Westminster Abbey Muniments Room, for her kindness during my visits between 1990 and 1993. Without her help I would not have found this valuable piece of evidence. A more detailed version of my argument appears as "Reading the Tombs of Elizabeth I," in *ELR: English Literary Renaissance* 26 (1996) 510–530.
8. Nigel Llewellyn, "The Royal Body: Monuments to the Dead, for the Living," in *Renaissance Bodies*, edited by Lucy Gent and Nigel Llewellyn (London: 1990) 218–240.
9. Thomas Millington, *The True Narration of the Entertainment of his Majesty from his Departure from Edinburgh till his Receiving at London* in *Stuart Tracts 1603–1693*, edited by C. H. Frith (New York: 1964) 15.
10. I did not come across Lewellen's essay until 1995.
11. H. M. Colvin, editor, *The History of the King's Works* vol. III 1485–1660, Part I (London: Her Majesty's Stationery Office, 1975) 210.
12. Stanley, 163–164.
13. Graham Parry, *The Golden Age Restor'd: The Culture of the Stuart Court, 1603–42* (New York: 1981) 9.
14. Parry, 9.
15. Parry, 9.
16. Parry, 9.

17. Parry, 9–10.
18. From *The Political Works of James I*, edited by Charles H. McIlwain (Cambridge, Mass., 1918) cited by Marie Axton in *The Queen's Two Bodies: Drama and the Elizabethan Succession* (London: Royal Historical Society, 1977) 133.
19. H. Neville Davies, "Jacobean *Antony and Cleopatra*," *Shakespeare Studies* XVII (1985), 124.
20. Davies, 125–126.
21. Axton, 133.
22. *Venetian State Papers 1603–1607*, 509–514, in *James I by His Contemporaries: And Account of his Career and Character as Seen by Some of his Contemporaries*, edited by Robert Ashton (London: 1969) 8.
23. Davies, 128–129.
24. Davies, 130.
25. Thomas Fuller, *The Church History of Britain: From the Birth of Jesus Christ until the Year M.DC. XLVIII*, edited by J. S. Brewer, vol. 5 (Oxford: 1845) 258.
26. Paul Johnson, *Elizabeth I* (New York: 1974) 438.
27. Anne Clifford, *Diary*, text from the Women Writers' Project, Brown University.
28. Millington, 15.
29. H. M. Colvin et al., editors, *The History of the King's Works* vol. III 1485–1660, Part I (London: Her Majesty's Stationery Office, 1975) 219. That Henry VIII was ultimately buried at Windsor does not mean that his son, Edward VI, ignored the burial plans stipulated in Henry's will. In an unpublished 1965 paper, "The Shrine of Edward the Confessor and Nicholas da Modena" (WAM 64299), Lawrence E. Tanner discusses the Modena being hired to build Henry VIII's tomb in Westminster and his housing there being paid for by Edward VI. But the Protestant "preestes of Westminstre," according the the artist's own account, kept throwing him out because he was a Papist, so he got nothing accomplished during Edward's reign. Tanner observes: "It is also evident that Edward VI had some qualms of conscience that this Father's solemn injunctions were not being carried out for in some notes he made for his own last Will there appears 'The King my father's tomb to be made upp.'

    "Queen Mary I was in a more difficult position. However much she might have wished to honour her Father's memory she could hardly, in the circumstances, erect an imposing tomb to the King who brought about the Protestant Reformation in England" (5).
30. Thomas Dekker, *The Wonderful Year, 1603*, edited by George B. Harrison, Bodley Head Quartos. no. 8 (New York: 1924).
31. William Camden, *Remains Concerning Britain*. The Seventh Impression, much amended, with many rare Antiquities never before Imprinted. by the Industry and Care of John Philipot ... London ... 1674. 523–525. [s/f modernized]

> Queen *Elizabeth*, a Prince admirable above her Sex for her Princely Ventures, happy Government, and long continuance in the same, by which she yet surviveth, and so / shall, indeared in the memory not only of all that knew her, but also of succeeding Posterities, ended this transitory life at *Richmond*, the 24. of *March*, 1602. the 45. year of her Reign, and seventy of her Age. Upon the remove of her body to the Palace of *Whitehall* by water, were writen then these passonate doleful Lines:

> The Queen was brought by water to White-hall,
> *At every stroake the oars did tears let fall:*
> *More clung about the Barge, fish under water*
> *Wept out their eyes of pearl, and swom blind after.*
> *I think the Barge-men might with easier thighs*
> *Have row'd her thither in her peoples eyes.*
> *For how so ere, thus much my thoughts have scan'd*
> *She'd come by water, had she come by land.*

32. College of Arms mss Vincent 151.
33. For accounts of the procession see: E. Arber, *The Passage of Queen Elizabeth* in *An English Garner* (Tudor Tracts, 1903), BL shelf-mark: 2324.c.9/1; and G. H. Chettle, *Englandes Mourning Garment* (1603), BL shelf-mark C.i16.b.13. Chettle proclaims "Shepheard remember our *Elizabeth*,/And sing her Rape, done by that *Tarquin*, Death" (no page: mark D3) and concludes:

    I Love as little as any man to come in print: but fleeing affection hath made me commit this fault, I pray you pardon it; and amend in reading the Printers errors; where being ill acquainted with Poetrie, he hath passed Heroes for Heroes; what euer else feems harsh, imagine I can write English, and make not the fault mine. Farewell. Hen: Chetle.

34. Dekker, 20, spelling modernized.
35. Writtine by *Infelice Academico Ignoto*. Printed for E. White. dwelling neere the little north doore of Paules Church, at the figne of the Gun. 1603. In *Expicedium: Funeral Sermons*, etc., R. Niccols (1603), BL shelf-mark C.121.b.5(2).
36. BL ad. mss 35, 324, folio 39. For a discussion of the hearse, see: Vicount Dillon, "The Hearse of Queen Elizabeth in Westminster Abbey," an offprint from *Middlesex and Hertforshire Notes and Queries*, Vol. ___ (19[05?])), 184–187, Westminster Abbey Library shelf-mark: 3.A.10*.
37. BL mss 6117 f.245.
38. This attitude is further confirmed by a letter from John Chamberlain to Dudley Carleton dated 12 April 1603. Although the letter runs three sides, fewer than seven lines are devoted to the queen's funeral plans: "The Queenes funerall is appointed the 28th of this prefent wth as much folemnitie as hath ben [yielded] to any former prince, and that by the kings owne direction ... the Lady Arbella is to be the chiefe mourner ... " PRO, State Papers 14/1 #9 [old numbering]/ #21 [new numbering].
39. *Westminster Abbey Official Guide*, 69.
40. *Official Guide*, 69. In *The History and Antiquities of Westminster Abbey* (London, 1856), however, I found the following statement about Elizabeth's tomb: "Walpole has stated, from an office book in the Earl of Oxford's collection, that the whole cost L 965 'besides the stone'" (110). Furthermore, Colvin sates that the artist, "Maximilian Powtrain or colt, a sculptor of French origin ... was paid £150 in 1605 and £570 in 1607. DeCritz, the Sergent Painter, was paid over £600 for painting the monument" (120). Colvin cites as his source M. Whinney, *Sculpture in Britain 1530–1830* (1964) 20, 236. Since the *Official Guide* cites no source, I would merely point out that, while the amount is open to debate, all sources agree that Mary Stuart's tomb cost significantly more.

41. *The Scottish Queen's Burial at Peterborough* (1589). Printed by AJ for Edward Venge, in *An English Garner*, vol. 8, edited by Edward Arber (Archibald Constable and Co., 1896).
42. *Official Guide*, 76.
43. *Official Guide*, 69.
44. *Calendar of State Papers* 1603–1610, edited by Mary Anne Everett Green (HM's Stationery Office 1858, rpt. 1967) 14/13, no. 8 .
45. Jonathan Goldberg, "Fatherly Authority: The Politics of Stuart Family Images" in *Rewriting the Renaissance: The Discourse of Sexual Difference in Early Modern Europe*, edited by Margaret W. Ferguson, Maureen Quilligan, and Nancy J. Vickers (Chicago: 1986) 5.
46. Goldberg, 4–5.
47. I am not suggesting that this burial of his own children's bodies with that of his mother was James' original intention. By the time Prince Henry dies, a large portion of James' available funds was tied up in the wedding of Princess Elizabeth, and at the time of her death, further Stuart building projects – notably the Banqueting Hall – had consumed most of his income.
48. *Calendar of State Papers* 1611–1618, no. 16.
49. The best example I've found of this strategy is a 1612 text by a Scotsman named James Maxwell. In the dedicatory epistle and introductory devices of *Queen Elizabeth's Looking-glass of Grace and Glory*, Maxwell makes a literary version of the statement made by James in Westminster. Addressed to the Princess Elizabeth, daughter of James I, and nominally lauding her father's predecessor, Maxwell's text (a collection of Bible stories) is actually dedicated to the glorification of Queen Mary Stuart; Maxwell turns the person and name of Elizabeth into a mere frame for his representation of the "matchless" Mary Stuart.
50. Davies, 142.
51. All references to the play cite *The Riverside Shakespeare*, edited by G. Blakemore Evans et al. (Boston: 1974).
52. Plutarch, "The Life of Marcus Antonius," translated by Thomas North in *Shakespeare's Plutarch*, vol. 2, edited by C. F. Tucker Brooke (London: 1909) 1–136.
53. Plutarch, 128.
54. Plutarch, 131–132.
55. Plutarch, 133.
56. Plutarch, 134–135.
57. College of Arms ms S.M.L. 30.
58. In 1999, complying with the Abbey's policy, I took a copy of the 1996 *ELR* issue containing "Reading the Tombs of Elizabeth I" to London with me, calling the Muniments Room and asking if I might drop it by in person. As I started to re-introduce myself to the Keeper, he cut in saying "Oh, indeed, I remember you." He went on to express his delight at the prospect of seeing the finished essay, and set a time for me to bring it by. When I arrived (on time), I was greeted by the ever-helpful Miss Reynolds, who told me that the Keeper had departed for the day soon after our phone conversation.
59. John Stow. *The Survey of London* ... Begunne first ... by Iohn Stow, in the yeere 1598. Afterwards inlarged by ... A.M. [Antony Munday] in the yeere 1618. And now completely finished by A.M. H.D. [Henry Dyson] and others, this present yeere 1633. Where-unto ... are annexed divers Alphabetical Tables,

etc. ... Printed by Elizabeth Purflow, and are to bee fold by Nicholas Borne, as his Shop, at the South Entrance of the Royall Exchange. 1633.

Even though the material I cite was added by A.M., H.D., and others after Stow's death, I will continue to refer to Stow as the author.

60. Helen Hackett, *Virgin Mother, Maiden Queen: Elizabeth I and the Cult of the Virgin Mary* (New York: St. Martin's Press, 1995).

61. Roy Strong, *Gloriana: The Portraits of Queen Elizabeth I* (Thames & Hudson, 1987) 164.

62. Strong, 164.

63. Stow, 826–827.

64. Stow, 854.

65. Stow, 840.

66. See: Andrew Belsey and Catherine Belsey, "Icons of Divinity: Portraits of Elizabeth I" in *Renaissance Bodies: The Human Figure in English Culture c. 1540–1660*, edited by Lucy Gent and Nigel Llewellyn (London: Reaktion Books, 1990) 11–35.

67. St. Martins Orgars, St. Michael Queenhithe, St. Michael Querne.

68. Hackett, 87.

69. Since Stow lists the dates for the restoration of All Hallows at the Wall as 1627–29, it is interesting to speculate whether this praise of Elizabeth was generated in relation to the reign of James or of Charles Stuart.

70. Frances A. Yates, *Astraea: The Imperial Theme in the Sixteenth Century* (London: Pimlico, 1993).

71. Roy Strong, *The Cult of Elizabeth: Elizabethan Portraiture and Pageantry* (Berkeley: University of California Press, 1977).

72. Hackett, 7.

1620–1660: The Shadow of Divine Right

1. For a variety of evaluations of the politics of the Spanish Match, see the following. Samuel R. Gardiner, *History of England, 1603–1642*, volumes IV and V (New York: AMS Press, Inc., 1965). Gardiner's strongly opinioned account – for example he speaks of James and Charles "signing away the independence of the English monarchy [while James'] subjects were regarding the proceedings of their sovereign with scarcely concealed disgust" (vol. IV, 399) – makes consistent reference to the various appeals to the memory of Elizabeth by both sides. D. R. Woolf, in "Two Elizabeths? James I and the Late Queen's Famous Memory," *Canadian Journal of History* 20 (1985) 167–191, offers equally strong, if divergent, evaluations of the role of Elizabeth's memory in the Stuart monarchy; while claiming that the "good Queen/bad King dichotomy" is far too simplistic (191), Woolf argues that many writers used references to Elizabeth's policies, not to denigrate James, but in an attempt "to set the king straight" (190). For less judgmental accounts of the issue see: Conrad Russell, *Parliaments and English Politics, 1621–1629* (Oxford: The Clarendon Press, 1979) and Thomas Cogswell, *The Blessed Revolution: English Politics and the Coming of War, 1621–1624* (Cambridge: Cambridge University Press, 1989); and for interesting archival discoveries, see: Glyn Redworth, "Of Pimps and Princes: Three Unpublished Letters from James I

and the Prince of Wales Relating to the Spanish Match," *The Historical Journal* 37 (1994) 401–409.

2. See A. C. Bald's discussion of Gondomar's influence in his "Introduction" to *A Game at Chesse* by Thomas Middleton (Cambridge: Cambridge University Press, 1929) 5–6.

3. Bald, 6.

4. Bald, 6. Bald cites a contemporary letter which recounts that Gondomar "'helpt to free some *English* that were in the Inquisition in *Toledo* and *Sevill*, and I could alledge many instances how ready and chearfuly he was to assist any *Englishman*'" 6 (quoted from Howell's *Familiar Letters* (1645), sec. 3, 80.

5. Conrad Russell, *Parliaments and English Politics 1621–1628* (Oxford, The Clarendon Press, 1979).

6. Russell, 85–86.

7. Russell, 86.

8. Russell, 119.

9. Russell, 119–120.

10. Russell, 121.

11. Russell, 130.

12. Russell, 131. Russell continues, making the point that even the anti-Spanish and often-quoted Sir Edward Coke "also wanted to get back to bills. Since Coke's long tirade about the abuses committed by Spain is more commonly quoted in arguments that the Commons were seriously anti-Spanish than anything else, it is worth stressing that this speech was a rambling collection of memoirs, and that Coke's only formal proposal was to get back to bills" (131).

13. Russell, 134.

14. Russell, 135.

15. B. L. Harley MS 1580, f. 430^r cited by Russell, 135.

16. Russell, 137.

17. Russell, 137.

18. Russell, 137.

19. Simon Schama, *A History of Britain: The Wars of the British 1603–1776* (New York: Hyperion, 2001) 60–61.

20. Russell, 138.

21. Gardiner, vol. IV, 246.

22. Gardiner, vol. IV, 257.

23. Gardiner, vol. IV, 349.

24. John Reynolds, "*Vox Coeli*, or News From Heaven," Elisium, 1624. The pamphlet is reproduced in *Somers Tracts*, II, edited by Walter Scott (London: T. Cadell and W. Davies, 1809), II, 555–596. For a summary of the debated authorship of this pamphlet see Levin's note 64 (213).

25. Woolf differs from my reading of the situation by refusing to see James using Elizabeth in a critical context. "He may have believed that there were those who misunderstood both the Queen and himself, but that is not the same thing. Respect for the memory of one monarch would carry with it readier obedience to her successor. Disrespect was nothing less than *lèse-majesté*, something which James would never brook" (180). Woolf, I must point out, praises James for the elaborate tomb he constructed for Elizabeth.

26. Woolf, 185.

27. Woolf, 191.

28. In the memorial in All Hallows at the Wall, Elizabeth is called a Judith who "Against Spaines Holifernes ... Dauntlesse gain'd many a glorious victory ... In Court a Saint, in Field an Amazon."

29. Woolf, p. 191.

30. John Donne, *The Sermons of John Donne*, edited by George R. Potter and Evelyn M. Simpson, 10 vols. (Berkeley: University of California Press, 1959–62). "As the Rule is true ... when men dare not speak of the vices of a Prince that is dead, it is certain that the Prince that is alive proceeds in the same fices; so in the inversion of the Rule is true too ... when men may speak freely of the vertues of a real Prince, it is an evident argument, that the present Prince practises the same vertues; for, if he did not, he would not love to hear of them. Of *her*, we may say (that which was first said to the Emperor *Iulian*) *Nihil humile, aut adjectum congitavit, quia novit de se semper loquendum;* she knows the world would talk of her after her death, and therefore she did such things all her life were worthy to be talked of. Of her glorious successor, and our gracious Soveraign, we may say; *Onerosum est succedere bono Principi,* It would have troubled any king but *him,* to have come in sucession, and in comparison with such a *Queen* " (1:217–218).

    All subsequent references to this sermon will be cited parenthetically by volume and page number.

31. "The faculties and abilities of the soul appeare best in affaires of State, and in Ecclesiasticall affaires; in matter of government, and in matter of religion; and in neither of these are we without example of able women. For, for State affaires, and matter of government, our age hath given us such a Queen, as scarce any former King hath eqlled" (10:190).

32. John Chamberlain, *The Letters of John Chamberlain*, edited by Norman E. McClure, 2 vols. (Philadelphia: American Philosophical Society, 1939) 2:140.

33. Jeanne Shami, "'The Stars in their Order Fought Against Sisera': John Donne and the Pulpit Crisis of 1622," *The John Donne Journal* 14 (1995) 28.

34. Shami, 28.

35. Remembering that Spenser dresses "fair Eliza" of the April eclogue in scarlet "like a maiden queen," we note that red is not associated with only the evils of sexuality (as in Revelation), but with sexuality in general, as sixteenth-century wedding dresses were often red. Queen Elizabeth's sexuality, of course, can never be discussed "in general"; for her the issue must always be very specific and very much under her own control.

36. See: M. J. Rodrîgues-Salgado and the staff of the National Maritime Museum, *Armada, 1588–1988: An International Exhibition to Commemorate the Spanish Armada: The Official Catalogue* (London: Penguin Books, 1988) 271–285.

37. Marshall Grossman, "Servile / Sterile / Style: Milton and the Question of Woman" in *Milton and the Idea of Woman*, edited by Julia M. Walker (Urbana: University of Illinois Press, 1988) 156.

38. John Milton, *The Reason of Church Government* in *The Works of John Milton*, vol. III, edited by Frank Allen Patterson et al. (New York: Columbia University Press, 1938) 237. All references to Milton's work, unless otherwise indicated, are taken from this edition and will be cited by volume and page number within the text.

39. See the labored reading by Albert C. Labriola in "Milton's Eve and the Cult of Elizabeth I," *Journal of English and Germanic Philology* 95:1 (1996) 38–51.

40. Michael Dobson and Nicola J. Watson, *England's Elizabeth* (Oxford: Oxford University Press, 2002) 67.
41. Dobson and Watson, 67.
42. Susanne Woods, "How Free Are Milton's Women" in *Milton and the Idea of Woman* 17.
43. David Loewenstein, *Milton and the Drama of History: Historical Vision, Iconoclasm, and the Literary Imagination* (Cambridge University Press, 1990) 83–84.
44. Loewenstein, 17.
45. John T. Shawcross, *John Milton: The Self and the World* (Lexington: University of Kentucky Press, 1993) 71. I heartily concur with Shawcross' judgment: "The Commonplace Book deserves certain considerations it has not been given, particularly its place in Milton's growing ambitions and its reflection of personal attitudes and biographical concerns" (71).
46. Mary Ann Radzinowicz, *Toward Samson Agonistes: The Growth of Milton's Mind* (Princeton: Princeton University Press, 1978) xv. Radzinowicz continues: "That he kept a further comonplace book, since lost, is clear from six cross-references in the existing notebook to a missing Theological Index" (xv). Shawcross disputes this, saying "there is no evidence that another miscellany had been kept. The matter of 'the other index,' as Milton calls it (CPB, 221), the theological index noted by Edward Phillips (CPB, 197), has been discussed elsewhere and need not divert us in the present study" (Shawcross, 77).
47. Radzinowicz, xvi.
48. Ruth Mohl, *John Milton and His Commonplace Book* (New York: Frederick Ungar Publishing Co., 1969) 165.
49. John Milton, *Commonplace Book* in *The Works of John Milton*, vol. XVIII, edited by Frank Allen Patterson et al. (New York: Columbia University Press, 1938) 185. All other references to Milton's work cite this edition as CE unless otherwise noted.
50. Henry V's great-great-grandmother, had she been a boy, would have ruled France. As it was, she was married to England's Edward II, while the French climbed back up the family tree in search of a male relation to occupy the throne. They passed the Salic Law after this dynastic debacle, to justify rather than authorize, their actions and political philosophy.
51. CE XVIII, 130.
52. CE XVIII, 185. Milton also mentions Elizabeth's good money management under the heading of "Property and Taxes" (201, 203).
53. Janet E. Halley, "Female Autonomy in Milton Sexual Poetics" in *Milton and the Idea of Woman* 235.
54. Julia M. Walker, "The Idea of Milton and the Idea of Woman" in *Milton and the Idea of Woman* 14.
55. Woods, 16.
56. Shawcross, 197–198.
57. Shawcross, 224, emphasis mine.
58. Ruth Mohl, editor, *Complete Prose Works of John Milton*, Douglas Bush, et al. general editors (New Haven: Yale University Press, 1953) vol. I, 425 n7.
59. Woods, 17.
60. Shawcross, 223.
61. Shawcross, 223–224.

62. Mohl, 167.
63. Woods continues: "He [Milton] could expect nothing from the unpopular queen, whom he knew at the time was probably soon to abdicate. Yet he produces an extended praise of her rule and learning and seems at ease with a female ruler and lawgiver whose sex is largely irrelevant" (17).
64. Woods, 17.
65. This is not, however, a distinction which saves any rightful queen from Milton's damnation. I include the passage on Cartismandua, Queen of the Brigantes, here because I find the language Milton uses to be very revealing.

> She who had betray'd Caractacus and her Countrie to adorne the Tryumph of Claudius, thereby grown powerfull and gratious with the Romans, presuming on the hire of her treason, deserted her Husband [not the king of the Brigante, although Milton suggests that he was "himself perhaps reigning elsewhere"]; and marrying Vellocatus one of his Squires, conferrs on him the Kingdome also. This deed so odious and full of infamie, disturbed the whole State: Venutius with other Forces, and the help of her own subjects, who detested the example of so foul a fact, and with all the uncomeliness of thir Subjection to the Monarchie of a Woeman, a peece of manhood not every day to be found among Britans, though she had got by suttle train his Brother with many of his kindred into her hands, brought her soon below the confidence of being able to resist longer. (CE X, 62)

What interests me here is not Cartismandua's crimes as a pro-Roman traitor and an adultress, but Milton's suggestion that Britians had "not every day" the "peece of manhood" to "detest" a woman ruler, even a bad one.
66. Buchanan, cited by Mohl in the Yale Prose, vol. I, 477–478 n4.
67. "Gynæcocratiam Reprehendit longa oratione ac rejecit Jacobus Kennedus Archiepiscopus Sanctæ Andreæ, Buchanan. Hist. Scot. L. 12. p. 403. Edit. Edinburgh" (CE XVIII, 200).
68. Mohl in the Yale Prose, vol. I, 477–478 n4. Mohl continues: "Writing shortly after the rule of a queen and a woman regent in Scotland and during the rule of a queen in England, Buchanan was doubtless struck by the difference between his own and Kennedy's times, a difference denounced in 1558 by John Knox's *Monstrous Regiment of Women.*"
69. Mohl, 165. She goes on to list these women. "In some thirteen other entries in the *Commonplace Book* Milton refers to women rulers: Mary Tudor, Mary Stuart, Mary of Guise, Queen Elizabeth, Queen Mother of Charles IX of France, Queen Martia of Britain, and the Empress Placida" (165). Most of these, of course, were after Kennedy's time, but not Buchanan's.
70. Mohl dates the entry in the 1650s with the Machiavelli entries, based on the hand of an amanuensis. But Shawcross makes a compelling case for Milton's use of his students in the role of amanuensis, which would allow the more logical dating of the early 1640s (Shawcross, 80).

1660–1837: The Shadow of a Golden Age

1. Simon Schama, *A History of Britain: The Wars of the British 1603–1776* vol. II (New York: Hyperion, 2001) 248.

2. Schama, 375.
3. Michael Dobson and Nicola J. Watson, *England's Elizabeth: An Afterlife in Fame and Fantasy* (Oxford: Oxford University Press, 2002) 82.
4. No author. *The Jesuites Ghostly Wayes* ... London: Printed for Will. Bowtel, at the sign of the Star new Mercers Chapel in Cheapside, 1679.
5. *Ghostly Wayes* ..., 18. To be a member of the Society of Jesus, of course, was not a goal to be revered in this context.
6. *Ghostly Wayes* ..., 18.
7. *Ghostly Wayes* ..., 18.
8. *Ghostly Wayes* ..., 22.
9. *Ghostly Wayes* ..., 23–24.
10. *Ghostly Wayes* ..., 24.
11. *Ghostly Wayes* ..., 25.
12. The first *Corante*, was printed (in English) in Amsterdam on June 6th of 1621; it was available in London after September of the same year.
13. Anon, *The Secret HISTORY of the Duke of Alancon and Q.Elizabeth. A True History.* (London, Printed for Will with the Wisp at the Sign of the Moon in the Ecliptic, 1671) 1.
14. *The Secret HISTORY*, 3.
15. *The Secret HISTORY*, 25–26.
16. *The Secret HISTORY*, 27.
17. *The Secret HISTORY*, 35–36.
18. *The Secret HISTORY*, 39.
19. *The Secret HISTORY*, 51.
20. *The Secret HISTORY*, 53.
21. *The Secret HISTORY*, 56.
22. *The Secret HISTORY*, 57.
23. *The Secret HISTORY*, 63–67.
24. *The Secret HISTORY*, 71.
25. *The Secret HISTORY*, 73.
26. *The Secret HISTORY*, 73–74.
27. *The Secret HISTORY*, 116.
28. *The Secret HISTORY*, 193 (but mis-numbered, should be 121. The last 100 pages are randomly numbered).
29. *The Secret HISTORY*, 190–191.
30. *The Secret HISTORY*, 193.
31. *The Secret HISTORY*, 198.
32. Dobson and Watson, 79.
33. These are the same three figures in the same order that we find in the *c.*1730 Temple of British Worthies, where Elizabeth's bust, stern of face and alone of all her sex, sits between those of Edward the Black Prince and William of Orange. See Dobson and Watson, 74–75.
34. Schama, 397.
35. Schama, 375–376.
36. Dobson and Watson, 80.
37. Ben Saddi, 6.
38. Ben Saddi, 56.
39. In his Introduction, written in Latin at a time when few women read Latin, Boccaccio claims that he is writing of famous and virtuous women of the

past because there are no virtuous women of the present. The present female population he claims to desire to instruct. Ben Saddi's postscript has much the same tone of disingenuous snarkiness.

40. Ben Saddi, 57–58.
41. *The Memoirs of Sir James Melvil of Halhill: Containing An impartial Account of the most remarkable Affairs of State during the Sixteenth Century, not mentioned by other Historians: More particularly relating to the Kingdoms of England and Scotland, under the Reigns of Queen Elizabeth, Mary Queen of Scots, and King James.* Published from the Original Manuscript by GEORGE SCOTT, Gent. The second Edition corrected (Edinburgh: Printed by T. and W. Ruddimans, 1785) 55.
42. *The Days of good Queen Bess. A new and Universal GARLAND Which contains My own, and the Days of my Grandfather, In the following new Songs, viz.* I. The Days of Good Queen Bess. II The Alteration of the Times, or the Days of George the Third! III. The Hardy Tar, or the Seaman's Complaint PRESTON, Printed and sold by T. Walker. [No pagination and no date, but the British Library notation says 1800.]
43. *The Days of good Queen Bess.* [No page number.]
44. Elizabeth Somerville's *Aurora and Maria: or The Advantages of Adverstiy, A Moral Tale, in which is Introduced a Juvenile Drama, Call'ed Queen Elizabeth or Old Times New Revived* (Brentford: Printed by and For P. Norbury, 1809) 92–93.
45. Dobson and Watson, 203.
46. Dobson and Watson, 201.
47. Dobson and Watson, 204.

1837–1910: The Shadow of a Paternalistic Queenship

1. See Dobson and Watson's discussion of a painting commissioned by Victoria to memorialize her own coronation; it was carried out by Chares Robert Leslie as Elizabeth hearing the news of her accession from Cecil at Hatfield House. Michael Dobson and Nicola J. Watson, *England's Elizabeth: An Afterlife in Fame and Fantasy* (Oxford: Oxford University Press, 2002) 148–149.
2. M. J. Franklin, *British Biscuit Tins, 1868–1939: An Aspect of Decorative Packaging* (London: New Cavendish Books, 1979) 23. See also: Peter R. G. Hornsby, *Decorated Biscuit Tins* (Exton, PA: Schiffer Publishing Ltd., 1984). For American tins, see: David Zimmerman, *The Encyclopedia of Advertising Tins: Smalls and Samples* vol. 1 and *The Encyclopedia of Advertising Tins: Identification and Values* vol. 2 (Paducah, KY: Collector Books, 1999).
3. I have the horrid feeling that this is something that an Englishperson would be able to figure out. At moments such as this, being an American scholar of English literature and history is a bit like having chosen a career as a one-armed paper-hanger.
4. http://www.imperial-tobacco.com/History/Chapter1_10.asp. See also: Douglas Dongdon-Martin, *Tobacco Tins: A Collector's Guide* (Atglen, PA: Schiffer Publishing Ltd, 1992).
5. See http://www.davesc.com/tins/list.asp and http://www.the-forum.com/ephemera/label/cigmfg.htm#s for more information. The following brands,

while having no place in this study, are simply too wonderfully ironic to leave unmentioned:

Casket – J. W. Pattriouex Ltd (UK)
Forbidden Fruit – National Tobacco Works (US)
Hygeia – T. C. Williams & Co. (US)
Jolly Tar – John Finzer & Bros. (US)
Life Ray – Ray & Co. Ltd (UK)
Lifeboat – United Tobacco Co. (South Africa)
Lipshuts Brand – T. C. Williams & Co. (US)
Red Cross – American Tobacco Co. (USA)

6. Dobson and Watson list many of these, with a reproduction of Stothard's Shakespeare's interview with Queen Elizabeth, 130–131.
7. This quote was taken from the whole text of the letter, found on an auction site for the letter itself. No permanently identifying reference material is available.
8. Dobson and Watson, 109. The authors identify this print as originally coming from an illustration in Friedrich Schiller's *Maria Stuart* (1800), later published by Currier and Ives of New York in the early nineteenth century (xi).

1910–1953: The Shadow of History

1. Martin Pugh, *The March of the Women: A Revisionist Analysis of the Campaign for Women's Suffrage 1866–1914* (Oxford: Oxford University Press, 2000) 19. Pugh's division, while extremely convenient, is – as he would acknowledge – too simplistic to be sustained in a close study of the history of the Movement. For the purposes of this chapter, however, the vocabulary is both clear and adequate.
2. Pugh, 19.
3. Pugh, 19.
4. Quoted in Pugh, 19.
5. Queen Victoria, quoted by Sir Theodore Martin in *Queen Victoria as I Knew Her* (Edinburgh and London: Wm Blackwood, 1908) cited by Constance Rover, *Women's Suffrage and Party Politics in Britain 1866–1914* (London: Routledge and Kegan Paul, 1967) 33.
6. Rover, 34.
7. Pugh, 43.
8. Parliamentary Debates, 3rd Series, vol. 99. c. 950), cited in Rover, 34.
9. Millicent Garrett Fawcett, *Life of Her Magesty Queen Victoria* Eminent Women Series (London: W. H. Allen & Co., Limited, 1895).
10. Fawcett, 14.
11. Edward III, who reigned for 50 years (1327–77) is currently in third place, after Victoria, Elizabeth II, and before Elizabeth I.
12. Fawcett, 9–10.
13. Fawcett, 10.
14. Fawcett, 11.
15. Fawcett, 14.

16. This was produced by the Women Writers' Suffrage League and the Actresses' Franchise League and first performed at the Scala Theatre in London on 10 November 1909.

17. Barbara Green, *Spectacular Confessions: Autobiography, Performative Activism, and the Sites of Suffrage 1905–1938* (London: Macmillan, 1997) 76.

18. Ford Madox Ford, *This Monstrous Regiment of Women* (1913) 19, quoted in Green, 76.

19. Green, 77.

20. Under the heading of "even Homer nods," Diane Atkinson, that prolific scholar of the Suffrage Movement follows the Protestant thinking of the time she studies and mistakes Beatification for Canonization: "the rhetoric of the movement used strong religio-militaristic imagery. Joan of Arc, who was canonized in 1909, was its patron saint. The WSPU leaders portrayed the fight for the vote as a holy crusade for women's freedom: they called each other comrades and holy warriors; their campaign fund was the 'War Chest'. It was a language which was attractive to many"(2). Atkinson later states, with perfect accuracy, "every WSPU member who had been to prison could identify with their patron saint, Joan of Arc" (124). Diane Atkinson, *The Suffragettes in Pictures* (London: Sutton Publishing, 1996).

21. Grace James, *Joan of Arc* (London: Methuen and Co. Ltd, 1910) 2–3.

22. James, 6.

23. Atkinson, 181.

24. Florence Dixie, *Gloriana; or The Revolution of 1900* (London: Henry and Company, 1880) no page number.

25. See: Ann Ardis, "'The Journey from Fantasy to Politics': The Representation of Socialism and Feminism in *Gloriana* and *The Image-Breakers*" in *Rediscovering Forgotten Radicals: British Women Writers, 1899–1939*, edited by Angela Ingram and Daphne Patai (Chapel Hill: University of North Carolina Press, 1993) 43–56; and Nan Bowman Albinski, "'The Law of Justice, of Nature, and of Right': Victorian Feminist Utopias" in *Feminism, Utopia, and Narrative*, edited by Libby Falk Jones and Sarah Webster Goodwin (Knoxville: University of Tennessee Press, 1990) 50–68.

26. Dixie, 2.

27. Dixie, 4–5.

28. Dixie, vii–x.

29. Dixie, 346.

30. Dixie, 347.

31. Dixie, 347–348.

32. Dixie, 350.

33. Atkinson, 153.

34. Cited in Atkinson, 258.

35. From *Woman's Effort: A Chronicle of British Women's Fifty Years' Struggle for Citizenship, 1856–1914* (1917) in *Mrs Broom's Suffragette Photographs: Photographs by Christina Broom, 1908–1914*, edited by Diane Atkinson (London: Dirk Nishen Publishing, no date [1992–93?]) 6.

36. See Marina Warner's *Monuments and Maidens* (London, 1985) for a thorough discussion of this topic.

37. Lisa Tickner, *The Spectacle of Women: Imagery of the Suffrage Campaign 1907–14* (London: Chatto and Windus, 1987) 208.

38. Tickner, 60.
39. Atkinson, 116.
40. Mrs. Henry Fawcett, *Some Eminent Women of our Times: Short Biographical Sketches* (London: Macmillan and Co., 1989).
41. Mrs. Henry Fawcett, LL.D. *Five Famous French Women* (London: Cassell and Company, Limited, 1905).
42. Margaret Wynne Nevinson (Mrs. H. W.), *Ancient Suffragettes* (London: The Women's Freedom League, 1913).
43. Nevinson, 2.
44. Nevinson, 2.
45. Nevinson, 2.
46. Nevinson, 2–3.
47. Nevinson, 3–4.
48. Nevinson, 5
49. Nevinson, 5–7.
50. http://www.bbc.co.uk/history/war/wwone/mirror02_04.shtml
51. Augusta Cook, *Queen Elizabeth: or Spies and Plots in the Sixteenth Century With an Introduction: History Repeating itself in the Events of Today* (London: Robert Banks and Son, 1915).
52. Cook, no page number.
53. Cook, 5.
54. Cook, 5.
55. Cook, 5,
56. Cook, 5–6.
57. See, among other works: *The Antichrist; the Man of Sin; the Beasts of the Revelation, etc.* (1932); *The Covenant Oath of Jehovah: its beginning, meaning and end* (1919); *The Divine Calendar; or, Studies of the Revelation from an Israelite standpoint*, 6 vols (1907–24); *Light from Patmos. The Apocalypse simply and concisely explained* (1916); *Light from the Book of Daniel on History, Past, Present, and Future. A course of twelve lectures, etc.* (1916); *The Near Return of Our Lord. A series of four lectures on the second advent of Jesus Christ* (1929); *Things that are coming on the Earth. A lecture, etc.* (1932); *What and Why? or, Anglo-Israel belief in questions and answers for young and old* (1914); *"The Whole Counsel of God" ... Three lectures, etc.* (1918); *The Wonders of Egypt. Its message to-day in the light of the Bible and modern discoveries and Protestant truth ... Lectures ...* Reprinted from the "Quarterly Notes," Protestant British-Israel League (1932); *The Story of the Light that never went out. A history of English Protestantism for young readers* (1904).
58. Cook, 6.
59. Cook, 6.
60. Cook, 6.
61. Cook, 21.
62. http://www.winstonchurchill.org (emphasis mine). All quotes from Churchill's speeches are taken from the documents on this site.
63. Michael Dobson and Nicola J. Watson, *England's Elizabeth: An Afterlife in Fame and Fantasy* (Oxford: Oxford University Press, 2002) 214.

1953–2003: The Shadows of Modern Imagination

1. Charles Williams, *Elizabeth I* Great Lives Series (London: Duckworth, 1936, rpt 1953) 140.

2. A. S. Byatt, *The Virgin in the Garden* (New York: Vintage Books, 1992) 10.
3. Byatt, 13.
4. Byatt, 12.
5. Byatt, 13.
6. Byatt, 239.
7. Byatt, 240.
8. Byatt, 243–244.
9. The Queen's Christmas Broadcast, *Christmas 1953*, in *A Queen Speaks to Her People* (Inglewood, Australia, 1977) 10.
10. See: Barbara Hodgdon's chapter entitled "Romancing the Queen" in *The Shakespeare Trade* (Philadelphia: University of Pennsylvania Press, 1998) and Michael Dobson and Nicola J. Watson in their chaper "Elizabeth Modernized" in *England's Elizabeth: An Afterlife in Fame and Fantasy* (Oxford: Oxford University Press, 2002).
11. *Mary of Scotland*, 1936, RKO, Katharine Hepburn and Fredric March, directed by John Ford. Turner Entertainment 1989, cassette cover.
12. *Elizabeth*, directed by Shekhar Kapur, Gramercy Films 1998.
13. Although this sounds unprofessional, calling her "Cate" (rather than the more conventional "Blanchett"), stresses both the personal immediacy she brings to the role and the parallel with Elizabeth the historical character, neither titled nor family-named in this production's credits, publicity, on-screen prose prologue or epilogue.
14. Famously, Sir Roy Strong and a team at the Victoria & Albert tried to reproduce the dress of the Ditchley portrait (significantly the model for the dress Cate dons in the film's last scene) and found it impossible to make real fabric sustain the weight of all those jewels.
15. For an entertainingly opinionated list of only the most egregious of these errors/revisions, see: http://www.elizabethi.org/faq/two.htm
16. For no apparent reason, when the Archbishop says "I present to the north …" he is shown standing in the crossing facing south-west; when he says "I present to the south," he actually faces north, toward the wonderful (but unseen) Five Sisters windows, with the more gaudy rose window of the rebuilt south façade in the background.
17. For texts of all the reviews cited here, with the exception of CNN, see the "reviews" link on the *Elizabeth* page of http://www.rottentomatoes.com
18. http://www2.cnn.com/SHOWBIZ/Movies/9811/04/elizabeth/index.html
19. Say what you will, the Harmony Ball manufacturers let me reproduce these for you without a fee, which is more than I can say for the second-richest woman in England.

Conclusion

1. http://www.bbc.co.uk/history/programmes/greatbritons/list.shtml
2. http://media.guardian.co.uk/mediaguardian/story/0,7558,953721,00.html
3. http://media.guardian.co.uk/firstnight/story/0%2C11131%2C627052%2C00.html
4. http://media.guardian.co.uk/broadcast/story/0,7493,778780,00.html
5. http://news.bbc.co.uk/1/hi/entertainment/tv_and_radio/2208532.stm
6. http://news.bbc.co.uk/1/hi/entertainment/tv_and_radio/2208532.stm
7. http://news.bbc.co.uk/1/hi/entertainment/tv_and_radio/2208532.stm

8. Of course, the fact that Wallace is there at all – pace Scotland, land of my ancestors – is largely due to the combined efforts of Hollywood and Mel Gibson.
9. http://www.bbc.co.uk/history/programmes/greatbritons/screensaver.shtml. Here, in case you are cut off from your lap-top, is the numerical listing of the next 90 Great Britons.

11	Ernest Shackleton – BBCi History
12	Captain James Cook – BBCi History
13	Lord Baden-Powell – BBC Radio 4
14	King Alfred the Great – BBCi History
15	Arthur Wellesley, 1st Duke of Wellington – BBCi History
16	Margaret Thatcher (Baroness Thatcher) – BBC News
17	Michael Crawford – BBC News
18	Queen Victoria – BBCi History
19	Sir Paul McCartney – BBC News
20	Sir Alexander Fleming – BBCi History
21	Alan Turing OBE – BBC News
22	Michael Faraday – BBCi History
23	Owain Glyndwr – BBCi History
24	Queen Elizabeth II – BBC News
25	Professor Stephen Hawking – BBCi Science
26	William Tyndale – BBCi Books
27	Emmeline Pankhurst – BBCi History
28	William Wilberforce – BBCi History
29	David Bowie – BBCi Music
30	Guy Fawkes – BBCi History
31	Leonard Cheshire (Baron Cheshire of Woodall) – BBCi H2G2
32	Eric Morecambe OBE – BBCi Cult
33	David Beckham – BBC Sport
34	Thomas Paine – BBCi History
35	Boudicca – BBCi History
36	Sir Steve Redgrave – BBC Sport
37	Sir Thomas More – BBCi History
38	William Blake – BBCi History
39	John Harrison – BBC News
40	King Henry VIII – BBCi History
41	Charles Dickens – BBCi Books
42	Sir Frank Whittle – BBCi History
43	John Peel – BBC Radio 1
44	John Logie Baird – BBCi History
45	Aneurin Bevan – BBCi History
46	Boy George – BBC Music
47	Sir Douglas Bader – BBC Radio 4
48	William Wallace – BBCi History
49	Sir Francis Drake – BBCi History
50	John Wesley – External: John Wesley Online Exhibition
51	King Arthur – BBCi Religion
52	Florence Nightingale – BBCi History
53	TE Lawrence (Lawrence of Arabia) – BBC News

54	Captain Robert Falcon Scott – BBCi History
55	Enoch Powell – BBC News
56	Sir Cliff Richard – BBC News
57	Sir Alexander Graham Bell – BBCi History
58	Freddie Mercury – BBC News
59	Dame Julie Andrews – BBCi Films
60	Edward Elgar – BBCi Music
61	Queen Elizabeth, the Queen Mother – BBC News
62	George Harrison – BBC News
63	Sir David Attenborough – BBCi Nature
64	James Connolly – BBCi History
65	George Stephenson – BBCi History
66	Sir Charles (Charlie) Chaplin – BBC News
67	Tony Blair – BBC News
68	William Caxton – BBCi History
69	Bobby Moore OBE – BBC Sport
70	Jane Austen – BBCi Books
71	William Booth – BBC Nottingham
72	King Henry V – BBCi History
73	Aleister Crowley – External: Biography.Com
74	King Robert the Bruce – BBCi History
75	Bob Geldof KBE – BBC News
76	The Unknown Warrior – BBCi History
77	Robbie Williams – BBC Radio 1
78	Edward Jenner – BBCi History
79	David Lloyd George (1st Earl Lloyd George of Dwyfor) – BBCi History
80	Charles Babbage – BBCi History
81	Geoffrey Chaucer – BBCi Books
82	King Richard III – BBCi History
83	JK Rowling OBE – BBC News
84	James Watt – BBCi History
85	Sir Richard Branson – BBC Radio 2
86	Bono – BBC Radio 1
87	John Lydon (Johnny Rotten) – BBCi Music
88	Field Marshal Montgomery – BBC News
89	Donald Campbell – BBC News
90	King Henry II – BBCi History
91	James Clerk Maxwell – BBC News
92	JRR Tolkien – BBCi Books
93	Sir Walter Raleigh – BBCi History
94	King Edward I – BBCi History
95	Sir Barnes Neville Wallis – BBCi History
96	Richard Burton – BBC Wales
97	Tony Benn – BBC News
98	David Livingstone – BBC World Service
99	Professor Tim Berners-Lee – BBC Oxford
100	Marie Stopes – BBCi History

Index